John Reid is chair of the Trimontium Trust in Melrose and has published and lectured widely on the Roman Iron Age. For two decades he has led the Trust's research projects, most notably at Burnswark Hill. Recent work has culminated in the complete renovation of Scotland's only museum dedicated to the period of the Roman invasion. Originally intending to study classics, he trained as a doctor specialising in diseases of the heart and lungs, but has now returned to his first love of Scotland's early history.

'*The Eagle and the Bear* is a fascinating account of the complex, and often violent, interactions between indigenous communities and Roman power in northern Britain. It is engagingly written and well-informed – a must read for anyone with an interest in Scotland's past.'

Manuel Fernández-Götz, Abercromby Professor of Archaeology, University of Edinburgh

'Probably the most complete history of Roman Scotland I've had the privilege to read. At once, scholarly, compellingly written and thought provoking, it brings a fresh perspective to the available evidence and provides genuine new insight into the study of the subject matter, with a forensic eye for detail. Most certainly a welcome addition to the genre.'

Douglas Jackson, author and creator of the Gaius Valerius Verrens series

Winter has come. Housesteads Roman fort on Hadrian's Wall, looking west.

The Eagle and the Bear

A NEW HISTORY OF ROMAN SCOTLAND

John H. Reid

BIRLINN

First published in 2023 by
Birlinn Ltd
West Newington House
10 Newington Road
Edinburgh
EH9 1QS

www.birlinn.co.uk

ISBN 978 1 78027 814 8

British Library Cataloguing in Publication Data
A catalogue record for this book is available
from the British Library.

Designed and typeset by Mark Blackadder

Printed and bound by PNB, Latvia

'*The eagle of the Roman army goes at the head of every legion – the king of birds, most powerful of them all . . .*'

Josephus, *Bellum Judiacum*,
on the First Romano-Jewish War

•

'*Laureolus gave up his naked flesh
to a Caledonian bear . . .*'

Martial, *Liber Spectaculorum*,
on the inaugural games of the Colosseum

To my parents, Watson and Jenny,
who first sowed the seed and to
Erica, Simone, Jonathan and Scout,
whose unconditional love
helped nurture it

Contents

Frontispiece. Artist's impression of the interior of a Caledonian settlement.

List of plates and figures

Plates

Figures

Acknowledgements

Most books are written with the generous assistance of others. For their scholarship, exchange of ideas and major contributions of time and energy, I am indebted to many people. With respect to previous works, I have tried to present here a broad perspective of early Scotland's experience of the Roman invasion by incorporating material gleaned from recent investigations and contemporary debate that builds upon a canon of fine scholarship stretching back many years. Pointers to some of the many publications are provided at the end of this book.

In response to the great asymmetries of power and existential crises that played out in North Britain at the time of the Roman occupation, this work documents something of what was a 300-year collision between two very different cultures. For stimulating my interest in that confrontation and in the potentially devestating effects of contact with Rome's seductive military machine, I wish to thank Manuel Fernández-Götz and Nico Roymans for their inspirational work in the field of conflict archaeology. Although this book is founded on fifty years of personal pursuit of the Roman army and its interaction with the peoples of ancient Scotland my horizon widened as my appreciation of non-Roman perspectives grew. For pointing me in the direction of a more balanced narrative, I am grateful to Kay Callander and Louisa Campbell, who introduced me to important indigenous themes I had not previously considered.

I am also grateful to those experts who have patiently tolerated my questions and challenges over many years. Knowingly or otherwise, their comments, arguments and contributions have allowed me to form many of the opinions expressed in this book (without them necessarily agreeing with any of its conclusions). I am particularly indebted to Fraser Hunter who has freely shared his prodigious knowledge of the material culture of Scotland's Iron Age. I would also like to thank the many other scholars who have taken time to answer my enquiries, either by correspondence or by allowing themselves to be button-holed at many archaeological conferences over the last decade. These include Ian Armit, Geoff Bailey, Jo Ball, Paul Bidwell, Mike Bishop, Andrew and Barbara Birley, Chris Bowles,

David Breeze, Richard Brickstock, James Bruhn, Dave Cowley, Andrew Fitzpatrick, Stephen Greep, Bill Griffiths, Bill Hanson, Nick Hodgson, Beccy Jones, Lesley Macinnes, Frances McIntosh, Gordon Noble, James O'Driscoll, Al Oswald, John Poulter, Tanja Romankiewicz, Eberhard Sauer, Niall Sharples, Matt Symonds, Richard Tipping, Alan Wilkins and Allan Wilson.

I wish to make special mention of colleagues from Germany who kindly provided information and access to important material from their areas of expertise. These include the late Sebastian Sommer whose genial personality and insightful perspectives of the Roman frontiers of Scotland and Germany will be sorely missed. Thanks also go to Ruth Beusing, Axel Posluschny, Regine Müller and Sabine Klein for generously providing much of the data that lies behind our improved understanding of events at Burnswark Hill and Trimontium. I am also grateful to Achim Rost and Susanne Wilbers-Rost for my initiation into the fascinating world of the Varusschlacht and the lessons to be learned from ancient battlefield debris, and to Holger von Grawert for helping me understand the intricacies of Roman military equipment. Great thanks also go to Jörg Sprave for his verve and ingenuity in ballistic experimentation.

I wish to particularly express my gratitude to Andrew Nicholson for his professionalism and archaeological rigour during our investigations at Burnswark, to Robin Edwins for his energy and logistical skills, to Derek and Sharon McLennan for their expert detecting survey, and to Sir John Buchanan-Jardine and Andrew Macgregor for their unstinting support and access to the site. Don Reid's slinging expertise was also fundamental to experiments that radically altered our appreciation of Roman assault tactics.

It has been a privilege to know and correspond with Lawrence Keppie on Romano-Scottish topics for decades. My relationship with Professor Keppie goes back to when he was director of my first dig at Bothwellhaugh Roman bathhouse in the 1970s (even earlier if it should count that we briefly shared the same Latin teacher) and he has been an inspiration since. His theories of events at Burnswark and the fate of the IXth Legion have been influential in my thinking and his helpful replies to many queries have been invaluable.

I wish to thank Strat Halliday for walking with me in the Borders hills to explore the nature of cultivation terraces and for opening my eyes to the myriad indigenous Iron Age settlements that dot the landscape of southern Scotland.

I am indebted to Danny Syon of the Israel Antiquities Authority who gave up a considerable portion of his time to introduce me to the archaeological wonders of Roman period Israel. The experience of hearing him read from the *Jewish War* atop the siege ramp of Masada and at Titus' breach in the wall of Gamla sparked a radical realignment of my thinking about the nature of siege warfare and the connectedness of contemporary events.

I wish to thank my children, Simone and Jonathan who have tolerated their father's behaviour for far too long and for allowing me to take them on innumerable Roman excursions, including two memorable expeditions to the West Bank and the Golan. They have not only borne my Roman fixation with fortitude but also openly encouraged it. And here's to you, Scout – for a decade of canine companionship, irrespective of the weather – as you cheerfully accompanied us over ditch and rampart.

My special gratitude goes to my exceptionally understanding wife Erica who has not only put her own projects on hold to allow this one to reach fruition but has also done a masterful job of editing out much superfluous material for which I am sure the reader will be grateful. Her resilient personality, which has propped me up on several occasions, is as solid as the foundation of the broch at the bottom of her family croft on the Isle of Lewis.

Finally, I would like to thank my editor and publisher, Hugh Andrew, for many helpful suggestions and for his own special insights into post-Roman and Early Medieval Scotland, and Andrew Simmons and James Rose at Birlinn for their help in guiding this work to completion.

Image credits

Many thanks are owed to Alan Braby (20, 23, 36b, 43, 55c, 70, 96, 99a & b, frontispiece and p.234) for his atmospheric artwork and to Jan Dunbar (1, 9, 15, 29a & b, 32b, 64, 74, 86) for her high-quality drawings and diagrams. Thanks also go to Margaret Wilson, picture librarian at NMS, and Sarah Dutch at HES archives for helping me source material from their image libraries. The author and publisher would also like to acknowledge thanks for permission to reproduce the following illustrations: AOC archaeology 80; Paul Bidwell 58a; M.C. Bishop 38; Ruth Beusing/RGK 77; Chester Museum (author photo) 32a; Dumfriesshire and Galloway Natural History and Antiquarian Society 41, 65; Christophe Finot, CC BY-SA 3.0 via Wikimedia Commons 31; Gerd Eichmann, CC BY-SA 4.0 via Wikimedia Commons 54; Mark Gerson (© National Portrait Gallery) 46; Hannes Grobe/AWI, CC BY-SA 2.5, via Wikimedia Commons 30; Historic Environment Scotland 19a, 56, 93; Historic Environment Scotland and courtesy of the Society of Antiquaries Scotland, 5, 6, 73b, 75; William Brassey Hole (photograph by Antonia Reeve) courtesy National Galleries of Scotland colour plate 1; LVR LandesMuseum Bonn 101; Pablo Llopis, SERF Project, University of Glasgow 50; Loescher & Petsch via Wikimedia Commons 2; Los Angeles County Museum Image © Museum Associates 104b; Derek McLennan 62; Myrabella via Wikimedia Commons 7a; Image © National Library of Scotland 12, 87; National Museum of Scotland (Images © National Museums Scotland) 36a, 51, 89, 108, and

Introductory note

This book is about early Scotland's contact with the Roman Empire and almost all the events described take place in the Christian era – dates are therefore AD unless otherwise stated. Since the names of areas of North Britain and the peoples who inhabited them were either not defined or were altered considerably during this period, specific titles are used only where possible and generic terms such as Scotland and Caledonians are employed for convenience. The term 'native' (literally meaning a person born in an area) where used, describes an indigenous inhabitant and carries no derogatory connotation.

When describing distances, Roman units of measurement, such as miles or paces, may be employed but wherever appropriate, measurements will be converted to metric units. Surface areas of camps and forts will be quoted in acres rather than hectares owing to the continued use of the former in a substantial body of modern scholarship.

1 Roman mile = 1,000 paces = 5,000 Roman feet
1 Roman mile = 0.92 Statute miles = 1.48km
1 Roman pace = 5 Roman feet = 1.48m
1 Roman foot = 11.65 inches = 296mm

Abbreviations
BAR   British Archaeological Reports
BM   British Museum
HES   Historic Environment Scotland
LiDAR   Light Detection and Ranging
NMS   National Museums Scotland
RGK   Römisch-Germanische Kommission
SAS   Society of Antiquaries of Scotland

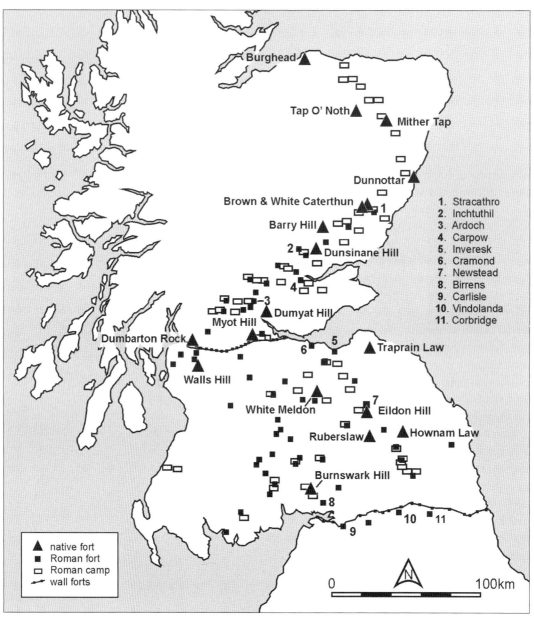

1. Map of Roman Scotland showing Roman military sites and native centres of power.

Legend (within map):

Burghead
Tap O' Noth
Mither Tap
Dunnottar
Brown & White Caterthun
Barry Hill
Dunsinane Hill
Dumyat Hill
Myot Hill
Dumbarton Rock
Walls Hill
Traprain Law
White Meldon
Eildon Hill
Ruberslaw
Hownam Law
Burnswark Hill

1. Stracathro
2. Inchtuthil
3. Ardoch
4. Carpow
5. Inveresk
6. Cramond
7. Newstead
8. Birrens
9. Carlisle
10. Vindolanda
11. Corbridge

▲ native fort
■ Roman fort
□ Roman camp
⌐ wall forts

0   100km

N

Foreword

Many aspects of Roman Scotland remain enigmatic – even the name itself is misleading. The country was never really 'Roman' at all, and certainly not colonised the way England and Wales were. At best, the empire managed to intermittently occupy the land to the south of the Highland Line and at worst, the Romans kept Scotland and its inhabitants at arm's length with, in the end, little attempt at civil development. But for over 300 years the Roman army, the most fearsome fighting force of the ancient world, was regularly pitched northwards, spurred on by imperial will. During this turbulent period at least six high-ranking generals, who either were or would become Roman emperors – literally masters of the ancient world – would take a personal interest in invading or annexing this small country. The onslaught of course was not directed against the landscape, but against the flesh and blood of the indigenous population. So why did the world's first truly intercontinental superpower expend so much time and resource directing its military might at what must have been a comparatively modest group of tribes?

It is not only this broad question of motivation that remains without consensus, but also much of the detail – such as the purpose of the Walls (Antonine and Hadrianic), the reasons for Roman advances and retreats and the causes of other singular events such as the apparent disappearance of the IXth Legion. In recent decades many scholars have proposed a variety of solutions to these conundrums, but modern explanations have a tendency to pacify the past and conflict has played a lesser role in the historical narrative. In contrast, early commentators were in little doubt about the nature of the relationship between Roman and native in the north of Britain. While acknowledging the superiority of Roman arms, authorities such as Mommsen (1885), Macdonald (1934) and Richmond (1955) suggested that the Caledonians and their successors, the Picts, represented a significant military obstacle to the invaders. Such an assumption appeared logical – since the indigenous peoples had been dispossessed of their ancestral lands, why wouldn't they resist? The story of this struggle appeared to be supported by comparatively reliable Roman literary sources such as the

2. Theodor Mommsen
(1817–1903) German historian
and early commentator on the
geopolitics of Roman Scotland.

great historians Tacitus and Dio. The physical evidence of centuries of frontier warfare was also there to see – the extraordinary offensive-defensive
engineering of the Walls of Hadrian and Antoninus Pius with their hinter-
lands bristling with forts and fortlets, which in turn supported a force of
Roman auxiliary soldiers unparalleled in the empire. Scotland also boasted
one of the highest concentrations of campaign camps in the Roman world,
silent testimony to numerous incursions by the Roman army. Now,
however, it is suggested that indigenous hillforts should no longer be seen
as strongholds, but simple farms with little defensive purpose. Multiple
ramparts, both Roman and native, are currently interpreted as status
symbols and formidable Roman frontiers have lost their military function
to be interpreted as imperial vanity projects. Wrecked forts and tumbled
brochs have become a long series of accidents or victims of shoddy renovation – the concept of concerted confrontation has become trivialised.
The warlike Caledonians and Picts whose resistance once precipitated the
wrath of Septimius Severus, have been converted into timid tribesmen,
desperate for imperial largesse, and eager to be 'Romanised'. The indigenous peoples are now represented as irritating cattle rustlers or dazzled
bystanders who looked on in awe as the legions came and went. In the
words of one modern author the northern tribes have been described as:
'an enthusiastic rabble' and 'such military action that did take place . . .
fell into the category . . . of cattle-theft and petty banditry' (Corby 2010).

   Is this perception biased? A book about Roman frontiers (Breeze 1982)
appeared to presage this phenomenon. It suggested that the ultimate insult
to the peoples of North Britain was for them to be written out of history
by others, something that not only had academic portent but also was
loaded with ideological consequence. In his landmark treatise *Ways of
Seeing* (1972), the art historian John Berger pointed out 'a people . . . which
is cut off from its own past is far less free to choose and to act as a people

---

Damnatio memoriae

The Latin term given to the systematic erasure of the records of existence
of an enemy of the state. The Romans believed the ultimate punishment
for opposing the will of Rome was not only to physically chasten an
individual by torture and death (often including the culprit's family) but
also to expunge any historical trace they had ever existed. Graphically
illustrated by the many defaced Roman images or stone inscriptions
from across the empire, *damnatio* was decreed to happen not only to
public records but to private property as well.

... than one able to situate itself in history'. It presented the chilling possibility that what may be happening, accidentally or otherwise, was a modern form of *damnatio memoriae*.

Indeed, it has been argued in a major journal that there are only polarised views of Roman Scotland, dependent on one's personal inclination and that this phenomenon colours all historical and archaeological interpretation: either pro-Roman in which Roman supremacy is always a given,

3. This painted panel – the so-called Berlin Tondo – portrays the Severan royal family. The face of Geta (lower left) has been erased by an act of *damnatio memoriae* ordered by his fratricidal brother Caracalla (lower right).

or pro-Caledonian where the northern tribes present a major threat to Roman interests (Breeze 2014). Unfortunately, this hypothesis invites one to subconsciously adopt a factional position and has the tendency to write off any argument as hopelessly flawed by personal prejudice. Is it possible then to disentangle, as Macaulay put it, the interplay between reason and emotion?

Prejudice aside, over the last half century, the paradigm has undoubtedly shifted from the ebb and flow of Iron Age warfare to one of cold cost-benefit analysis, making it appear that Roman aggression was only checked by the calculation of a poor financial return for the effort involved in annexing a wild and apparently worthless land. This viewpoint, which veers uncomfortably towards inferiorism, is at the very least unhelpfully Romano-centric.

So is there anything new to say? There are numerous scholarly works focused on specific areas of Roman Iron Age archaeology to which I am greatly indebted, and I acknowledge much has already been written about Roman England. However, the recent narrative of Roman Scotland, with a few exceptions, is affected by something of a colonial bias when assessing the impact of the empire on northern peoples and vice versa. A way of viewing the history of North Britain that arguably skews our perception of events by concentrating on details of Roman military process and culture at the expense of a wider synthesis and by diminishing what was likely to have been a prolonged and exceptionally violent period of confrontation. So, for me, there are several reasons to offer a new history of Roman Scotland: to provide a less Roman-centred overview of the period; to share new insights into some particular controversies based on recent discoveries; to challenge some current concepts; and, finally, to make a small contribution to restoring the voice of a lost people from a time and a place that are dear to me.

John H. Reid

CHAPTER ONE

What's in a name?
How we tell the story of Scotland's past

One of the earliest links in classical literature between Scotland and the Roman Empire is a reference to *urso Caledonio*, the Caledonian bear that had been transported to Rome to provide one of the Colosseum's gory entertainments. The no-doubt distressed animal, which was to execute a prisoner bound to a stake, made its literary appearance in *Liber Spectaculorum*, a collection of epigrams produced by the poet Martial. These made reference to 100 days of games given by the Emperor Titus to mark the official opening of the Roman world's largest amphitheatre in the year 80. Martial (40–104), a Spanish provincial who made a precarious living in the capital by associating with rich patrons like the doomed Seneca, recognised the importance of inserting references to remote lands. This vignette, however, reveals more than his grip on geography or Rome's morbid fascination with public bloodletting – it suggests that within a year of the first Roman incursions, the empire was exploiting Scotland's natural resources and that Caledonia had already entered the public consciousness.

Anyone writing today about Caledonia, the Iron Age land we now call Scotland, walks into an etymological minefield. It is easy to forget that before the construction of Hadrian's Wall there was no border and that the concept of Scotland as a single country (which would initially become known as Alba) would not emerge until much later when it was unified under Kenneth MacAlpin in the ninth century.

If consensus for the name of the land is difficult to achieve, agreement on the origin of the people who inhabited it is even more elusive. From the eighteenth century, scholars recognised there was at least a linguistic link between the ancient peoples of north-west Europe and those who still inhabited Scotland. However, their concept of a unified Celtic nation, which encompassed the peoples of the western seaboard of Europe, has been seriously challenged in recent years with some justification – the Romans, for example, never used the term Celt to describe any of the peoples of the British Isles. It is probably more appropriate to see the 'Celts' as Atlantic-facing regional groupings who at some point shared significant cultural

4. A mosaic from a Roman villa at Nennig, Germany, shows *bestiarii* fighting with a bear. The animal has terminally wounded one of its attackers.

and trading crossflow, rather than a unified mass who swarmed out of Central Europe to take refuge on the west coast.

The word Scot is also problematic – the original Scotti, who appeared in Roman literary sources in relation to the 'Barbarian Conspiracy' in the 360s, and from whom the country now takes its name, were fourth-century (or even earlier) Gaelic speaking invader-settlers from Ireland who blended with the other indigenous peoples in the west of Scotland.

Rome itself, certainly initially, considered mainland Britain and its smaller islands a single entity called Britannia. The word seems to have originated via a Greek form *Pritannike* from an ancient term used to describe the island as a whole. This desire for semantic unity was probably partly driven by Roman familiarity with insular geography and partly because successive emperors for the next 300 years considered total subjugation of the whole island as a work in progress. Roman prose and poetry made frequent references to northernmost Britain as Caledonia, particularly when an author, for literary effect, wished to emphasise the area's wildness. As far as we can tell, the Caledonia of the Romans more specifically referred to the country north of the Forth–Clyde isthmus. For ease of use however, this name will occasionally be employed for the whole area north of Hadrian's Wall and for variety, the term North Britain will also be used despite its geographic vagueness and its previous pro-Hanoverian connotations.

From the earliest contact with the peoples of the Mediterranean basin, Caledonia and Caledonians appear to have had a niche in classical geomythology. So how do the relative latecomers, the Picts, fit into this story of proto-Scotland? Although the word Picti was introduced in Latin literary sources from the end of the third century to describe the tribes or confederation of peoples of northern Scotland, there has been considerable speculation about the origin of the word itself with suggested derivations of varying levels of complexity. However, it probably simply represented the slang Latin term for the 'painted ones' alluding to body decoration, possibly tattooing.

To further confound the nomenclature, Roman writers frequently did not differentiate between the ethnic origins of their foes and the subjugated peoples, and often employed the single blanket term 'Britons'. This is not very different from the habit of modern Americans, who when referring to the Scots and Welsh often describe them as English. In the *Agricola*, the modern name given to the work by the Roman historian Tacitus about his father-in-law's life and his campaigns in Scotland, there are eleven direct references to indigenous peoples living north of the Forth–Clyde isthmus. In three, he uses the term 'the inhabitants of Caledonia' but in eight he describes the enemy, i.e. Caledonians, simply as 'the Britons'. Putting aside any cultural sensitivity, it is easy to see why the agent of a superpower would take this casual semantic approach. However, the flexible Roman use of the terms 'Britannia' and 'Briton' has a consequence for interpretation. Modern scholars have occasionally understood 'war in Britannia' to refer to more southerly parts of the island although on the evidence of troop dispositions, Roman writers were likely to be referring to warfare in North Britain. Other specific opportunities for this confusion are: what was inferred by the Roman term *Expeditio Britannica*, the 'British campaign', prosecuted sometime during Hadrian's reign; or the demeaning term *Brittunculi* ('little Britons') used on one of the Vindolanda tablets? Both of the above are equally likely to have referred to the place or peoples of modern Scotland.

Even the term Iron Age is open to interpretation. Broadly speaking, it represents the epoch when iron began to supplant, or be used alongside, bronze, the earlier utilitarian alloy of copper and tin, but the acknowledged timing of this transition is different depending on where in the world it took place. For North Britain, scholars have suggested it extended from approximately 800 BC to the epoch we now call the Early Medieval. More specifically, the period on which this book is primarily focused is the Roman Iron Age, which for Scotland spanned the first 400 years of the first millennium.

Literary sources

Aphorism or not, history is always influenced by zeitgeist and the prejudices of the writer. It is important therefore to acknowledge from the outset that all contemporary literary evidence for Iron Age Britain is derived from a few highly biased Roman sources. Although there is some evidence from inscriptions on indigenous coinage from southern Britain that the tribes there were at least symbolically acquainted with Latin before the Roman invasion, the peoples of North Britain did not use coins and they had no written language. Consequently, none of what would have been their oral history has been preserved to present their view of the Roman occupation.

Apart from works by Tacitus, Cassius Dio and Herodian, little survives of what may have been written by the Romans themselves about Scotland. Most likely this is due to Caledonia's marginal importance to the Roman world, but it must be partly the result of the serendipity by which ancient texts are preserved. All modern translations of the *Agricola*, for example, are derived from a single medieval copy that was sequestered in a German monastery. If it had been lost to the ravages of fire or hungry mice, we would have no detailed references at all. Barbarian destruction, accidental conflagrations and cutbacks in maintenance budgets of the Roman world's fabulous libraries, such as those at Alexandria and Pergamum, have created huge lacunae in our knowledge. The result is, that although several works mention the existence of Caledonia, few other than the *Agricola* and Dio's history of the Emperor Severus, provide any detail of Roman strategy or everyday accounts of the struggles on the north-west frontier. Even Hadrian's visit to Britain in 122, is barely covered in the *Augustan Histories* with only a single sentence making direct reference to the initiation of his Wall, despite it being by far the largest physical manifestation of almost 400 years of Roman rule.

Josephus' history of the First Romano-Jewish War (66–73), another fortunate accident of literary survival, is an exceptional example of this type of historical discordance. He produced a singularly detailed account of the tumultuous events of this period of the Roman occupation of Judea (modern Israel), which is still used extensively by scholars today. And yet, the same interlude to which it pertained, received relatively scant mention by other Roman historians. If Josephus had committed suicide, as his compatriots had urged him to during the siege of Jotapata, and his book had never been written, there would be an even greater gap in our knowledge of how Rome dealt with recalcitrant subjugate peoples.

So how else do we gain further insight into the empire's impact on the indigenous population of Scotland? To supplement the relative paucity of literary sources we must turn to the discipline of archaeology. Although it would seem a logical next step towards our understanding of what life was like for both sides of this clash of cultures it is worth noting that archaeology has occasionally been misused by historians and populists as a means of vindicating their theories or nationalistic viewpoints. The symbiosis between history and archaeology is a natural one and when utilised with care, this marriage of disciplines can be one that is made in heaven. However, to avoid the union from hell, one must be wary of allowing confirmation bias to shape the narrative.

Cognitive bias

As with most disciplines that rely on interpretation of data, archaeology is prone to a number of cognitive and perceptual biases. Confirmation bias is when an observer selectively emphasises data that confirm a particular theory while failing to gather or consider evidence that challenges it. Cognitive dissonance may be thought of as one step higher in the bias hierarchy, where an observer, uncomfortable with the implications of conflicting evidence, develops a variety of excuses or a blind spot for the offending data.

The archaeology of Roman Iron Age Scotland

One definition of the discipline of archaeology is the study of past human culture by the systematic examination of its physical traces. In modern times, this systematic examination is made up of many associated subspecialties which include pottery, coinage and other material cultural analyses, landscape archaeology, aerial photography, geophysics (assessing

5. The 1927 excavations at the Antonine fort of Mumrills near Falkirk.

subterranean structures by non-invasive techniques), dendrochronology (securing dates and climate information from tree-ring analysis) and taphonomy (studying how things decay) to name but a few.

Today, archaeology is perceived as a science that adopts a painstakingly careful approach to investigating sites and artefacts, utilising intricate techniques to produce reliable results. This has not always been so. A significant proportion of the archaeological investigation of Roman Scotland took place in the transitional period between the age of antiquarians (enthusiastic Georgian and Victorian amateurs) and the scientific revolution of the early twentieth century. Antiquarians often record the 'turning over' or 'clearing' of a site, in effect ransacking and plundering it for prominent stonework, inscriptions and pottery, with foremen directing labourers who used picks and shovels rather than trowels, hand brushes and microscopes. Hence many of the early investigations of Roman Scotland, while well-intentioned and energetic, lack detail or accurate recording. The best of this period's publications is crude by modern standards and even Edwardian excavations often overlooked many subtleties such as wooden structures and organic residues.

Allied to archaeology, and important to the story of Roman Scotland, are three other disciplines. The first is epigraphy, a term used to describe the study of inscriptions. The Romans were prodigious inscribers, writing on buildings, altars, memorials, gravestones and milestones – right down to items of equipment and even scraps of pottery. On rare occasions civil or military inscriptions, particularly military diplomas, are discovered which can shed light on a very specific time period, such as the year of the tribunician power of an emperor, making them invaluable for accurate dating of associated objects or sites.

The second is prosopography, which in the context of this history is a technique used to make historical assumptions based on the expected career pathways of groups of Roman military or political personnel. For example, by knowing the average age of promotion of a Roman politician to the governorship of a province, one can use his inscribed curriculum vitae (the posts he held and the military units he commanded), to work backwards to determine the presence or absence of that unit from a theatre of war. Notably, this process has been used in assessing the mysterious movements of the IXth Legion.

Since history is often said to simply consist of a series of battles, the story of Scotland's Iron Age is inextricably bound to the exploits of the Roman army. Consequently, the last of this group of disciplines, conflict archaeology, offers novel insights into the army's interactions with the indigenous population that would otherwise have remained invisible. Employing methods such as large-area prospecting by metal detectors, conflict archaeologists can extrapolate from positional data of battlefield detritus to help them understand the choreography of episodes of warfare. Using these techniques it may be possible to build, for example, an impression of an individual engagement such as at Burnswark Hill, or by locating marching camps, a whole campaign such as the Severan invasion. However, it is more challenging to identify ephemeral events like famine or pestilence that complete the picture of the devastating consequences of what conflict with Rome may have brought to Scotland.

No matter how large the gaps are in our knowledge, there are strong indications from surviving Roman literature and modern archaeology that the land which was to become Scotland was exceedingly turbulent during this period. Combined evidence suggests North Britain remained a thorn in the flesh of Rome for more than 300 years of partial conquest – an incomplete occupation requiring the empire to introduce unique measures and make extraordinary commitments in resources and manpower to keep its northern frontier under control.

It is perhaps equally remarkable that for the last half-century or so, contrarian interpretations of that same evidence have come to the fore, suggesting that Scotland was a backwater to which the Romans were almost indifferent. Syntheses have been framed that propose Rome was almost the sole agency at work, minimising the effect of the empire on the indigen-

6. Sir George Macdonald (1862–1940) gives a characteristic scowl as he looks up from the bottom of a recently excavated ditch at Mumrills.

ous peoples and vice versa. In contrast to the previous narrative of almost continuous warfare, it became fashionable to portray conflict in Caledonia as inconsequential, with much softening of causality, such as 'misguided Roman venture', 'political expediency' or 'imperial vanity'. Theories that, although closely argued, went against the grain of Roman historians themselves. What in the mid-twentieth century caused this shift of emphasis away from an earlier conflict-centred account of Roman Scotland supported by such figures as Curle and Macdonald? Was it personal prejudice or a rejection of militaristic views of history, society and archaeology as a response to the devastating effects of two world wars?

To help explore this, it may be worth considering a possible bias which it has been suggested permeated the twentieth-century study of Roman Britain in its broadest sense – how a significant proportion of effort favoured, until relatively recently, the detailed investigation of the actions of the Roman state alone. Perhaps it is as David Mattingly, Professor of Roman Archaeology in Leicester, succinctly put it in *An Imperial Possession* (2006): 'in pursuing this agenda over the last 100 years or so, archaeologists have consciously or unconsciously implanted a basic sympathy with Rome and its elite culture at the core of Romano-British studies'. Much of the light cast on previous endeavours appears to have been refracted through this Romanocentric prism.

Imperialism and nationalism

Philosophers have asked for centuries if there is such a thing as disinterested enquiry? Regarding those with pro-Roman sympathies, I am inclined to think not, as the hammer tends to regularly seek out the Roman nail. However, the diametrically opposite perspective, where invincible woad-covered freedom fighters engage in guerrilla warfare until the Romans are forcibly expelled at the end of the fourth century, is equally damaging to the integrity of historical understanding. This is particularly true today when xenophobia is again on the rise and where any foreigner is seen as an enemy. Britain is not unique in adopting this conflicted position. France and Germany in the last 300 years have had imperial aspirations of their own, with leaders such as Napoleon borrowing strongly from Roman motifs.

The old European powers saw themselves as natural inheritors of Rome's legacy: Roman things good, barbarian things bad. Post-imperial Paris, London and Berlin are rich in monumental classical architecture. Columns and pediments abound, and Roman symbolism of eagles, standards and laurel wreaths is everywhere. However, in the recent past (from about the 1850s), France and Germany have also experienced a growing historical nationalism. Arminius in Germany and Vercingetorix in France are revered as anti-Roman freedom fighters with the erection of huge statues and considerable investment in systematic establishment-backed archaeology and historiography of these local heroes. In Britain however, Boudicca's stand against Rome (finally and controversially immortalised in bronze by Thomas Thornycroft on the Thames Embankment) presented problems

7a. The 7m-tall statue of
Gaulish resistance fighter,
Vercingetorix, at the site of
Alesia, attacked by Caesar in
52 BC. He was captured,
imprisoned and then ritually
strangled on the Capitoline
Hill in Rome.

b. The statue of Hermann
(Arminius) in heroic pose at
the Teutoburg Forest near
Detmold in Germany. It was
originally thought that the site
of his victory over the Roman
general Varus in AD 9 was near
here.

for Victorian historians and social commentators. Celebration of her bellicose response to Roman oppression caused some embarrassment for those
who were already employing apologetic language for Britain's imperialist
actions in overseas dominions.

Scotland is perhaps particularly guilty of (or to be admired for?) a
neglectful attitude to its own local hero. Nowhere can you find a statue to
Calgacus, immortalised by Tacitus as the leader of the Caledonian forces
at the fateful battle of Mons Graupius in 83. Despite being the first ever
Scot to be named and commemorated as a heroic figure by his Roman
adversaries, he is totally unrecognised by the vast majority of his modern
countrymen. To my knowledge, apart from Calgacus' place in the stunning
processional frieze of William Brassey Hole (1846–1917) in the National
Portrait Gallery in Edinburgh, where he is glared at malevolently by Agricola, there is not a single depiction of Scotland's first folk hero (plate 1).

8. Thornycroft's imposing bronze of Boudicca and her Roman-defiled daughters, riding forth in their chariot on the Embankment in London.

In contrast to this apparent self-inferiorisation, many continental European scholars have been happy to see the Caledonians as a match for the legions and to identify them unequivocally as the principal cause for the imposing scale of Hadrian's Wall and the other traces of prodigious Roman military activity in North Britain. In the 1880s, the venerable German historian, Theodor Mommsen (1817–1903), was firmly convinced that the impressive engineering of the Hadrianic frontier was proportionate for defence 'against the Highlanders of Britain, in whose presence the province was always in a state of siege'.

Time frames

The nomenclature for the episodes of Roman occupation generates its own difficulties. For ease of use and understanding, historians and archaeologists bracket time periods: such as Flavian (69–98) or Antonine (139–92). Although these can be helpful to conceptualise broad sequences, they create artificial boundaries that can stand in the way of a more comprehensive synthesis of events. For example, because of a lack of written sources between the withdrawal of the governor Agricola in 84 until the sketchy details of Hadrian's involvement with the province of Britannia in 122, there appears to be a gap in the record and indeed the archaeology of Scotland. One could be forgiven for thinking that nothing happened in Caledonia at all during the reign of the Emperor Trajan (98–117). Even on the grounds of day-to-day military necessity irrespective of enemy incursions, this simply cannot be the case. Thankfully, the extraordinary information gained from the Vindolanda writing tablets has shone a little light on this dark period. There is an equally large lacuna in our knowledge during the reign of Hadrian (117–138) when it has been implied there was in effect a military moratorium creating a power vacuum north of the new Wall. Is it right to assume that there was complete Roman withdrawal from Scotland lasting for four decades from the end of the first century until the northern advance of Antoninus Pius in 142? It is hard to believe that the Romans, or indeed the Caledonians, were inert for two generations.

And so, to fill these and even larger gaps, it seems the story of Roman Scotland must be unavoidably fashioned from a complex blend of patchy stories bequeathed by ancient writers, mixed liberally with narratives provided by modern archaeology, and seasoned by zeitgeist, cultural politics, ethical judgement and a veneer of personal prejudice. Cognitive biases may seem a modern spin, but as we shall see with regard to Roman Scotland they have a long tradition stretching back to the birth of antiquarian enquiry.

CHAPTER TWO

Lost and found:
the rediscovery of Roman Scotland

Melrose, a small picture-postcard town, nestles beside the River Tweed in the Scottish Borders. Above the burgh, the three Eildon hills rise majestically as a backdrop. Artisan shops, hotels and gourmet restaurants line its fetching Victorian streets – it even boasts its own Cistercian Abbey partially ruined by the forces of Henry VIII. Facing Market Square, and more relevant to this history, lies the Trimontium Museum, the only museum in Scotland dedicated to the Roman Iron Age.

A committed band of volunteers has staffed the museum for over thirty years and each morning, as they switch on the audio-visuals, they prime themselves for newcomers to Scotland's Roman past. 'Did they really get this far north?' is perhaps the most frequently asked question. The enthusiastic docents explain how the Roman army not only battled into the Lowlands, but built strongpoints along the way, including the great fort at Trimontium just outside the town. Taking command of the Forth–Clyde isthmus, the legions then marched northwards up Strathmore skirting the Highlands – the museum's audio-visuals map the invasion with upwardly curving arrows and a long string of forts and camps that penetrate as far north as the Moray Firth (overleaf).

Things, however, have not always been so clear-cut. For centuries the story of Roman Scotland lay lost beneath the soil, opaque to the enquiries of early historians. In the time of Bede (*c.*673–735), the venerable monk of Jarrow, writing only 300 years after the departure of the last Roman official, the facts were already becoming hazy. Soon, the stories behind the Roman walls and camps would become lost in the mists of time.

The early chroniclers

With the awakening of Renaissance enquiry, Britain began to emerge from the blank pages of its own history, and scholars turned their attention to the still visible remains. William Camden's (1551–1623) topographical and historical masterpiece, *Britannia* (1586), a shining example of the energy of the Elizabethan age, was seminal in drawing attention to Rome's rich

9. Schematic of the incremental nature of the Roman invasion that reflects the literary evidence. It is however uncertain how far north some earlier governors reached before the time of Agricola.

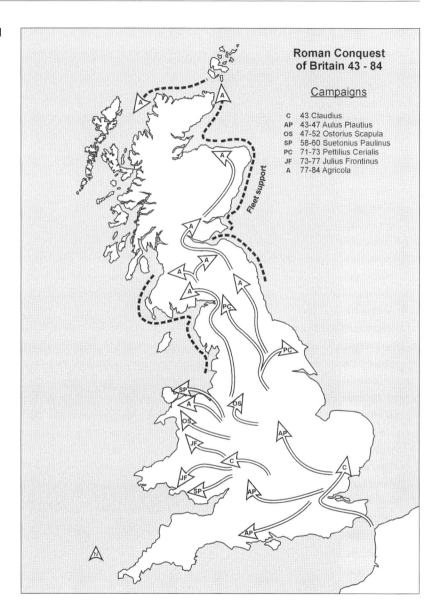

residue. His stated ambition was to 'restore antiquity to Britaine, and Britain to his antiquity', and judging by his book's popularity it struck a chord of antiquarianism that resonated through contemporary academia, encouraging several authors to follow suit.

Camden, however, wasn't the first to be moved by the spirit of historiography – a few Scottish scholars had set out years before to investigate the profusion of military works scattered across the northern landscape. To them, the walls, roads and earthworks were indicative of Rome's considerable preoccupation with Caledonia. One such writer was the chronicler,

John of Fordun (1330–84), an Aberdeenshire cleric, who collated a considerable corpus of Scottish history derived from folklore and earlier scholars.
He listed several wars between the Caledonians and the occupying Roman
forces, most if not all of which were likely to have been invented or embel-
lished by the passage of time. In his principal work, *Chronica Gentis Scoto-
rum* we have the first mention of the Antonine Wall, which he called
Grymisdyke (Graham's Dyke). He indicated this Graham or Gryme was a
Caledonian warrior who had broken through the turf wall as part of an
uprising of the northern peoples. Although much of Fordun's writing has
a fabulous ring to it, the strength of folklore surrounding Gryme is difficult
to dismiss completely, with many places in the Falkirk area still bearing
the local hero's name.

   Stories of resistance, however, are a powerful unifying force and consequently politics never lie far from historiography. A country's history is
rarely untainted by current events, particularly during periods of religious
and political upheaval. Such challenges were to confront the Renaissance
scholars of Scotland.

   As Scotland's pursuit of its own history gathered pace with the rebirth
of intellectual enquiry, early writers and poets busied themselves with laying
the literary foundations that would underpin the notion of a romanticised
Caledonian opposition to Rome. The historian Hector Boece (1465–1536),
who was to become the first principal of Aberdeen University, borrowed
liberally from the work of John of Fordun. He skilfully interwove many
of his predecessor's confabulations with more trustworthy material gleaned
from the recently recovered writings of Tacitus. Although much of his
history concerning Roman Scotland is also considered to be fantastical,
Boece was probably one of the first to correctly ascribe the building of the
Tyne–Solway Wall to Hadrian and also to suggest that Caracalla had later
refurbished it.

   By the time George Buchanan (1506–82), another literary giant and
Latin scholar of the period, became the tutor of James VI he was already
an influential figure with a stellar academic career behind him that stretched
from Paris to St Andrews. One of the most frequently cited examples of
his pro-Caledonian writings was the marriage-poem he dedicated to Mary
Stuart and Francis, Dauphin of France. In it he reflected that Rome 'drove
other peoples from the lands of their ancestors' or condemned them to 'vile
slavery', and the Scots were the only people against whom Rome fortified
its borders with 'walls and ditches'. The Antonine Wall (which he ascribed
erroneously to Septimius Severus) and Arthur's O'on (the remarkably
preserved domed Roman building which stood near Falkirk) feature in
detail in his great history of Scotland – *Rerum Scoticarum Historia* –
published in the year of his death. Later scholars such as the barrister and
politician, James Dalrymple (1619–95), 1st Viscount Stair, were also happy

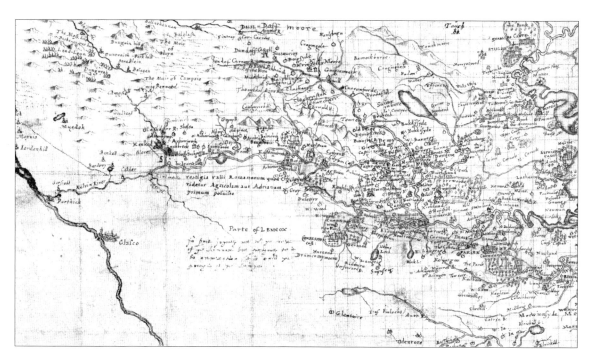

10. Timothy Pont's early 17th-century map displaying the Roman structures on the Forth–Clyde isthmus. The text ascribes the vestigial remains to Agricola or Hadrian.

to fuse ideas of history, religion and the politics of the day. In the preface of his magnum opus concerning the laws of Scotland, he hinted strongly at similarities between the threat of ancient Rome and the dangers posed by the contemporary Roman Catholic Church.

The political atmosphere of Scotland was to become even more highly charged as the Union of the Crowns under James I in 1603 gave way to the more contentious Act of Union in 1707, with its real and perceived loss of sovereignty. Consequently, the seventeenth- and eighteenth-century prism of Scottish history began to project the period of Roman occupation as a spectrum of interactions: from the imperialist vision of a beneficent and civilising foreign power to the more patriotic view of resistance to outside interference and a longing for freedom from an oppressive invader.

However, it was from a more scientific perspective that a man called Timothy Pont (c.1560–c.1614), a Scottish minister by calling and a cartographer and mathematician by inclination, began plotting the positions of the Roman army's structural remains, many of which could still be clearly identified in the Scottish countryside. As a result of what for his day was meticulous fieldwork, Pont produced – with the patronage of King James VI – the first detailed map of Scotland, which included details of the course of the Antonine Wall, 'vestigia valli Romanorum', across the Forth–Clyde isthmus. He is also known to have produced the first plan of the constituent elements of the Antonine Wall, even suggesting there were interval fortlets and signal towers. It is clear from his annotations that he was aware of the close spacing of some of the structures ('within a call one of another') and the construction detail of the Wall base. Pont himself almost became lost to history but by good fortune, a hundred years later, he and his work were, for a time, rescued from obscurity by Robert Sibbald, one of the greatest intellects of the era.

Robert Sibbald

Robert Sibbald (1641–1722) was undoubtedly one of the most important figures in the antiquarian investigation of Roman Scotland. An Edinburgh physician, and by any standards a prodigious polymath, he is credited with playing a leading part in a number of innovations, including the founding of the Royal College of Physicians of Edinburgh, the Royal Botanical Gardens of Edinburgh and the first Chair of Medicine at Edinburgh University. He also produced fine works of natural history and it is claimed he produced the first full description in the English language of the blue whale, which was for a time named 'Sibbald's rorqual' in his honour.

From the number of royal institutions he was associated with, it's not difficult to deduce how he positioned himself in contemporary society and it is also no surprise his productive final years were spent coeval with King George I. Crucially, Sibbald was also appointed Scottish Geographer Royal in 1682, and as an ardent antiquarian, he proved as energetic in his pursuit of the landscape vestiges of the Romans in Scotland as he had been with his other obsessions. He consequently developed a viewpoint that was to be a significant departure from previous pro-Caledonian writers, of attempting to show that early Scotland had been a civilised Roman province. With little actual evidence, his pro-Roman stance enabled him to write: 'By all which is made clear, that the Romans stayed long in the Country: They did introduce Order and Civility wherever they came, and by the Arts and Policy they taught our Ancestors, they tamed their Fierceness, and brought them to affect a civil Life'. Today, we view this concept of the improving nature of Roman colonisation as a somewhat naïve model that is overtly imperialist in its origins. However, it was further developed in the thinking of a succession of more recent historians, probably reaching an apogee in Francis Haverfield's (1860–1919) view of the 'Romanisation' of Britain. Even though Sibbald saw himself as a Scottish patriot and a promoter of the nation's interests, his words can also be seen as an apology for the commercial aspirations of the Georgian state and as a foundational myth of the British Empire which was undergoing aggressive expansion at the time. Although they were of their time and now sound outdated and condescending, one can still find faint echoes of these sentiments in contemporary enquiry and popular belief. Sibbald's objective, to carve out an imperial past for Scotland, has residual energy and it continues to seep into the collective psyche where, as we shall see, it competes with the equally dubious concept of the noble savage.

The Antiquarians

Shortly before Sibbald's death, the great English historian and physician, William Stukeley (1687–1765), also contributed to Romano-Scottish history when he published in 1720 an essay which described the details of Arthur's O'on. He too was greatly impressed by what he saw as the civilising effects of Rome and although he never personally visited Scotland, he populated his vision of the Romanised Lowlands with triumphalist architecture. Sadly, the object of his Scottish treatise, the little temple on the banks of the River Carron, was not to survive the brutal onslaught of Scotland's industrial revolution.

Stukeley was followed by an expanding group of antiquarians interested in Scotland's Roman remains including the young Alexander Gordon (1692–1755) from Aberdeen. Painter, musician, singer and historian, he wrote the notable *Itinerarium Septentrionale* (1726), a major feat of fieldwork and scholarship in which he meticulously catalogued extant Roman sites. Although initially grateful for his predecessor's observations, he became increasingly sceptical of Sibbald's imperialist conclusions, and he went on to deduce that the Roman occupation of Scotland was relatively fleeting and ultimately unsuccessful. In the words of the modern historian Alan Montgomery (2017): 'Gordon's intention was to present Scotland not as a stable and settled Roman province, but rather a war zone, its Roman remains evidence not of civilisation, but of ongoing failed attempts to subdue an indomitable people.' Gordon was also at pains to expose English antiquarians (while diplomatically not naming them) who suggested that the Roman failure to conquer Scotland was due, not to the level of indigenous resistance, but because it was a profitless exercise. Gordon's detailed and relatively accurate compendium of Roman sites in Scotland, became an indispensable reference work for eighteenth- and nineteenth-century students of Roman Scotland, and was the same book immortalised in Sir Walter Scott's novel *The Antiquary*.

The great patron of the youthful Gordon, Sir John Clerk of Penicuik (1676–1755), demonstrated it was possible to maintain a diplomatic foot in both camps by enthusiastically supporting the patriotic work of Gordon, while occasionally espousing unionist and pro-Romanist views. A keen and gifted antiquarian, Sir John managed in his ideological balancing act, to offer a pro-Caledonian face in public, once commenting that the magnitude of Hadrian's Wall was symbolic of Scotland's desire for independence, while in private writing an essay on the Union in which he says: 'the descendants of the Caledonians today should take care not to boast of their resistance

. . . for their refusal of Roman rule means admitting that one's ancestors were barbarian'. However, the essay remained unpublished at the time of his death. Sir John was succeeded in the baronetcy of Penicuik by his son James, who had antiquarian leanings of his own. It was James who provided the only cheering sequel to the sorry story of the destruction of Arthur's O'on by making an exact copy of the building from Gordon's drawings. This he created as a dovecote crowning the stable block of his Palladian mansion at Penicuik House, where it can still be seen to this day.

John Horsley (1685–1732) was an English antiquarian and nonconformist minister, who subscribed to the concept that 'North Britain was worthless' as an explanation for Rome's failure to secure Caledonia. He consequently became one of the unnamed targets of Gordon's invective. Nurtured in Newcastle and educated in Edinburgh, Horsley wrote his famous *Britannia Romana*, which was published posthumously in the year of his death. This book, in three volumes, covered in detail the Roman antiquities of Britain and, notable for its time, the archaeologically attested deployment of individual legions and auxiliary forces and a catalogue of Roman inscriptions and sculpture. He also utilised epigraphy to determine the disposition of Roman troops and place names along the line of Hadrian's Wall ('*per lineam valli*' as he put it). Book III featured a geography of Roman Britain which is remarkably modern in its approach to surviving Roman cartography such as the *Ravenna Cosmography* and the *Peutinger Table*, which contain elements specifically relating to Britain. To Gordon's

11. Sir James Clerk's Georgian reconstruction of Arthur's O'on Roman temple (as a dovecote) atop the stable block of Penicuik House.

annoyance, Horsley had also made some improvements to Gordon's own data.

Paralleling Gordon's life was the notable eighteenth-century Jacobite poet Allan Ramsay (1686–1758) who, as a collector of Scottish folklore, ballads and folk songs, was well placed to put some of the 'resistance' theme into verse. He was however, like his friend Sir John Clerk, more balanced in his approach to Rome, which allowed him to admire the great works of Roman literature, art and architecture while simultaneously rejecting the empire's bellicose interventions in Scotland.

The remainder of the eighteenth and nineteenth centuries saw a growing awareness of the historical and archaeological vestiges of the Roman invasions in Scotland and was populated with men like William Maitland (1693–1757) whose pro-Roman stance allowed him to outrageously suggest that the kilt and bonnet were adapted Roman garments, and that Scots Gaelic contained many residual Latin words. However, all endeavours of this period were not quite as honestly deluded as Maitland's. The mission of rediscovery was to be tainted by the fraudulent activities of two men, one English, the other a highlander.

Charles Julius Bertram and James Macpherson

The first was Charles Julius Bertram (1723–65), an English expatriate living in Denmark. He invented a 'lost' memoir of Agricola, allegedly translated by a fictitious medieval Benedictine monk, Richard of Westminster (conflated with a real monk, Richard of Cirencester), which he published in his *De Situ Britanniae*. Bertram began leaking the fabrication, which included a fake map and an Antonine-style itinerary listing over a hundred previously unknown sites, to Stukely in 1747, who accepted it as genuine and published an abridged version in 1757. It would take another hundred years of scholarship for the deception to be fully uncovered.

The second, more successful, fraudster was James Macpherson (1736–96) who invented the third-century bard *Ossian* and his cycle of epic poems. He gave his creation the persona not of a wild northern barbarian but of a civilised Caledonian living in a fabulous age of noble heroes fighting their Roman foes, and passed his forgery off as a new-found translation of an ancient Gaelic text. Macpherson cleverly managed to restrict references to contemporary Romans or actual historical events sufficiently stylised or vague, allowing him to offer his own interpretations as glosses. It was a successful formula that was eagerly snapped up by those who wanted the best of both worlds: romantic and cultured forebears who also valiantly resisted Rome. Among those who were won over by the heady mix were Thomas Jefferson and Napoleon Bonaparte. Although there were contemporary critics like Samuel Johnson, who instantly suspected subterfuge, there were enough important figures who were at least partially duped, like the esteemed historian Edward Gibbon (1737–94) who fuelled a continued interest in the bard well into the nineteenth century. Although many modern Scots will have no idea of his origins, Ossian the son of Fingal, this romantic figment of Macpherson's imagination, retained an impressive cult following for over a hundred years, inspiring books, operas and artwork.

The Hanoverian generals

A review of antiquarian interest in Roman Scotland would be incomplete without a mention of two military men who contributed significantly to our understanding of the Romans in Caledonia. Generals Melvill and Roy, both of Scottish descent, played supporting roles in the Hanoverian suppression of the northern clans in the wake of the Jacobite rebellion of 1745. One of their previous commanders, Field Marshal George Wade (1673–1748) had famously constructed a network of roads throughout Scotland, which was intended to facilitate rapid troop deployment against the highlanders. Wade's approach to snuffing out resistance was in fact inspired by Roman ideals, going so far as to insert a Latin inscription on his military bridge at Aberfeldy, emphasising that its position lay 250 miles north of Hadrian's Wall.

Although the brutal Hanoverian military response immediately after the Forty-five uprising added in no small way to the already negative attitude of Scots to foreign invaders, the antiquarian inclinations of the two younger officers, Melvill and Roy, were considerably more benign and allowed them to recognise the cultural importance of Rome's rapidly disappearing archaeological legacy.

Captain Robert Melvill (1723–1809), later Lieutenant General Melvill, had fought in Flanders as ensign in the King's Own Scottish Borderers. He is credited with inventing the short smooth-bore cannon, the *carronade*, which was employed so successfully by Nelson's flagship HMS *Victory* at Trafalgar. Ironically the gun was named after the same River Carron that Arthur's O'on had been torn down to dam, thereby providing a ready water supply for the ironworks that produced the cannons. Melvill became an accomplished antiquary in his later years making a study of Roman camps in Scotland and even suggesting the most likely route of Hannibal across the Alps.

It is Major General William Roy (1726–90), born in Carluke in the Scottish Lowlands, whose name is synonymous not only with the introduction of techniques in cartography (triangulation) which led to geodetic mapping and ultimately the creation of the iconic Ordnance Survey, but also with inspired early draughtsmanship of Scotland's Roman remains.

12. The remarkably accurate map of the Roman siegeworks at Burnswark Hill in Dumfriesshire drawn by General Roy and published in 1793 in his *Military Antiquities of the Romans in North Britain* (compare with Fig. 64).

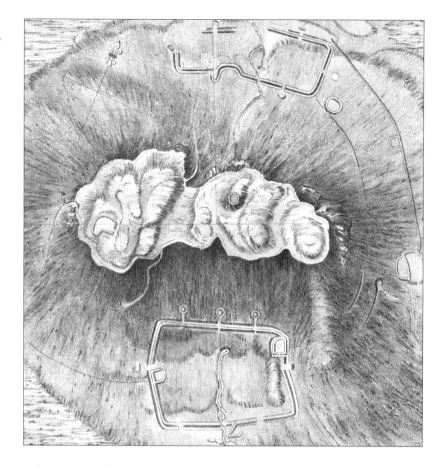

Whenever possible, during his appointment as Surveyor General of Scotland, he made time to record any upstanding Roman fortifications and plot them accurately on his maps. His faithful hand drawings, included in his posthumously published *Military Antiquities of the Romans in North Britain* (1793), were not to be bettered for several generations.

The sages of the Renaissance in Scotland and the Scottish Enlightenment adopted firm and often polarised views of Roman involvement in Caledonia, and it is possible to suggest that many current orthodoxes have their origin in the heyday of the antiquarian. One can also argue that some of what appears to be scholarly debate about Roman Scotland is a surrogate discourse allowing more modern commentators to express their personal opinions of Scotland and the Scots in general. Equally importantly, popular perspectives of this period reflect to some extent how the Scottish people themselves envisage their origins within the history of Europe.

And so, having paid our respects to the masters of Scotland's antiquarian past, it is time to look forward to some of the more recent discoveries that help piece together the narrative of the first 400 years of Caledonia's history.

CHAPTER THREE

Scotland before the Romans

On a miserably wet and windy morning in Peebles, a silver-bearded academic stands before a gathering of over a hundred local history enthusiasts who have braved the elements to learn about their ancestors in the Tweed Valley. Richard Tipping is a self-confessed hybrid: an environmental scientist and an archaeologist. His presentation is convincing in its clarity and scientific authenticity as he expounds on our deep past. He demonstrates by way of pollen profiles and landscape assessments how early peoples exploited Scotland's challenging environment to optimise their chances of survival, and then, when they found a niche, put down long-lasting roots in areas suitable for human habitation. He persuasively argues that attachment to the land is a greater anchor than the attractions of a footloose and nomadic way of life. He points out that superficial survey of this early period of settlement in southern Scotland does not adequately reflect the thriving population he believes lived in the rolling hills between the Highland Line and the Tyne–Solway isthmus. He also tells us that far from the deep dark forests of our imaginings, the landscape was largely cleared for arable farming and pasture. His explanations of the techniques and patterns of ancient agriculture make sense of the abundant lynchets and swathes of improved land that can be found closely related to the traces of Bronze and Iron Age settlements, so generously scattered across the Border hills.

Until relatively recently, these cultivation terraces were seen by some as evidence of medieval improvements produced by population-pressures of the last 500 years, thereby removing any link with the deep past. This freed Iron Age Scotland to be portrayed as if the Romans had burst into a virtually empty landscape, populated by nomadic groups of impoverished natives. This model tangentially supports the colonialist view that the barbarian north depended on the imperial south to channel innovations from the continental classical world and also props up the notion of a beneficent Roman foreign policy. Tipping persuades us otherwise, arguing that the archaeological evidence, which has its roots in the Bronze Age, points to a complex agricultural system with its origins long before the Romans ever left the Mediterranean basin.

Literary sources

Before exploring the archaeology of pre-Roman Scotland, some background descriptions of North Britain's early geography may be gleaned from a small number of classical authors. Mentions of Britain beyond its value as a quasi-mythical place, first began to appear in third-century BC travel writing. Pytheas of Massalia (*c*.350–285 BC), an intrepid Greek explorer from what is now modern-day Marseilles, is reputed to have circumnavigated the island and recorded his observations in a work called *On the Ocean* and despite the book itself not surviving, it is often referred to in antiquity. Details are sparse, and although Pytheas is unlikely to have been sailing single-handed, no information on his travel arrangements has come down to us. He is credited with providing the first account of Britain and describing the meteorological conditions at high latitudes, including the long summer days (an observation referred to repeatedly by subsequent classical authors), and names Orkas as the most northerly point. Pytheas also introduced the place name of Thule, which was said to lie six days' sail to the north of Scotland near the 'frozen ocean'. In recent times, Thule has been tentatively identified with a number of places including Shetland, Norway and Iceland.

Pliny the Elder (23–79) in his encyclopaedic work *Natural History* provides remarkably accurate dimensions for Britannia as a whole and mentions some of its satellite islands including Orkney and the Hebrides. Although he tells us nothing of the indigenous population, he makes this interesting observation: 'it is barely thirty years since any further knowledge of it [Britannia] was gained by the force of Roman arms, and even as yet

OPPOSITE.

13a. An ancient field system merges with more recent rig and furrow around the base of the hillfort at Chatto Craig (left background).

b. Massive cultivation terraces at the foot of the hillfort at Hownam Law in Scottish Borders. These agricultural structures probably had their origins in the Bronze Age.

Orkney

Despite its apparent remoteness and small size, Orkney (*Orcades*) appears to have had a disproportionate prominence in the earliest records, perhaps reflecting something of its under-appreciated importance, highlighted by the emerging archaeology of the area. The king of Orkney, for example, is reputed to have been one of the eleven British kings to pay homage to Emperor Claudius immediately after his invasion of 43. It has been suggested that references to the islands were a device used by Roman writers to define the edge of the known world and to emphasise the reach of Roman power, but a few finds of unusually early Roman material from Orkney hint that its status was greater than the distant geography suggests.

they have not advanced beyond the area of the Caledonian forest'. This segment of text has given scholars food for thought as to when the first Roman advance into Scotland took place. Since it is well recorded that Pliny died in the eruption of Vesuvius in 79, and he probably wrote his *Natural History* in the early 70s, it would suggest that Roman forays had been made into the far north significantly in advance of Agricola's governorship which commenced in 77.

The direct references to Scotland made by Tacitus, Cassius Dio and Herodian will be considered in later chapters but suffice it to say here that North Britain's inhabitants were subjected to the standard Roman descriptions of 'barbarian' peoples with the expected allusions to nakedness, skin decoration, fabled fierceness and lack of civil development. It is interesting to note in passing that Tacitus suggests that prevalence of red hair and large physiques among Caledonians and Germans reflected a common ancestry.

Another important figure in the early description of Caledonia was Claudius Ptolemy (*c.*100–*c.*170) a Graeco-Egyptian polymath working in Alexandria in the first half of the second century. He contributed to many areas of science including optics, music and cosmology – his *Almagest* for example influenced the field of astronomy for over a thousand years. But it was his accomplishment as a geographer that has contributed most to our understanding of the ethnography of Scotland in the Roman Iron Age. As part of a much larger work, Ptolemy gathered data (presumably acquired from old Flavian military sources) with which he populated the earliest known survey of Britain. He himself did not draw the map but bequeathed coordinates which were transformed in the Middle Ages to the illustration

---

Who were the barbarians?

The word βαρβαρος, 'barbaros', was originally coined by the Greeks to describe anyone who did not speak Greek – the word is said to be onomatopoeic for the 'bahrbahr' sound of the guttural speech of non-Greeks. The term quickly assumed pejorative connotations, and the Romans expanded the meaning to apply to anyone who was a 'foreigner' and 'uncivilised'. In literary works, Romans could occasionally equate barbarian with the ideal of the 'noble savage' – Tacitus' generally positive view to the Caledonians in the *Agricola* is a good example. It is nevertheless predictable, based on examples from more modern frontiers, that on the margins of the Roman Empire – where civil law gave way to harsher military rule – the general treatment of barbarians had the potential to be exceptionally unpleasant.

we are familiar with today. He also provided coordinates for a list of proper names, a mix of peoples and places, many of which we hear of for the first and last time.

One of the most striking visual features of Ptolemy's map is how North Britain above the Tyne–Solway line is rotated right through almost 90 degrees. There are several theories for this vertiginous stoop including: a classical scientific unwillingness to accept that life could exist above 60 degrees north; Ptolemy's most northerly coordinates being derived from a single erroneous observation made at sea; scribal error; and deliberate deception. It is interesting to note that on his larger map Denmark is similarly tilted suggesting there is an inherent fault in the coordinates calculated at higher latitudes.

While over twenty Scottish tribes were named at the time the data was collected, probably in the late first century, subsequent writers significantly reduced that number to three or four with only the Caledonians being common to earlier and later works. Ultimately the names in Roman sources were reduced to the Maeatae and Caledonians, and eventually only the Picts and Scots. It has been convincingly argued that this consolidation of Scottish tribes over a considerable period was a stress response to the prox-

14. The 'Dying Gaul', a Roman marble copy of a Hellenistic bronze, which is now displayed in the Capitoline Museum in Rome. The courageous way he accepts his fatal wounds, his nakedness, his neck torc and his Celtic hairstyle typify the romanticised barbarian warrior.

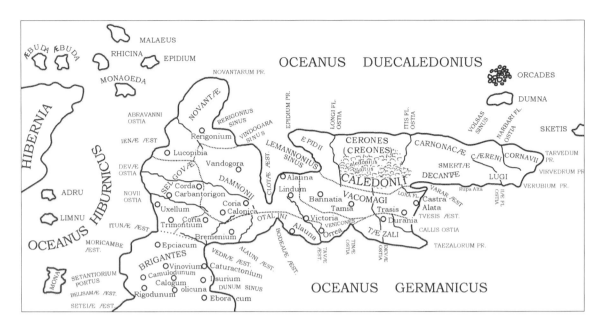

15. A map of northern Britain reconstructed from Ptolemy's coordinates – these identify various places and peoples that may have been familiar to Roman troops.

imity of Roman power with the same explanation being advanced for a similar coalescence of tribal units in free Germany.

'Celtic cowboys'?

Whatever the true name and number of the indigenous tribes, it is clear that prior to the Roman invasion there were thriving communities distributed throughout most of the accessible areas of Scotland. Aerial imaging has revealed extensive field systems, large annexes and probable stock corrals around many hillforts and enclosed farmsteads that point to a firmly anchored society dependent on a mainly mixed farming economy.

These signs of a fixed population go some way to refute the concept of the 'Celtic Cowboy' first put forward in the 1950s by Stuart Piggott (1958) whose dominant influence on Scottish archaeology ensured its currency for decades. His conviction that the south of Britain was a bucolic haven while the north was populated by rambunctious nomadic tribes who lived a hand-to-mouth existence, may have been more to do with his distaste of the Highlands and love of Wessex than the observable evidence (Sharples 1996).

Perceptions and archaeology of the indigenous peoples

It could be argued that compared with the situation on the Continent, the status of the peoples of early Scotland could be improved in the popular imagination. This is especially true when undertaking major heritage pro-

jects. The presentation of the Roman frontier across the Forth–Clyde isthmus serves as a good example of how one perspective can come to dominate the narrative. Since its inscription as a World Heritage site in 2008, significant energy has been directed at raising awareness of the Antonine Wall as a major monument. The multi-agency 'Rediscovering the Antonine Wall Project' has been successful in winning grants for community engagement ventures and has systematically upgraded information panels and delivered several public-facing initiatives, such as creating Roman-themed play parks and recreating Roman military sculpture in public places.

However, the culturally important content and overarching symbolism could be viewed as decidedly Romanocentric. The project website sets the tone: 'Imagine what life was like for the Romans posted on this remote frontier?' and 'Built by the Romans . . . to mark the north-west frontier of their empire, the Wall was a mighty symbol of their power and authority.' On one of the new information boards near the fort on Croy Hill can be found a quotation from W.H. Auden's 'Roman Wall Blues'. Originally written about a soldier on Hadrian's Wall, it is used here to sympathise with a hapless auxiliary stationed in such a miserable place: 'I've lice in my tunic and a cold in my nose.'

The project succeeds well in portraying a vivid depiction of life on the Wall from a Roman military perspective, and it punctuates the line of the

16. Woden Law hillfort high in the Cheviots. The concentric rings of defensive ditches are themselves surrounded by what may have been extensive cattle stockades.

frontier with a number of interesting artworks. The overall message, however, is one-sided. 'The biggest, most awe-inspiring building project the people of Scotland had ever seen' is unlikely to have been among the initial reactions of the people whose land this leviathan sliced in half. It could be argued that the initiative may have benefited from more sensitive consideration of the effects of aggressive invasion, population displacement or trauma for those who originally lived in the occupied territories. Nor is this phenomenon unique to the Antonine Wall: few information panels throughout the length of Hadrian's Wall attempt to say anything about its consequences for the indigenous population.

There continues then, to be something of an antiquarian hangover that sees Rome as a protecting force, a view probably borrowed from an age when Britain aspired to be a benevolent empire. There is also a subtext of Roman frontier soldiers being prime movers in what is often portrayed as a cultural goodwill exercise, coupled with a distracting emphasis on the minutiae of Roman military infrastructure. The consequence of this is eloquently summed up by Dennis Harding, Emeritus Abercromby Professor of Archaeology at Edinburgh University, in his book *The Iron Age in Northern Britain* (2004): 'It is as if recent historians were to study the Berlin Wall on the basis of its construction and design, its checkpoints and watchtowers, without reference to the daily trials of a divided community or the personal tragedies of those who vainly tried to escape.'

It would however be wrong to suggest that historians and archaeologists have ignored the indigenous Iron Age culture of Scotland. Some later twentieth-century scholars eschewed the lure of rich Roman sites with their copious finds and focused on more challenging native settlements within the 'contact zone'. The legendary figures of Peggy Piggott and George Jobey who championed the numerous Iron Age sites of the Borders and the Cheviot massif in the 1950s and 1960s are a good place to start. Although some critics have suggested they may have been unduly influenced by more southerly models or outdated concepts of *Pax Romana*, they did bring this less glamorous group of sites from 'between the Walls' to academic and public attention.

They were succeeded by later figures such as MacKie in the 1970s with his interest in Lowland brochs resulting in the important dig at Leckie near Stirling (1982, 2016). The near-complete excavation of the hillfort at Broxmouth in East Lothian by Hill in the late 1970s, has now been published by Armit and colleagues (2013), with C-14 results filling a much-needed gap in the dating evidence. It has broadened our understanding of the longevity of such sites in North Britain and adds further weight to counter the suggestion that Scottish hillforts were abandoned by the time of the Roman invasion. Excavations at Birnie (Hunter 2008) and Traprain Law (following seminal Traprain investigations by Curle in the 1920s and Bersu

17. The left-hand panel of the sculpture found at Bridgeness at the eastern end of the Antonine Wall. Although something of a Roman sculptural trope, the messaging is unambiguous.

in the 1940s), and the research by Macinnes (1984, 2020) and Campbell (2016) has investigated the uptake – or otherwise – of alien material culture to help shed more light on the impact of Rome. Results are also still coming in from Glasgow University's SERF Project (Strathearn Environs and Royal Forteviot) and AOC's work at Black Loch of Myrton (an Iron Age loch village in Dumfries and Galloway), which continue to supplement our wider understanding of the indigenous peoples. The natural continuum into the Early Medieval period has also been embraced by several investigators including the wide-ranging evaluations by the Alcocks in the 1980s augmented by Carver's investigations (2008) at Portmahomack in the early 2000s and the current work on the northern Picts led by Noble (2019).

The results of all these endeavours, topped by Toolis's recent review (2021) of the culture of first millennium Scotland, show that Iron Age North Britain had a thriving population within a developed society that seemed to be largely independent of southern influence. The message is that the peoples of Caledonia were present in the landscape in all their unique complexity well before the Romans – they just take a little more effort to find.

Settlement patterns

At the time of the Roman invasion, a few broad groupings of native peoples can be defined by the geographical distribution of their architecture, while acknowledging significant overlap of site types – loch dwellings for example are found in the Lowlands, the south-west and the Western Isles, and hill-forts, so prevalent in the south-east, extend into the north-east and south-west.

These architectural styles make sense when seen in the context of their landscape and available natural resources. Neal Ascherson, in *Stone Voices* (2002), his lyrical journey through Scottish history, crystallises the harsh realities of Scotland's geography: 'The land eventually named Scotland was always in some sense a poor country, in that geology and climate put tight limits on the size of the population and its standard of living.' The slender tracts of farmland in the north-west gave rise to smaller clan-based groups and restricted dun-style architecture while the wider more arable straths of the south and south-east favoured larger communities capable of creating major settlements of roundhouses within monumental hillforts.

Although the word 'dun' when prefixed in a Gaelic place name means

18. Approximate distribution (with some significant outliers) of indigenous settlement architecture. The pattern probably reflects a combination of natural resources and local political arrangements.

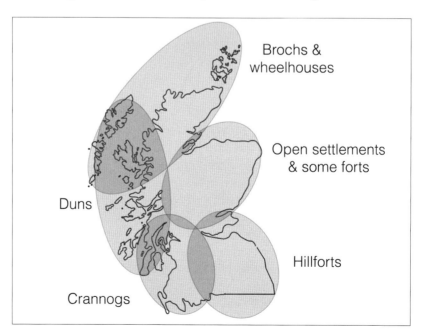

just about any kind of ancient 'fortified site' (Dundee, for example), architecturally the term refers to a small low-level drystone-walled fortification, usually found on a knoll or promontory. Although duns are common on the Atlantic-facing aspects of Scotland, they are in other respects indistinguishable from other compact stone-walled hillforts.

The peoples of the Northern Isles and the Atlantic coastal areas were generally represented by what is sometimes called the Atlantic roundhouse culture, their architecture dominated by drystone roundhouses which were up to 10m in diameter, most often found in village-type settings but occasionally solitary. Incorrectly characterised as simple dwellings, they eventually evolved into intricate structures, possibly two storeys high, with their interiors compartmentalised by radial internal walling, a form typified by the wheelhouses of the Western Isles. The evolution of these structures took many centuries and wheelhouses were still in use well into the first millennium.

The more complex derivative of the Atlantic roundhouse is the multi-storey broch. Built without mortar, these spectacular towers are among the tallest surviving drystone constructions in the world and are unique to Scotland. They are a predominantly northern phenomenon with concentrations in the Northern and Western Isles and in the north-east, particularly Caithness (plate 2).

Brochs usually have a set of distinctive architectural elements that include featureless external walls, low main doorways with guard chambers and internal stairways which, turning in a clockwise direction, rise within the thickness of the hollow walls. These common defensive characteristics and their frequent situation in ditched enclosures suggest they were constructed primarily for security. However, like the medieval towers of Tuscany, their variability in size, height and visibility suggests an element of display by a people who were culturally linked in some way. Some brochs occur in isolation with virtually no outbuildings, while others are found at the centre of a nucleated settlement where the broch is almost surrounded by a cellular village. The more unusual and violent history of the small number of architecturally similar Lowland brochs, whose foundations seem to postdate the first Roman incursion, will be considered later (plate 10).

Crannogs, the freestanding loch dwellings built on log piles, are located predominantly in the west of Scotland and Ireland and the more Atlantic facing areas of the Lowlands, particularly Dumfries and Galloway and Ayrshire, with a further prominent cluster in Perthshire. Within the crannog style can be found a subtype of stone-built island dun particularly in the Western Isles, presumably because of the large numbers of small lochs and the relative scarcity of timber.

Crannogs demonstrate distinctive woodworking techniques and represent one of the few examples of early construction in Scotland where suffi-

19a. Vertical view of a
wheelhouse at Grimsay on
Uist. Note the spoke-like
supporting walls and the
cellular living spaces.

b. Broch village at Gurness on
Orkney. There is extensive
surrounding settlement and
multiple defensive ditches.

cient organic material survives to reveal the skill and artistry of elaborate
craftsmanship. Recalling what has been said earlier about conscious or
subconscious Romanocentricity, it is not surprising that this indigenous
carpentry was previously identified, like the adoption of rectangular buildings, as another example of Roman influence. However, we now know
from radiocarbon dating that both styles considerably pre-date the Roman
invasion of Britain.

Hillforts are found throughout Scotland but those with multiple concentric rings of ditches and ramparts predominate in the south-east, which has
one of the highest concentrations of hillforts anywhere in Europe. Many

20. Reconstruction of what a crannog may have looked like. Probably sited on lochs and inlets for defensive purposes – although it is worth noting that midges (more prevalent in the west) avoid travelling far from the bank!

of these were founded in the Bronze Age on suitable hilltops, promontories, ridges and knolls. Fort ramparts, which could be impressive drystone walls or simple but robust dumped-earth constructions topped by a palisade, offered protection to a variable number of large roundhouses built on scooped platforms. Many hillforts are relatively small and represent what may be thought of as defended farmsteads built to shelter extended family groups, but in several large forts like Hownam Law in the Scottish Borders, traces of hundreds of these hut platforms can still be seen under favourable conditions.

It is often said that the hillforts of Britain were mostly abandoned by the time of the Roman conquest but in North Britain archaeology appears to suggest the opposite. Results from virtually all the hillfort sites in Scotland that have undergone modern excavation point to continuous occupation at least until the early years of the invasion. The overlapping radiocarbon dates at Broxmouth underscore Tipping's comments about the strong attachment early peoples had to place and land.

Oppidum, the generic word used by the Romans to denote a tribal 'capital', could be used to describe at least four of the largest hillforts in southern Scotland: Eildon Hill North and Hownam Law in the Borders (40 and 20 acres respectively), Burnswark Hill in Dumfriesshire (17 acres) and Traprain Law in East Lothian (40 acres). There is good literary evidence from Caesar's campaigns on the Continent, that these *oppida* represented key objectives for the Roman army. Controlling them by force or diplomacy was a primary requirement when a new territory was annexed. The former was probably the case where Eildon Hill North and Burnswark were concerned – the aggressive juxtaposition of the Roman fortress of Trimontium, one of the largest and best defended forts in Scotland is a good

21a. Chesters hillfort near
Drem in East Lothian. Multiple
layers of defences are well
preserved, as are the
foundations of the
roundhouses in the nucleus of
the fort.

b. One of the largest hillforts in
North Britain, Eildon Hill
North is encompassed by
massive lines of defence. The
'dimples' in the interior are all
that remain of nearly 500
scooped platforms for
roundhouses.

example of the Roman proclivity for establishing impressive strongholds
adjacent to centres of indigenous power. Burnswark is an even more
extreme case that will be considered in a later chapter.

The converse appears to be the situation at Traprain Law, where there
is plentiful evidence from hilltop excavations that the indigenous people
were engaged in commerce with the occupying forces. To date, not a single

Roman military installation, permanent or temporary, has been identified in the whole of the fertile East Lothian plain pointing to the local tribe, the Votadini, being a client kingdom. Judging by the wide chronology of the material assemblage at Traprain, this symbiosis, which is so far unique in Scotland, was to last for virtually the whole of the Roman occupation.

There are several shortcomings with the above generalisations about the distribution patterns of the indigenous societies of Iron Age Scotland, not least because of the natural tendency to investigate and describe upstanding structures. It is becoming increasingly clear that the landscape was significantly more densely populated, as shown for example by the cropmark surveys of East Lothian and the Northumberland Coastal Plain. These reveal a myriad of archaeologically ephemeral habitations confirming that much if not most of the population was widely dispersed between the larger defended settlements.

There is also a problem in terms of assessing social hierarchy. In less wealthy societies that had no means of mass production and relatively little durable material culture, any residual artefacts or 'monumental' buildings probably reflect a social elite, which in themselves create a biased narrative. If one tried to paint an ethnographic picture of the people of modern Scotland by looking only at the structure and contents of Premier League footballer's homes for example, it would provide a very skewed impression of what society was like.

There are other glaring gulfs in our knowledge. How was tribal society governed? Do high numbers of defended settlements indicate that intertribal warfare was endemic? Did the Roman invasion precipitate unified resistance or was there opportunistic compliance? What traditions did the tribes possess, who were their gods and what did they think of the afterlife? The latter point highlights a particular problem for our understanding of Iron Age Scotland – the rarity of indigenous funerary structures and associated grave goods. This is a significant disadvantage since mortuary paraphernalia provide much of our knowledge of other ancient civilisations who otherwise have left no literary sources. Most of what we know about the Etruscans, for example, the great pre-Roman culture which arose in ninth century BC in what is modern day Tuscany, comes from their funerary remains. The Etruscans left virtually no written records and almost everything important we know about them is derived from the study of the contents of their cemeteries.

It is clear from the relatively small number of intact Iron Age graves which have been located so far in Scotland that there was little if any Roman material being placed with the indigenous dead to accompany them to the afterlife. This contrasts with the rich burials from even pre-invasion southern England that frequently contain Roman luxury goods. The absence of Roman grave goods in pre-Roman Scotland tellingly carries

22. Circular tombs and exotic grave goods – here at Cerveteri, 50km north of Rome – are the enigmatic remains of the great Etruscan civilisation. No written history has survived to supplement the archaeology.

over into the period of the occupation.

Status envy?

As highlighted above, Roman artefacts found on indigenous sites in Scotland (apart from caches of coins and occasional solitary high value objects which may be seen as diplomatic gifts to purchase armistices) are at best fragmentary. Exhaustive surveys by Wilson (2010) and Campbell (2011) independently suggest that the everyday material culture of Rome, even in relation to the universal preoccupations of feasting and adornment, was either made difficult to access or actively spurned, Traprain being the notable exception. Most lower-status native sites have no significant Roman material at all, with a few having only tiny pieces of pottery or glass such as thumbnail-sized fragments of red samian ware, so carefully curated almost to have a talismanic significance. Peggy Piggott's landmark excavations in the Scottish Borders at Hownam Rings (1948) for example, uncovered only minuscule fragments of Roman pottery, so nondescript they could not be illustrated in her reports. Even at Burnswark Hill, which is within a day's walk from the Hadrianic frontier, Jobey's excavations (1978) uncovered only small segments of Roman ceramics, many of which were so worn they proved difficult to date. 'Normal' indigenous sites in Caledonia are also devoid of signs of everyday use of Roman coins – such hoards that have been found are compatible with high-level targeted Roman diplomacy or bribery. The occasional metalwork cache, such as the Ruber-

23. A reconstruction of the Roman bronzewear hoard found by Victorian ditch diggers close to the summit of Ruberslaw hillfort near Hawick. The two scabbard fixings hint at a military origin.

slaw hoard of Roman pans and sword accessories, may just as easily be interpreted as war booty, loot or a Roman cultic offering.

This lack of evidence of commonplace material crossflow, which Wilson (2010) suggests may represent 'a positive rejection of all things Roman', does little to counter persistent assertions that trade was a feature of cross-frontier Roman–native interaction. Trade of what, and with whom? Comparison with other areas of the empire indicates that the opposite was true. The relative paucity of Roman finds from Scotland stands in stark contrast to the rich Roman material culture found in comparable zones north of other Roman frontiers, such as in Germany, reflecting negatively on the relationships in North Britain. Material envy, however, continues to be invoked as a driver in theories that portray the Walls as customs controls, keeping aspiring immigrants out, rather than representing deterrents to significant military threat.

Funerary practices

As indicated above, we can be certain that in Iron Age Scotland there was a substantial population who required some form of postmortem ritual, but we can only speculate how the bodies were disposed of and how past lives were commemorated. Did the indigenous peoples of Scotland practise excarnation by exposing the deceased on platforms for wild birds and animals to consume? Or was the corpse deposited on a mountainside to be scavenged by vultures like the Tibetan sky burial practice? Perhaps the

predilection for carrion by the sea eagle, a large native bird closely related
to the vulture and recently reintroduced to Scotland, came in useful in
coastal areas, creating unusual artefact assemblages like those found in the
Tomb of the Eagles in Orkney?

The scarcity of complete inhumations from Scotland's Iron Age is problematic, but with respect to disarticulated body parts, there is a relative
abundance. Not infrequently archaeologists encounter segments of human
remains buried, apparently without ceremony, in and around settlements.
For example, at Broxmouth, Armit highlighted that despite the presence
of a small 'cemetery' outside the fort, a considerable quantity of fragmentary
human skeletal material was deposited across the interior of the site, some
of it in what appeared to be random domestic contexts. These finds have
a fascinating variety of possible explanations ranging from war-trophies,
executions, residual excarnations and cannibalism. At some sites, body
fragments are common in the foundations of roundhouses suggesting a
possible sacrificial origin, such as the butchered twelve-year-old boy found
distributed among four pits below an Iron Age roundhouse at Hornish in
the Outer Hebrides. Complex belief systems now completely lost to us,
almost certainly had a strong part to play in these activities that appear so
macabre to the modern eye.

We also know that in common with other Celtic nations, some ritual
significance was associated with the human head. Stone representations
have been found in archaeological contexts in Scotland and complete or
partially dismantled skulls have been found on many native sites, often
accompanied by other selected body parts. Armit (2012) and others have
highlighted that head-hunting was practised not only by barbarians but by
the agents of Rome itself as depictions on Trajan's Column graphically
demonstrate. When James Curle (1911) excavated Newstead, enough
disconnected crania or parts of skulls were found in the pits and ditches of
the fort to suggest that the Roman practice of decapitation and display was
commonplace. Gruesome as it is Armit also reminds us, by citing several
close modern parallels, that such rituals are not confined to the distant
past.

Universal motivators?

The prevalence of ditches and ramparts, the Iron Age equivalents of razor
wire, suggests a concern for security in a society where some level of warfare
must have been endemic and defence considered a prerequisite. Tacitus,
Herodian and Cassius Dio all describe the ferocity of northern tribes,
despite attempts by modern authors to diminish their military reputation.
Later history tells us that inter-clan violence was likely to have been a
constant and it comes as no surprise to learn from Tacitus that warring

24. A Roman auxiliary wearing mail armour uses his mouth to carry a trophy head by the hair in this vignette from Trajan's Column.

factionalism was one of the reasons for early Roman success in Britannia (*Agricola*:12). Defensive architecture aside, it is, however, difficult to prove by direct archaeological means that Iron Age Scotland could be a potentially dangerous place even for the indigenous population let alone unpopular intruders. Methods including osteology have been successful in exemplifying and quantifying endemic violence in other early societies but the absence of skeletally intact inhumations from Iron Age Scotland has so far hampered this approach.

A current archaeological trend, which views defensive works primarily as symbols of prestige (e.g. Hill 1995), possibly overplays this interpretation and may unduly pacify the past. As an alternative approach, it may be useful to introduce the concept of 'hierarchy of need' that can offer a helpful framework to allow us to evaluate the incentives behind the architectural features and artefactual assemblages. This concept, first put forward by the psychologist Abraham Maslow (1943) as a model of human motivation, may be adapted for archaeological interpretation, and provides an alternative perspective for why we should not see prestige and display as immediate priorities.

But whatever the level of aggression of Iron Age Scotland's inhabitants in time of war, they certainly weren't naked savages living a primitive existence as portrayed by Strabo and Herodian. One way of evidencing this is to focus on a few of the durable residues of their society such as bronze utensils or jewellery which confirm a highly developed sense of cultural identity. The design and craftsmanship of individual pieces demonstrate a

25. Maslow's 'hierarchy of need' (left) as it might be applied to certain archaeological phenomena (right). In this framework, security and physiological imperatives take precedent.

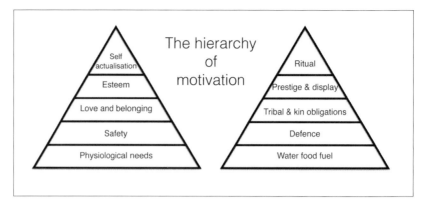

clear familiarity with art forms and an expertise with high-level metalworking, and it is noticeable how many of the larger indigenous sites in Scotland show traces of metal production in one form or another. Metalwork in terms of personal adornment also reveals early Scotland's connectedness to the rest of Britain and the Continent. Items such as the gold torc terminal from Netherurd and the group of torcs from Blair Drummond speak to the long-distance connections of Caledonia's elite with their far-flung counterparts (plate 3).

And so archaeology continues to slowly reveal how northern society was flourishing and getting on with the business of inter-clan politics in the first millennium, even if contact with the south was patchy and so-called luxury goods were in relatively limited supply. The coming of the Roman army was about to change all that.

CHAPTER FOUR

The gathering storm:
a warning from the East

The aromatic air is still as I walk alone through the security gate and wend my way up the dusty road towards the base of the hill which looms massively in the new-moon darkness. It is almost midnight, and it is still over 25 degrees Celsius, but at 1 mile below sea level, the heat radiating from the rocks around the hostel is dry and comfortable. I am taking a private moment to consider the following day's activities when I will fulfil a childhood dream, preparing to behold a sight I have seen in my mind's eye for nearly fifty years. For on the summit of the great rock of Masada which rises before me, stand the awe-inspiring remains of a stronghold with no ordinary history. The gravity defying fortress-palace of Herod the Great, clinging dizzyingly to the cliffs, witnessed the final episode of an insurrection against Rome that had spanned eight bloody years. We are told that 960 Zealots, including their families, had overpowered the token garrison in late 73 and taken refuge on the summit: their vain hope to fan flames of support from the embers of the First Jewish Revolt. But the governor Vespasian and his son Titus had already ruthlessly quashed the rebellion, and help would never come. As the massive Roman siege ramp inexorably rose to penetrate their refuge, the Zealots would deny their tormentors the ultimate humiliation and take their own lives, to the last man, woman and child in a final act of defiance.

So why is this sun-bleached, blood-drenched mountain, towering over the Dead Sea at the other end of the empire, at all relevant to the story of Scotland's Iron Age? The reasons are simple and threefold. Firstly, the above-mentioned Titus, Vespasian's son and heir, was the same Titus who authorised the first Roman invasion of Caledonia less than a decade after he had crushed this uprising in Judea. Secondly, it permits an introduction to Flavius Josephus, the legendary Jewish historian who, as a combatant on the losing side (and subsequent defector) chronicled the First Jewish War at very close quarters. As one of the very few non-Roman scholars able to provide an articulate and vivid first-hand account of what it was like to be on the other side of the Roman military machine, his testimony is invaluable. And thirdly, it lays a foundation that helps us understand the

26. The great Roman siege ramp rises up to the western rampart of Masada.

tactics of another confrontation linking Palestine to far-off Caledonia sixty years later.

In modern descriptions of the Roman occupation of North Britain, relatively little attention is paid to what might be loosely termed Roman foreign policy. This perhaps conceals a little awkwardness among some scholars to admit to what the Romans may have done *to* us rather than *for* us. Which seems a missed opportunity since a work like the *Jewish War* provides a unique insight into a whole catalogue of common themes of Roman–native interaction in an empire celebrated for the uniformity of its infrastructural systems – systems that allowed personnel, materiel and standard procedures to be applied consistently across great distances.

Roman expansionism

Before considering Josephus in more detail, it may be helpful to explore some general questions about the nature of Rome's aggressive incursions into new territories. Was there, for example, a unifying geopolitical strategy

for imperial growth or was it simply an opportunistic, state-by-state acquisition at the whimsy of each emperor? Much scholarship has gone into this
debate and although the matter is not yet settled in academic circles, it
would seem that the latter was more likely. Was there also a more deep-
rooted idealogical or spiritual motivation – *'imperium sine fine'* ('empire
without end') as Virgil styled it in the *Aeneid*? This fundamental belief,
which amounted to divinely sanctioned expansionism, was explicit in
Tacitus' polemic in the *Agricola*: Rome was intent on acquisition for acquisition's sake, irrespective of the size of the prize. This may have been a
significant contributing factor for why successive emperors considered
North Britain unfinished business despite the baffling lack of immediate
financial benefit. Retaliation for perceived threats to Roman sovereignty
of neighbouring states was another useful *casus belli* and could provide
emperors with a quick war and subsequent victory to bolster their legitimacy – the concept of 'if there is trouble at home start a war abroad'
remains a potent weapon in the arsenal of tyrants even today. Finally, even
a lean country like Scotland might eventually produce a small but positive
tax base and will have had some natural resources worth coveting. Slaves,
minerals, hunting dogs, comestibles – particularly beef cattle and cereals

Josephus

Flavius Josephus (37–100) was a Jewish aristocrat who serendipitously
found himself in command of rebel forces in Galilee at the beginning of
the First Jewish War (66–73). He had been schooled in the three traditional philosophies of Judaism and was also an articulate chronicler of
the period, but he was no soldier. He narrowly escaped mass suicide at
the end of the siege of Jotapata and controversially resolved to change
sides and join Roman forces against the rebels. He also cemented his
relationship with the Flavian dynasty by presciently prophesying that
Vespasian (who had been only one of a number of legates vying to
succeed Nero during the dying days of his reign) would ultimately
become emperor and founder of the Flavian dynasty. Josephus provided,
among other things, a uniquely detailed account of how the Roman
army operated on campaign and how it interacted with resistant native
peoples. He wrote two major works, *The Jewish War* and *The Antiquities of the Jews*. He also wrote a shorter autobiography known as the
Vita. Written in Greek, these were produced during his later life in Rome
and survive intact as an indispensable resource for students of the early
principate.

are all quoted as potential attractions for the state-sanctioned avarice of Roman procurators.

The First Jewish War, however, as recorded by Josephus, was a reaction to a rebellion in what was already a conquered and 'Romanised' province, rather than a primary invasion of a hitherto unknown people. But because Roman military personnel and units were rapidly interchangeable, his detailed descriptions give us useful pointers to some of the specifics of the empire's tactics, weaknesses, and responses during periods of insurrection (an imperialist term used for when indigenous peoples have had enough):

- Rome, while successful in rapidly adding to its conquests, not infrequently underestimated pent-up resentment within occupied territories. Often led by short-term politicians, Roman forces were susceptible to initial major setbacks from a sudden eruption of resistance, like the catastrophic losses suffered by Gaius Cestius Gallus, the governor of Syria, early in the First Revolt. The ambush at Beth Horon, during Cestius' disastrous retreat from Jerusalem, cost him many of his senior commanders, most of his heavy equipment and more than a legion's worth of men. At this point, the whole province slipped from Roman control and was at the mercy of what Josephus described as a rag-tag force of untrained Jewish militia.
- In the case of planned assaults against rebels, the Romans always sought numerical superiority and had no problem in calling in very large numbers of additional troops stationed in neighbouring provinces. It is estimated that at least five additional legions took part in putting down the First Revolt including the XVth from Alexandria. This has resonance with the three additional legionary detachments called into Britain from Germany (VIIIth and XXIInd) and Spain (VIIth) under Hadrian to reinforce the existing three British legions to deal with trouble in the north at the start of his reign sometime around 120.
- Roman commanders and forces had no issue whatsoever with total annihilation of whole cities or ethnic groupings who were brave enough to resist. Groups would be rounded up en masse and slaughtered, or cities besieged until their populations were ground down and exterminated (Caesarea, Gamla, Jotapata, Jerusalem and Tiberias to name only a few of those listed by Josephus). However, it seems that the Romans perpetrated mass slaughter on a case-by-case retaliatory or personally vindictive basis rather than by sweeping ideologically driven genocide that has been the case in more recent periods of history. This probably had as much to do with Rome's skill for retaining a rump of population to support the taxable infrastructure, as its innate morality.

- Mass enslavement was also no problem to Roman thinking and had its own financial rewards. It is said that the Colosseum in Rome, the Flavian Amphitheatre as it was known, was built by Vespasian and Titus on the proceeds from the sale of Jewish prisoners as slaves.
- Those who capitulated early were occasionally spared and allowed to carry on as tangible assets if their defences came down under Roman supervision (such as Gischala and Jerusalem).
- Josephus detailed the standard terror tactics of marauding Roman forces 'relentlessly devastating the cultivated plains, pillaging people's property and killing anyone fit enough to bear arms and then enslaving the weak'. These same tactics would be used by Agricola in Scotland only twenty years later to bring the Caledonians to pitched battle.

27a. Vespasian's greatest architectural legacy, the Colosseum, was reputedly paid for by the spoils from the First Jewish War, including the sale of slaves.

b. Detail of the looted menorah on the interior of the arch of Titus. He accompanied his father on the Jewish expedition and was personally present at the sack of Solomon's temple in Jerusalem.

On reading the *Jewish War*, one can readily see that Josephus' account is biased in favour of Rome, which is unsurprising given his eventual status as a useful sage to the Flavian dynasty and given his position as a defector from the Jewish resistance. However, his reports of Roman atrocities against the native population are not particularly sugar-coated, such as his matter-of-fact description of Vespasian's cold and calculated butchery of 1,200 of the 'useless' old and infirm in Tiberias, perhaps reflecting his Roman readership's exceptional tolerance for institutional violence on a grand scale.

No matter how we view the moral complexity of Josephus' allegiances, the details of interactions from the First Jewish War remain a key resource which sheds useful light on the apparently arbitrary nature of Roman aggression, and they reintroduce something of the human stories lost by the unavoidable sanitising and mollifying effect of academic archaeology. It is also worth emphasising once more that Josephus' Jewish rebels were drawn from the 'civilised' stock of the Levant and were not typical of barbarians encountered beyond Rome's western frontiers. Consequently, the treatment of northern 'savages' was highly likely to have been considerably less sympathetic.

How does this grim tale from the East add further to our understanding of events still to come in Caledonia? Like all the world's great empires, Rome's attitude to belligerent foreigners differed slightly from region to region and from period to period. Clearly Rome's approach to rebellious Hellenic or Latinised Jews in Palestine, or tax riots in Alexandria, could differ generally and in detail from its dealings with, say, the barbarian tribes of Germany or North Africa. Generally speaking there were likely to have been three possible outcomes for the people of Caledonia: complete conquest and subjugation leading to acculturation if possible; interim containment by Roman-controlled buffer states; or a decision that the bulk of the indigenous population were recalcitrant barbarians and, since for tactical and geographic reasons they couldn't all be exterminated, a 'frontier' would be needed – a frontier beyond which official policy would oscillate between bribery to keep the peace and chronic intermittent punitive expeditions resulting in occasional exemplary mass slaughter and enslavement.

Josephus tells us that, on many occasions, slavery was the destination for tens of thousands of Jewish prisoners even in his 'civilised' province of Judea. It is highly likely therefore, that the widely acknowledged dehumanising attitude Rome showed to its slaves, that group of 'human machines' who were embedded in their Roman masters' day-to-day lives, would be extended with vigour to 'sub-human' frontier peoples. It is equally likely that when circumstances were aligned, the Roman military response to native resistance could be brutal beyond our modern imaginings. The extensive array of random body parts found around the perimeter of Newstead Roman fort bears silent testimony to the fate of 'troublesome' indigenous peoples.

If Roman actions here appear extreme, it is perhaps useful to conclude this section with a brief reflection on the more recent and better recorded frontier policy of the nineteenth-century United States as it drove west into the Great Plains and its effect on the indigenous peoples. The powers implementing this policy were the political and military elite of a so-called beneficent and Christian Western civilisation. And yet, this modern nation, not steeped in the obligatory militarist and bloodthirsty culture of the Roman

Empire, was able to perpetrate genocide on a scale that today's Americans find hard to come to terms with. And short of mass slaughter there are further lessons from North America, recorded in tragic detail, which perhaps can be applied to Iron Age Scotland, of how civilian carpetbaggers and militant settlers conspired under the protective umbrella of the army to purge native peoples from their ancestral homes in newly won territory. The appalling story of the 'Trail of Tears' (1830–50), the forced displacement of tens of thousands of indigenous Americans which resulted in incalculable hardship, may perhaps reflect the suffering of the hapless native population of Iron Age Scotland.

Of course, this sad commentary upon the treatment of subjugated people is not unique to Rome or indeed North America or to any period. As unmet contemporary UN resolutions will testify, the phenomenon of blatant privation, is happening even now in many parts of the globe as indigenous people are dispossessed and 'ethnically cleansed' from their homelands in full view of the world's media. We seem to have learned little over the last 2,000 years since the bloody siege of Jotapata, when Josephus, thankful to be alive, was led from the charnel-cave of his compatriots, and emerged blinking into the Galilean sunlight.

CHAPTER FIVE

Tracking the tempest

The early morning sun hurts my eyes as I drive past the first warning sign at Otterburn. I stop to read it quickly for I must reach my objective while the late winter shadows are still long. The crimson information board tells me that under no circumstances should I pick anything up. Point absolutely taken – everything from small arms ammunition to howitzer shells have been lobbed over this British army firing range for years. The red flags are not flying, and as I press on with a mixed sense of excitement and foreboding, this high moorland which forms the border between Scotland and England begins to strike me as bleakly attractive.

After five miles of single-track road with bored-looking sheep watching from the unfenced margins (how do they manage to not get blown up?), I drive over a low hill and see Chew Green for the first time. Even after 2,000 years of weathering, the ramparts of the vast Roman transit camps and forts are so impressive that I spontaneously gasp.

Stretching off into the distance, arrow straight, are the parallel ditches and mounds expertly thrown up by Roman troops, for shelter and defence. And squatting in the middle, a small but perfectly formed Roman fortlet with such prominent walls that it instantly reminds me of a fortified police station I once saw in Belfast many years ago.

Quickly, eyeing the height of the rising sun, I park and unpack the drone. I calibrate its compass and watch it acquire sufficient satellites to lock the GPS. Memory card in, aircraft safe-fly-zone checked, 4K camera on and ready to lift off in four minutes flat. Once airborne, I take it up to just short of its maximum ceiling of 120m. And there it is. The patchwork of ridges and furrows at ground level suddenly makes sense as the array of Roman camps unfold in all their preserved glory. I have seen a lot of Roman earthworks in my time, but these are truly impressive – and to top it all, Dere Street, the main Roman road into Scotland, passes straight through heading resolutely northwards towards the heartland of the Selgovae. The fort is at least two days march beyond the Wall, and the soldiers who built this complex must have been confident in their powers, for even now in this isolated spot I can feel the hairs beginning to stand up on the back of my neck.

The story of Scotland's Roman Iron Age is largely derived from archaeo-logical survey of military installations such as Chew Green and so is quite unlike the southern narrative. In place of villas, towns and Romano-British farmsteads, the ancient landscape of Caledonia, thanks to decades of pioneering aerial photography by scholars such as St Joseph, Maxwell and Hanson, is littered with dozens of Roman army camps, like burned-out tank hulks scattered across the Eastern Front. These 'marching camps' of Rome's Scottish expeditions represent one of the highest concentrations of such structures per square mile anywhere in the Roman world. There is a general perception that they were built for a single night, but evidence has now been uncovered that shows they may have been occupied intermittently for long periods, thus bearing silent witness to over 300 years of countless campaigns. Each incursion would have involved colossal movements of men and equipment and represents what would have been a signifi-cant shock to native resources. The north during this period was without doubt a turbulent zone.

In stark contrast, there are no definite Roman civilian sites in Scotland, other than the *vici*, the small defended paramilitary settlements of depend-ents and camp followers, huddled in the lee of the more permanent Roman forts. Apart from the anomaly of Traprain Law hillfort mentioned above,

28. The vast network of Roman forts and campaign camps at Chew Green that lies on the modern Scottish Border.

29a. A schematic of the approximate distribution of Roman military installations compared to b. Roman 'civilian' settlement (excluding the *vici* surrounding forts). Note the complete absence of civic activity north of the Tyne–Solway isthmus.

and a couple of brochs, there is little evidence of substantial material exchange between Roman and native from sites in the Scottish Lowlands. And in Dumfries and Galloway and the north-west, the situation is even more striking, with almost complete absence of Roman artefacts.

It has been argued the Romans used a 'gloved fist' approach in Caledonia, suggesting that the residue of Roman material culture is evidence of local tribes trading food surpluses with the army in return for high status objects. In reality, Roman finds are exceptionally sparse on ordinary native sites, and it is equally possible to interpret what finds there are as booty or the detritus of opportunists. The investigations by Hodgson and colleagues (2012 and 2022) at indigenous sites on the Northumberland Coastal Plain confirm this observation, showing a distinct paucity of Roman material goods. Furthermore, there seems to be a significant change in land use and a dislocation of indigenous society after the start of the construction of Hadrian's Wall.

An ability to track the movements of the Roman army with some precision has placed Scotland in a strong position to contribute to the understanding of Roman expansionism and frontier policy at the zenith of its empire – the time when Rome's hitherto irresistible storm of aggressive acquisition was about to run out of wind. Many military sites, like Chew Green, stand in splendid isolation and have been barely touched in the 2,000 years since they were abandoned. Here there is no confusing layer cake of superimposed architecture that complicates urban sites, or 300 years of continuous rebuilding and repair as on Hadrian's Wall. Minimal agricultural activity in the intervening years has failed to erode the remains of usually ephemeral structures, such as ditches that can still be easily followed on the surface or remain detectable by aerial photography or LiDAR. Roman military sites in the north are like insects stuck in amber, frozen in time with helpfully narrow chronologies locked in.

Discoveries from the Borderlands have provided revelations that explain some of the puzzling thirty-six-year gap between the Claudian invasion of the south in 43 and the first attested push into Scotland in 79, a delay in total conquest remarked on by Pliny the Elder in his *Natural History*. Until a few years ago, scholars of the *Agricola* accepted Tacitus' assertion that his father-in-law, appointed governor of Britannia in 77, led the first invasion of Caledonia. However, work on early Roman ceramics at Luguvalium, the fort which would ultimately become Carlisle, had raised the suspicion that all was not well with the accepted dating sequence. Pottery analysis suggested the fort had been founded by a previous governor, possibly Quintus Petillius Cerialis or even the governor before, Marcus Vettius Bolanus (69–71), and by implication, Roman forces had at least reconnoitred the borders of Scotland several years in advance of Agricola. The debate remained unresolved until excavations as part of Carlisle City Council's Millennium Project encountered the waterlogged gate timbers of the earliest fort. Dendrochronology of these well-preserved timbers was a game-changer, confirming a felling date of late 72 and clinching the Cerialis

AD 79

The year 79 was to be bountiful for newsworthy events in the Roman world: the Emperor Vespasian died, to be succeeded by his son Titus; Pompeii and Herculaneum were obliterated by the cataclysmic eruption of Vesuvius (Pliny the Elder (?23–79) was asphyxiated while evacuating survivors); and the new Emperor Titus sanctioned his general Agricola to proceed with the invasion of Caledonia.

30. The technique for obtaining wood samples for dendrochronology. The faint ring lines can be seen in the cores.

connection. This also added weight to the previously contentious theory by Hoffmann and Woolliscroft that the chain of Roman signal towers in Perthshire, known as the Gask Ridge may too have significantly pre-dated Agricola (2006).

The seeds of this new information have taken root and some other observations of the northern Iron Age begin to make a little more sense. It is now thought that the first Roman forts and settlement at Carlisle were probably much larger and earlier than had previously been imagined, which would be logical in view of the geopolitics of the area. A fort of up to 8 acres during this period is likely, prompting the suggestion that the base may have been built to house part of a legion, possibly the IXth, whose stamped roof tiles have been found in the city. It is generally accepted that much of the indigenous opposition experienced by the Romans early in Hadrian's reign likely came from south-west Scotland, and so, creating an early, powerful fortress on the Solway would have been a prudent strategic move (Graafstal 2012).

It was rare, however, especially during the early empire, for Rome to hold back on its expansive military strategy, believing as it did in a divinely inspired and limitless gift for global conquest. So, even if the northern peoples were more fierce and more numerous than previously suspected, the dating information from Carlisle tends to confirm what some have previously deduced from early coins and pottery: that significant numbers of Roman troops had been probing the far north of Britain in the late 60s and early 70s. This in turn suggests that the tempest that was to blast the northern tribes in the late 70s was not entirely unexpected.

CHAPTER SIX

Enter Agricola

A bronze statue of a man in classical Roman armour stands to attention in the small square under the sweltering sun of the Côte d'Azur. He is Gnaeus Julius Agricola (40–93), Fréjus' much-loved son who moved on from this provincial town to do well among the Roman elite. Immortalised by his son-in-law, the great historian Tacitus, he was guaranteed a place in posterity, unlike his forgotten Caledonian opponent, Calgacus. But, despite the kudos of eponymous plazas and streets, Agricola, according to some scholars, was no great shakes either as a governor or as a general. In fact, significant energy has gone into rubbishing his reputation and the authenticity of Tacitus' book.

Before considering these contentious views, and what evidence or prejudices lie behind them, there are several facts about Agricola's life and career that can be established without much controversy to provide a useful backdrop when gauging his achievements. His curriculum vitae also affords an insight into the staggering mobility of Roman military personnel, and the scope of their operational shuttling. Mounting evidence from frontier forts shows, for example, that the dependents of even relatively junior officers could travel with them to foreign postings involving long-distance translocation of whole households.

Agricola was born into a reasonably wealthy Gallo-Roman family in Forum Julii, now Fréjus, in Provence. After a promising start as a young military tribune serving in Britain in the service of the imperial governor, Gaius Suetonius Paulinus, he assisted in crushing the Boudiccan rebellion in 60. This suppression was reputedly so brutal, even by Roman standards, that after an inquiry, Nero recalled Paulinus and replaced him with a more benign figure, Petronius Turpilianus.

Agricola too returned to Rome to take up a series of increasingly senior administrative posts in the years following the rebellion. Then, in 69, during the chaotic civil war precipitated by the death of Nero, he shrewdly backed the soon-to-be victorious Vespasian. The new emperor rewarded him with command of the XXth Valeria Victrix back in Britain under the governor Vettius Bolanus. Tacitus described Bolanus as 'a man too mild mannered

31. Modern bronze statue of
Agricola in the square of Fréjus
in the Côte d'Azur.

to govern such a fierce province [*provincia ferox*]' and he was soon replaced
in 71 by someone altogether more aggressive, Quintus Petillius Cerialis.
The appointment of this man is interesting: it shows that a previous disaster
was no bar to subsequent promotion, since he was the same Cerialis who
barely escaped with his own life when he led the ill-fated IXth Legion into
their first near annihilation at the hands of the Iceni during Boudicca's
revolt ten years previously – of course, being the emperor's son-in-law may
also have helped his advancement.

Agricola seemed to have developed a rapport with his new superior and
distinguished himself, or at least held his own, during episodes of heavy

32a. Lead waterpipe stamped with the name of Agricola, imperial legate, on display in Chester Museum.

b. Schematic of Agricola's campaigns in Scotland likely culminating at Mons Graupius somewhere north of the Mounth. He probably returned to Rome in 84.

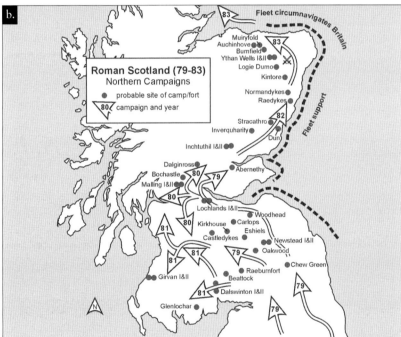

fighting against the Brigantes. Described by Tacitus as the largest tribe of northern Britain, Brigantian territory extended north and east from York to what is now the Scottish Borders. After completing his tour of duty with the XXth, Agricola was given the governorship of Gallia Aquitania (Western France), and after two or three years moved back to Rome to become consul in 77, by which time he had already been elevated to patrician status. Possibly then seen as something of a 'British specialist', he returned to Britannia as imperial governor with responsibility for the whole province – and so into the pages of history.

Before we consider modern criticism of the man, or the record of his exploits, it is worth noting that Scotland has been given a rare, if under-valued, gift in the form of the *Agricola*. Few countries are privileged to have been the focus of one of the world's acknowledged masters of history and benefit from an ancient book at least partly devoted to describing the activities of Roman forces within its borders. Probably even more aston-ishing is the dramatic quality of Tacitus' writing that features a number of memorable vignettes and includes the famous pre-battle speech placed in the mouth of Calgacus, the Caledonian leader. Words and emotions so powerful that they have sufficient impact today to raise the blood and guar-antee partisan admirers and fierce critics in equal measure.

The Agricola

The book, written in the closing years of the first century, is titled *De vita et moribus Iulii Agricolae* (*On the Life and Character of Julius Agricola*), and Tacitus delivered exactly what he promised: a eulogy for his kinsman, extolling his virtues from his earliest days as a junior officer, to his alleged poisoning at the hands of the reviled Emperor Domitian. For scholars of early Scotland, the work also illuminates the otherwise obscure period of the country's transition from prehistory and provides us with descriptions of potentially dateable events from Agricola's arrival as imperial governor in 77 until his final return to Rome in 84.

The book adopts a standard formula beginning with a general descrip-tion of the province in which Tacitus outlines something of the country's geography, ethnography and its natural history, including the standard

Calgacus

Even the name of the Caledonian leader, Calgacus, meaning the 'Swords-man', has the feel of the theatrical, and indeed we have no proof he ever really existed, which would place him in the same category as many other great figures from history. It is fair however, to assume there were leaders within the Caledonian tribal confederacy gathered on the hill called Mons Graupius and in the mouth of one of these chieftains Tacitus placed what has come to be recognised as one of the finest rallying calls ever written. Using a technique honed by previous authors such as Thucydides, Tacitus allows the antagonists, Calgacus and Agricola, to reveal in their grand orations some of the historian's own thoughts on what he considered to be the malignant effects of empire and the loss of the 'simple life' of a less tyrannical epoch.

Roman topoi of gloomy weather and long summer nights at high latitudes. As well as portraying Britannia as a 'fierce province' Tacitus reveals his admiration for the fighting spirit of the indigenous peoples 'who had not yet been softened by subjugation'. It has been suggested by some modern authorities (e.g. Campbell 2010) that the authenticity of his descriptions point to Tacitus personally accompanying his father-in-law on at least part of the campaign in fulfilment of his own military tribunate. Tacitus follows up the rich preamble with a detailed season-by-season account of Agricola's northern campaign:

- 77. Although Agricola arrived late in his first year as governor he wasted no time in pulling his forces together to deal a genocidal blow ('*caesaque prope universa gente*' – '*he slew almost the whole nation*') to the Ordovices in north Wales as retribution for their daring attack on a Roman cavalry squadron. He then rounded off his debut year with a successful full-scale assault on the Druidic heartland of Anglesey thereby crowning the conquest begun by Paulinus almost two decades before.
- 78. Over the intervening winter, Agricola focused his attention on correcting some of the administrative laxities and corruption that had developed at the centre of provincial government and stamping out the more extreme exploitative practices of his senior staff. Geographic details are lacking for his second campaigning season but it seems likely that Agricola busied himself with consolidating gains in the north of England by a combination of diplomacy, fort building and force of arms.
- 79. After a winter of overseeing construction and welfare projects in the south of Britannia, the better weather brought a renewed impetus for Agricola to force his way northwards by all means possible. Tacitus tells us that the standard Roman tactics of shock and awe were employed as the new governor 'ravaged the territory of the tribes as far as the Tay'. We are also alerted to Agricola's singular talent for personally choosing impregnable fort sites – 'no fort of his choosing was ever taken by storm'. Paradoxically, the details supplied in this section hint that Roman strongholds were indeed occasionally stormed and besieged for Agricola commanded that all his new forts 'were sufficiently provisioned to withstand a siege of up to a year' suggesting that things had not always gone to plan for the occupying force.
- 80. The fourth campaign season was spent further consolidating areas that had recently been overrun, with a particular emphasis on fortifying the Forth–Clyde line. Indeed it has long been suspected that some of the forts (e.g. Castlecary) on the later Antonine frontier

that runs across the isthmus, had been built on Agricolan foundations. Tacitus concludes that the enemy had been pushed northwards
'into what was almost another island' conjuring up images of local
militia and refugees streaming northwards to escape the oncoming
onslaught.

- 81. In his fifth season, Agricola prudently decided to deal with residual enemy forces in the south-west of Scotland previously bypassed
by the rapid Roman advance. Tacitus makes it clear that Roman
troops eventually penetrated Dumfries and Galloway as far as the
sea, by telling us that Agricola personally surveyed Ireland from the
Scottish coast. We are informed that the new governor predicted
(probably rashly) that should he be given the go ahead to snuff out
Hibernian support for the northern tribes, he would be able to
conquer the whole of Ireland with a single legion and some auxiliaries.

- 82. Intelligence gathered at the opening of the sixth season caused
Roman high command to fear a coordinated uprising of the northern
tribes which Agricola pre-empted by instructing his navy to make
multiple coastal forays using marines in close support of his rapidly
advancing land forces. Although the ploy seemed initially successful,
Tacitus tells us that the Caledonians soon recognised they had no
other option but to turn to armed resistance on a major scale and
were emboldened to begin attacking some of Agricola's permanent
installations. The governor had some difficulty quelling the nerves
of his more skittish generals who advised a strategic retreat south
of the River Forth and so he decided to push on more rapidly by
splitting his grand army into three columns. Once the Caledonians
became aware of the impending Roman counter-attack, they
suddenly changed their tactics and opted for a night assault on the
encamped IXth Legion. The outcome of this audacious confrontation hung in the balance for a short time, with battles raging in the
camp gateways until Agricola came to the rescue with overwhelming
reinforcements drawn from the other legions in the battle group.
The native levies, realising they were about to be trapped in a pincer
movement, melted into the night with minimal casualties thus
preserving their strength to fight another day.

- 83. In the opening months of his seventh and final campaign season,
a personal tragedy – the death of his infant son – caused Agricola
to immerse himself in his efforts to bring the Caledonians to pitched
battle, something they had prudently avoided until that point. It is
unclear if it was the provocative Roman shock tactics (Tacitus repeatedly uses the word 'terror' when describing Agricola's modus
operandi) of laying waste to native homelands or sheer exhaustion

precipitated by the protracted war, which eventually led to a grand coalition of native tribes gathering on a hilltop called Mons Graupius to do battle with the Roman army. Although Tacitus gave the numerical superiority to the Caledonians, who additionally had the advantage of higher ground, the outcome of the battle was never really in any doubt. After preliminary skirmishes and outdated chariot displays, the carnage began. Like the wild charges of the highlanders 1,700 years later, the sheer courage of lightly armoured and undisciplined troops was no match for the steely resolve of a better-equipped and seasoned army, which butchered its way up the slope. The Roman auxiliaries did most of the fighting with their cavalry ultimately closing in from the wings and causing a rout of the native infantry. The slaughter went on until nightfall, with dawn the next day finding the battlefield strewn with 10,000 native dead. The Romans had lost less than 400 auxiliary troops.

- 84. After overwintering his victorious battalions in their southern quarters Agricola returned to Rome where Tacitus recorded that the ungrateful and increasingly unstable Emperor Domitian 'immediately let go' Agricola's hard-won gains in Britannia. By choice or subterfuge, Agricola was subsequently denied the usual trappings of a successful general and he lived out the last few years of his life in Rome in relative obscurity.

Fact or fiction?

The overtly positive light Tacitus shone on his father-in-law has encouraged some scholars to trivialise the complete work as a family tribute devoid of historical value. Conversely, some commentators cherry-pick the *Agricola* for selected references that support or refute whatever point they are trying to make. Others are more generous and suggest the book provides a rare framework on which to drape our understanding of events of this period and acts as a foil to some of the archaeological data. It is certainly not a dispassionate, detailed and temporally accurate history but what eulogy from this period is? Although Tacitus is vague in lots of areas, place names for example, he does provide exhilarating descriptions of the Roman army's movements in Scotland, which simply cannot be obtained from any other source.

Although brimming with flattery for his departed relative, it is perhaps disingenuous to suggest, as some historians have done, that there is no basis for much of Tacitus' detail. Yes, Agricola could do no wrong in Tacitus' eyes, from the firm but fair way he disciplined his men to how he sent away his horse before the great battle. But why fabricate everyday events of a whole campaign – confabulation that could easily be exposed by well-connected contemporary figures who would have been embedded in Agricola's high command as eyewitnesses? He undoubtedly exaggerated the numbers of the opposing forces and their prowess, as most Roman authors did, and of course Tacitus utilised an old literary technique, of placing artificial speeches in protagonists' mouths to score moral points. But, equally surely, the historian will have gained an account of actual events as an eyewitness or over the dinner table from his father-in-law after his return to Rome. How could Tacitus have published a fictitious year-by-year account of the Roman army's progress through Caledonia? It is unlikely Agricola was at liberty to fabricate an alternative reality since there were tens of thousands of soldiers and staff to balance any account. There is no doubt the Romans themselves considered Britannia a dangerous province, and as we shall see, the cream of its military establishment fulfilled their obligation before the standards in North Britain. So, can we really suggest that all these senior people, many of whom would have been well respected, highly educated and exceedingly literate, were complicit in a grand conspiracy?

It may be helpful to look for other motivations behind this counterintuitive position – an explanation that may have less to do with an assessment of the data, and more to do with simply not liking the implication that Caledonia, even if temporarily, was a credible threat to Rome. It may also be useful to compare similar scholarly reactions to the implications of the northern expeditions of the emperors Hadrian, Septimius Severus and Constantine.

Placing biases and theories to one side, one of the real delights of the *Agricola* is the insight provided by the asides and anecdotes Tacitus laced through the work and by the hidden meaning and allusions contained within his protagonist's speeches.

Although it now seems highly unlikely that Agricola was the first Roman general to set foot in Scotland, he was certainly the best publicised and one of the best resourced. There is little doubt his force included sizeable elements drawn from the Roman army in Britain but apart from the ill-fated IXth Hispana, and possibly the XXth Valeria Victrix, we are not quite sure if the two others, the IInd Adiutrix and the IInd Augusta, were represented. Accompanied by many thousands of auxiliaries, Agricola led his battlegroup northwards. Marching camps can be traced at approximately 15-mile intervals as they traversed north-east Scotland skirting the Grampians to penetrate as far as Muiryfold near Keith in Aberdeenshire. A further camp has been suggested to lie within 4km of the Moray coast at Bellie, just north of Fochabers, but the data from that site remains somewhat equivocal (Jones 2011).

Scholars are, however, reasonably confident these northernmost camps, several of which were discovered by aerial photography, belong to the same early incursion because they have near identical surface areas (110 acres) and similar ditch profiles. The total force, as calculated from the camp dimensions, was probably about 25,000 men. This appears to correspond with the invasion army described by Tacitus comprising legionary detachments plus 10,000 or 12,000 auxiliaries and cavalry. Clearly a considerable number to provision and keep in the field for a whole campaign season.

But it is not just size which suggests that this sequence of camps belongs to Agricola's campaign: the camp at Kintore near Inverurie was threatened by housing development and subsequently underwent extensive area excavation. Numerous Roman field ovens were identified and radiocarbon dates from cooking charcoal cluster around the late first century, which fits well with the Agricolan expedition. This is a rare positive outcome for investigation of such large, often featureless, marching-camp sites that used to be regarded as archaeologically sterile.

The search for Mons Graupius

The site of the battle of Mons Graupius, the cataclysmic finale to the Agricolan invasion, has not been so easy to pin down and has eluded historians and archaeologists for literally hundreds of years. Some commentators consider identification of its location an irrelevance but in comparison with other countries, there is no sound reason to deny Scotland the same public, historical and national interest there is in pivotal conflict sites such as Austerlitz, Hastings or Waterloo.

For once, the usually geographically vague Tacitus provides us with some helpful clues. He states that Agricola mustered the legions in reserve battle order just outside the ramparts of their campaign camp and positioned his force of auxiliaries in front of them, directly opposite a hill, Mons Graupius, on which an estimated 30,000 Caledonians had gathered. Tacitus also states that the battle took place towards the close of the campaigning season, suggesting it may have been reasonably far north. This is also hinted at in Agricola's speech when he talks of the great distance they have travelled into enemy territory. However, it is just possible that Agricola was marching and countermarching his army, laying waste to the countryside for a whole season in a last attempt to precipitate a pitched battle. Tacitus describes the annoyance of Agricola and his men at the reticence of the locals to engage in conventional field warfare (quite rightly as it turned out). For Agricola, a major battle was a necessary culmination of the campaign, for it would provide him with the decisive victory and head count that would allow dispatches to go to Rome trumpeting the complete subjugation of Britannia.

Several hills close to known Roman marching camps of the required size have been put forward as the battle site and at least ten candidates are

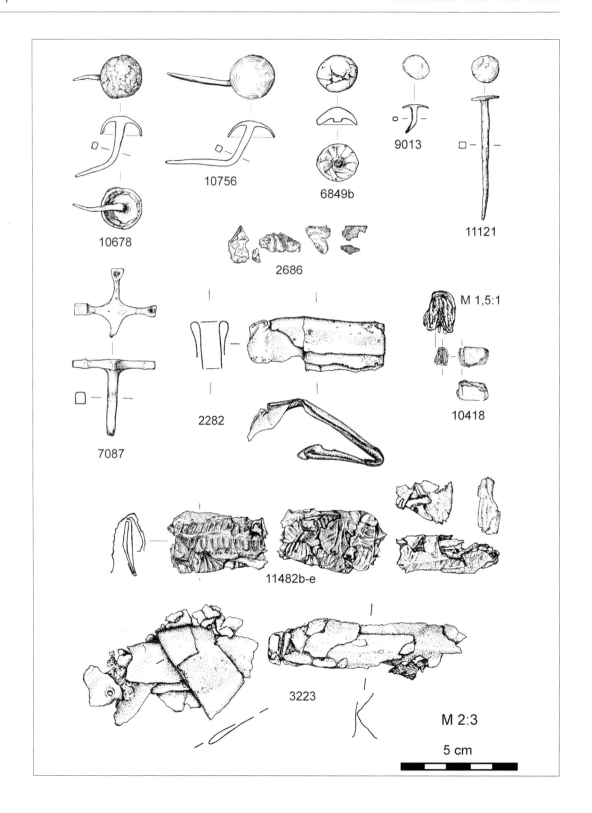

10756

10678

6849b

9013

11121

2686

M 1,5:1

7087

2282

10418

11482b-e

3223

M 2:3

5 cm

currently in contention. Field surveys have so far drawn a complete blank. This is not surprising – despite the reputed magnitude of the Roman victory with 10,000 native dead versus only 360 Romans, most of whom would have been auxiliaries, the asymmetry of the struggle will have left little residue. This is especially true when battle detritus is widely scattered over a very large area and once body stripping and plundering had been completed. Exposed body parts will have decayed easily within a decade and all accessible weaponry and jewellery will have been removed by the Roman forces as booty or to construct a *tropaeum*, an impromptu victory monument made from captured gear.

Only tiny fragments of military equipment (buckles, studs, fragments of harness, etc.) are likely to remain in the ground, particularly from sparsely armoured Caledonian warriors. It could be hoped that expendable missiles such as lead sling bullets may have remained buried as potential markers, but clay rather than lead bullets seem to have been the missile of choice during this period.

Two examples emphasise that confidently identifying ancient battlefields is no easy task: a) the largest defeat Rome ever suffered at the hands of a foe, in this case Hannibal, at the battle of Cannae (216 BC), where Roman losses on the field are estimated to have been as high as 70,000 men, one of the largest single-day losses of life on any battlefield ever, has never been confidently traced; b) by the time that British army officer, detectorist and amateur historian Major Tony Clunn discovered the site of the Varus Disaster, the so-called Varusschlacht, in the Teutoburg Forest near Osnabruck in Germany in 1988, it had been searched for in vain by numerous historians for centuries. Only his initial lucky find of a few coins and three lead sling bullets led him to the site of the slaughter of thousands of Varus' heavily armed Roman legionaries who perished in AD 9.

Probably the most favoured candidate for the site of Mons Graupius is situated at Bennachie, the mountain near Inverurie. And for good reason, as the physical presence of the hill is striking in the landscape and the proximity of the very large Roman campaign camp at Logie Durno immediately opposite, discovered by St Joseph in the 1970s, would be a prerequisite. At this location, however, the slopes of Bennachie are generally steep, which may render the sort of infantry battle Tacitus described problematic and well-nigh impossible for the native chariot display that he says took place immediately prior to the battle. There is also a tactically troublesome and unmentioned river between the Roman camp and the proposed battle site.

Tacitus, however, helpfully outlined the order of battle, which provides some additional clues. We are told specifically that Agricola ordered four Batavian and two Tungrian cohorts to close with the enemy – seasoned troops drawn from the more warlike Germanic tribes. However, this is a relatively small force, constituting between 5,000 or 6,000 men, assuming

OPPOSITE. 33. Metallic battlefield debris from the Varusschlacht at Kalkriese near Dortmund. Mostly what remains of three legions are tiny shreds of re-processed metalwork including studs, hobnails and fittings.

34. A schematic for the suggested arrangement of opposing forces at Mons Graupius, here identified with the hill of Tillymorgan. The Roman forces are shown to the north, drawn up in front of their camp.

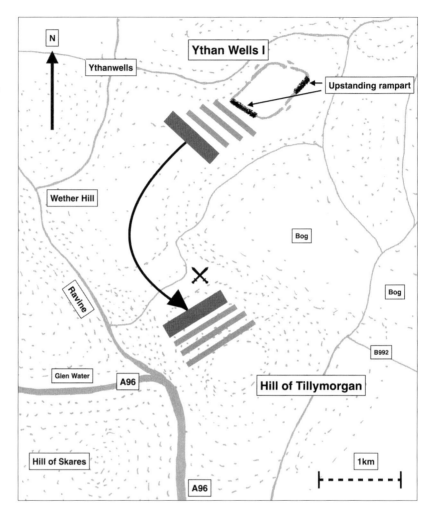

the battalions were all miliary (1,000 strong) cohorts, to face an enemy host of 30,000. This suggests that there may have been a limiting topographic factor that dictated a relatively narrow front.

On reviewing Tacitus' description and the terrain, it may be that the battle as described favours a site further west along the chain of '110 acre' marching camps. Tillymorgan, another prominent hill but with more amenable slopes than Bennachie, has a relatively flat saddle which joins it with the elevated land to the north where, less than 2km away, lies the large Roman camp of Ythan Wells. This generous spur of land is almost a kilometre in width, has no troublesome watercourses, and would perhaps be a better setting in terms of the described choreography of the engagement. To add to this topographic feature, the Tillymorgan-facing rampart of the Roman camp at Ythan Wells still stands to a height of a metre, even after 2,000 years of weathering and agriculture, and as such it represents

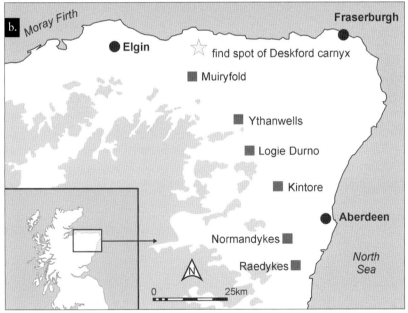

35a. The hillward-facing rampart of the Roman campaign camp at Ythan Wells, the most northerly upstanding earthwork of the Roman Empire. Scout for scale.

b. Map showing the probable campsites of Agricola's army as it moved towards the Moray Firth. The findspot of the Deskford carnyx lies remarkably close to the line of advance.

the most northerly upstanding Roman structure in the empire. The importance placed on this section of the rampart by the Roman engineers was revealed by Macdonald and Haverfield in 1913 when they found its surviving dimensions to be 2m high and 5m wide. This chimes with the entreaty by the first-century Roman author Pseudo-Hyginus to particularly exaggerate defences when in the presence of the enemy – thus adding weight to the assertion that the circumstances here were special.

So, is there anything new to say about the site of the battle? To date, despite the efforts of six seasons of detecting surveys, not a single shred of military debris has come to light. However, less than 30km away, one extraordinary object has been found which may cast further light on the mystery. In 1816, while digging drains through peaty subsoil, farm labourers uncovered what looked like a bronze boar's head. This object, now painstakingly restored by the National Museum of Scotland, represents the sound bell of Britain's only surviving carnyx.

Much respected by the Romans, the carnyx was the battle trumpet of the Celtic tribes (Hunter 2016). Often depicted on coins and monuments, an example can be seen among war booty on the base of Trajan's column, and it is also shown being sounded by the figures on the Gundestrup cauldron (the large silver feasting vessel found in a peat bog in Denmark). And so this exceptionally rare relic of Celtic warfare was found buried at a hamlet called Deskford, two days march from Tillymorgan. Excavation around the find site showed evidence of early settlement but no other clues as to why it was buried there. Was this a votive offering to appease the war gods after a major defeat, or concealment of the standards for safe keeping after a rout until forces recovered sufficiently for the next rebellion? Whatever the reason for this astonishing object's burial, the proximity to Agricola's likely invasion route gives one pause for thought.

Apart from Tacitus' terse statement, *perdomita Britannia* ('Britain was completely subdued') what did Agricola's unusually long governorship of seven years, much of which was spent on active campaign, bring to the indigenous population? Here, where Tacitus glorifies Agricola's personal attributes, is perhaps the place to reprise the Monty Python sketch of 'what did the Romans ever do for us?' Tacitus makes it clear that there was little humour in the Roman army's progress to Mons Graupius and considerable resultant misery for the northern peoples. As we have seen from evidence in other theatres of conflict, the use of massive, overwhelming and genocidal force did not present a moral dilemma for the Roman army. When faced with concerted opposition and directed by their political masters, the army could exterminate all resistance to the last woman and child. Josephus' detailed account of the bone-crushingly brutal expedition into Judea by Titus and Vespasian, which had ended only a decade earlier, helps us visualise what Roman forces could do to people from a rebellious frontier state. It is true that in context, Roman cruelty was, in its individual horrors, no more extreme than any other culture of its time, but it was more systematised and persistent, and was orchestrated on an unimaginable scale. By the second century, the Romans had honed the use of state-sponsored exemplary violence to perfection.

And what specifically of Scotland? What would Agricola's legacy be for Caledonia apart from the chain of forts designed to block off the High-

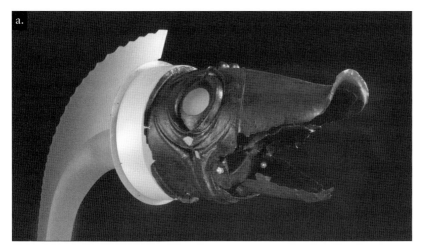

36a. The Deskford carnyx, found close to Agricola's invasion route in north-east Scotland, remains Britain's only example of an ancient Celtic war trumpet. The eyes of the boar-head sounding bell would have been inset with enamel.

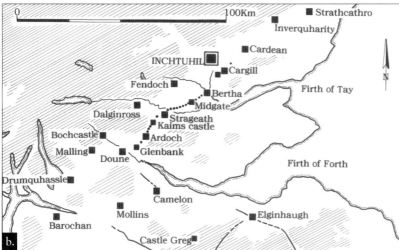

b. The distribution of Roman strongpoints in the immediate aftermath of Agricola's victory. Note the series of northerly 'glen-blocking' forts and the dotted line of watchtowers from Ardoch to Bertha.

land glens? In addition to the 10,000 reported dead on the battlefield at Mons Graupius, Tacitus describes the collateral damage resulting from vanquished warriors killing their families to prevent them falling into Roman hands. There will also have been the longer-term effects of enslavement of the survivors and the impact of subsequent widespread famine because of the loss of several seasons' crops and the manpower to manage them. The destruction of tribal society on a scale never previously experienced by the indigenous population will, in a culture whose identity relied on oral tradition and storytelling, possibly have reverberated for many generations. It is also likely that the 'shock and awe' advantage enjoyed by the Romans in their first major military contacts with Caledonia, would lead to profound changes in the battle tactics of the warrior class of Scotland. It may have convinced subsequent generations of angry young men to approach Rome very differently the next time the carnyx was sounded.

CHAPTER SEVEN

Smell the smoke:
the post-Agricolan black hole

37. The triangular plateau of Inchtuthil – the military complex of legionary fortress and construction camps lie within the distant encircling tree line.

The Coach House at Inchtuthil, 10km east of Dunkeld, is an attractive destination lying in a broad loop of the Tay as it meanders lazily towards Perth. Every comfort is catered for and even Scout has his own space beside the log fire. But for Roman enthusiasts this is an even more special place – for rising immediately behind the house is a wide plateau, on which rest the remains of a massive legionary stronghold, virtually undisturbed since it was abandoned 2,000 years ago. Carefully dismantled only a couple of years after construction began, it provides a perfect blueprint for a first-century Roman fortress. Here, in the 1950s, Richmond was able to trace the ghostly outlines of barrack blocks, granaries, headquarters building and even an infirmary, so completely that Agricola (who may have commis-

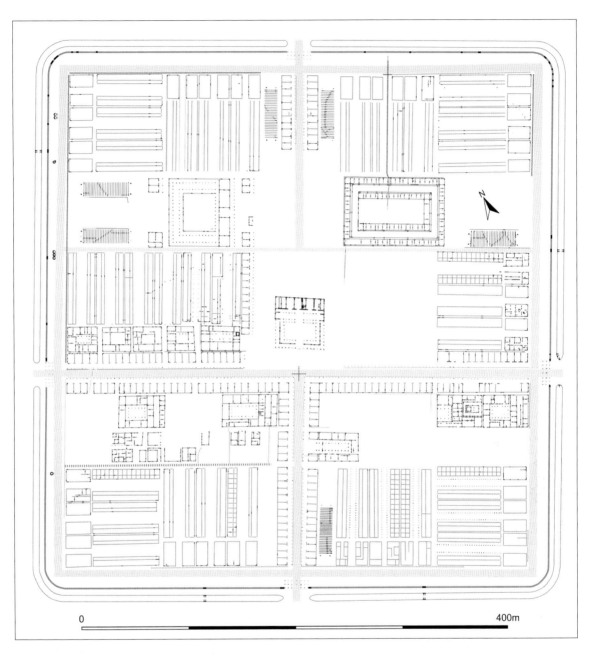

38. The plan of the fortress at Inchtuthil showing that the central range of buildings was not yet complete at the time of abandonment. Note the regimented rows of barracks. (Drawn by Mike Bishop).

sioned it) would have recognised it. And it is to here I retreat for inspiration to ponder one of the yawning gaps in the history of Roman Scotland – the time between the recall of Agricola in 84 and the next recorded Roman activity – Hadrian's excursion to the province in 122.

But a forty-year hiatus, in effect two generations, cannot go unremarked, even if historical sources are silent. Current thinking assures us that after

Agricola returned to Rome there was a rapid withdrawal of Roman forces to the Lowlands of Scotland in 87–8, the '*statim omissa*' ('immediate abandonment') of Tacitus' narrative. It has become accepted wisdom that this retreat south was precipitated by the removal of troops, particularly the withdrawal around this time of the whole of the IInd Adiutrix, one of Britain's four legions, to supplement Domitian's forces after a succession of military disasters at the hands of the Dacians, in what is now modern Romania.

Using archaeological data from northern forts such as Inchtuthil, Cardean and Stracathro, particularly the recovery of a handful of mint condition coins of 86, a pattern of strategic abandonment builds up which supports this suggestion. Systematic dismantling and clearing of sites with no evidence of chaotic *in situ* burning indicates that the Roman army was very much in control when it was packing up. There was even a set of table crockery, presumably too bulky to transport easily, of high-status samian ware, deliberately smashed up and sealed with a layer of clay in the ditch-terminal of Cardean fort.

Perhaps the most impressive and in many ways forlorn memorial was the huge, unfinished, fortress of Inchtuthil itself – a spectral testament to failed imperial whim. The massive 50-acre site with its attendant outworks was nearing completion when the orders came to decamp southwards. Ditches were filled in, half-timbered buildings pulled down and pits were dug to bury and deny asset strippers what the army did not want to haul southwards. Perhaps the caches were marked in some way for rediscovery if the imperial gaze turned northwards once more. Probably the most remarkable, if not iconic, find from Richmond's excavation was the hoard of several tons of unused iron nails. From finger size to the length of a forearm, they came from a clay-capped pit in their hundreds of thousands, many in useable condition after nearly 2,000 years beneath the Perthshire soil.

Many of the nails were donated to museums and there can be few schoolchildren in 1970s Scotland with a serious interest in the Romans who did not receive one or two for their collection. As a nice touch, a 1960s presentation box of four can still be seen on the lounge wall of the Coach House.

It is interesting to speculate what would have happened to the geopolitical map of Scotland if Inchtuthil had not been abandoned and returned to agricultural serenity. When they had fulfilled their immediate military purpose, most legionary fortresses such as London, Lincoln, Chester and York, were transformed into *coloniae* for veterans and ultimately became regional centres. If Domitian's attention had not been so distracted, perhaps the capital of Scotland would have been on the banks of the Tay rather than the Forth.

39. The heap of nearly 1 million unused nails excavated from a pit within one of Inchtuthil's workshop buildings.

The Flavian withdrawal from Scotland

Once the withdrawal from the northern forts was complete, it is said that a few Lowland installations, notably Camelon near Falkirk and Newstead near Melrose, were held for a brief period until about 105 and then these too were abandoned in favour of creating a line across the Tyne–Solway isthmus. This line, defined by the Roman road known as the Stanegate, and its handful of attendant forts, is still accepted by many to represent the frontier for virtually the whole of the reign of Emperor Trajan (98–117). But this theory did not go unchallenged.

Sir George Macdonald (1862–1940), a doyen of Roman archaeology in Scotland and a leading expert in Roman numismatics, began a feisty correspondence in the pages of *The Journal of Roman Studies* – backed by the coin evidence he had reviewed for James Curle at Newstead – with two other great Roman army scholars of that period, T. Davies Pryce and Eric Birley. The debate, which lasted from 1935 to 1939, ended in stalemate at the time of Macdonald's death, but scholars slowly accepted Birley's viewpoint of the earlier evacuation date, and this has now become an accepted fact. But this seemingly trivial academic disagreement over a chronological misalignment of two decades is representative of a multitude of other controversies. Although the date of 105 has become canonical for the orderly withdrawal to the Stanegate from all Scottish Lowland forts, there remain some important inconsistencies, not least the fact that coin finds from Newstead and Camelon support the theory that both were held almost until the accession of Hadrian in 117.

The map of the immediate post-Agricolan withdrawal period shows

40. A complete *spatha* (cavalry sword) from the early second century levels of the Vindolanda excavations – an exceptional find.

that if all the forts in southern Scotland are suddenly removed from the picture, it leaves a relatively thin bulwark against potential incursion from the north: Corbridge, Vindolanda, Nether Denton and Carlisle. Four forts and a road to police a frontier that just two decades later would require 15 large forts, 80 milecastles, 160 turrets and a very large wall.

We do know for certain from the landmark work at Vindolanda that things were reasonably peaceful in the Stanegate area in the late 90s since dinner-party invitations were still being sent out by non-combatants like the commandant's wife, Claudia Severa. But by their very nature, frontier dynamics can shift dramatically over short timescales, and within a couple of decades, by the end of the 110s, there is mounting evidence of a major upheaval with ominous signs of destruction and abandonment, not just of the forts of southern Scotland but also those of the Stanegate itself.

As recently as 2017, Andrew Birley's team working in a cavalry barracks at Vindolanda, in a context dating to this period, made the surprise discovery of weapons strewn over the floors of several rooms. These included two *spathae* – cavalry longswords – in good condition, together with spears, arrowheads and ballista bolts. The immediate impression is one of sudden abandonment. The loss of valuable serviceable weapons like these cannot be casually dismissed, particularly when they join a constellation of other similar fragments of contemporaneous evidence from Roman military sites across the Scottish Lowlands and the Borderlands.

There is a growing body of evidence to support the assertion that there was a major wave of violence that enveloped the south of Scotland and extended into the north of England to include sites like Birrens and Carlisle. Sites where there are peculiar signs of desertion such as at Vindolanda and even as far south as Ribchester where there is concealed cavalry gear, including a precious face mask, and slaughtered cavalry horses left to rot on the surface of the fort (Buxton 2001).

These signs of rapid evacuation have been interpreted in various ways but counterintuitively the orderly extraction of troops to support further wars in Dacia is the current favourite. However, the circumstantial evidence of uncharacteristically messy desertion is at odds with the careful dismantling quite evident a few decades earlier in the Flavian period, at sites north of the Forth–Clyde isthmus such as Stracathro and Inchtuthil. In contrast, significant burning has been attested archaeologically at Trajanic-period forts from Newstead, Cappuck and Oakwood southwards as far as and including Carlisle, Corbridge and beyond. This burning is not the methodical 'dismantle and take to offsite bonfire' type we see associated with the northern forts, but a considerably more disorganised form which involves *in situ* conflagration. The evidence is pronounced at forts like Newstead, Glenlochar and Birrens where the latter demonstrated a burned layer up to 20cm thick right across the fort.

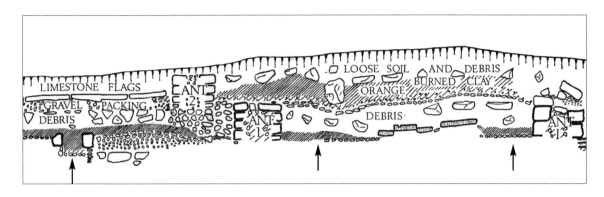

41. A diagram showing an excavated section through a range of buildings that lay near the centre of the fort at Birrens. A thick layer of ash (indicated by arrows) permeates the cutting confirming extensive burning.

This pattern of conflagration is not a new observation. Hanson in his *Agricola and the Conquest of the North* (1987) pointed out that the *in situ* burning confirmed archaeologically on numerous occasions at Corbridge is particularly difficult to dismiss as planned demolition by Roman troops. He concluded that a 'rash of "accidental" fires would be rather suspicious' as a tenable explanation. While not definitively endorsing enemy action, he cautiously concludes his analysis of the burning of forts of this period by pointing to a parallel in Tacitus' *Histories*. We are told that two auxiliary garrison commanders in Germany burned down their forts as part of a policy of forced evacuation to deny their occupation by the enemy. This seems a plausible alternative scenario to one of outright destructive assault by rebellious northern tribes.

Most of Newstead's famous pits contained a rich assortment of abandoned material also potentially belonging to this Trajanic period if Macdonald's coin dating referred to above is correct (plates 4 and 5). In the pits were undamaged tools, cavalry equipment, armour, querns and trophy heads, interpreted by the excavator, James Curle, as all the hallmarks of a catastrophe. If not an all-out episode of barbarian destruction, then at least a hasty abandonment under duress (Curle 1911).

Of course, the picture is unlikely to be uniform across the whole of the country as not all forts or fortresses would necessarily have succumbed to an uprising at this time. Tacitus recounts that in the rebellion of the 60s, after losing all his infantry, Cerialis managed to retreat to the safety of his fortress where he was able to survive Boudicca's onslaught. There does, however, appear to be enough firm evidence to argue for a period of widespread trouble in the north, evidenced by the presence of patchy abandonment or destruction horizons, which cluster to the second decade of the second century. Modern excavations that cover this time period are rare but wherever they do take place, such as at Vindolanda, they continue to add significant supportive new evidence.

The suggestion of a wave of violence in southern Scotland in the Trajanic period has previously been put forward by historians and archaeologists

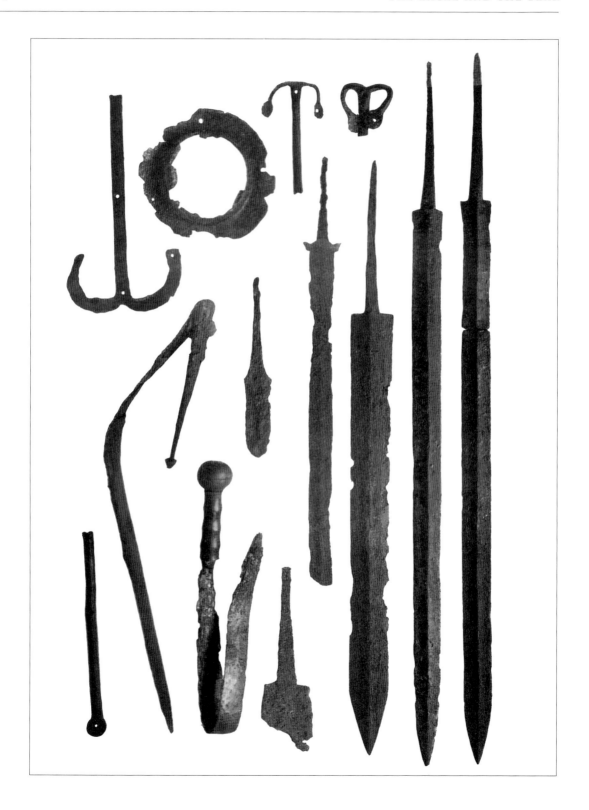

from Mommsen to Frere: 'a serious setback – perhaps a disaster – occurred. Excavations at Newstead, Dalswinton, Glenlochar, Cappuck, Oakwood, High Rochester and Corbridge have shown that these forts perished by fire', although Frere (2000) here still subscribed to the 'not long after 105' date for all this and suggested that it was largely Roman negligence which was the root cause rather than the strength of opposition.

Hadrian's biographer tells us that at the time of the new emperor's accession 'the tribes could not be kept under Roman control', making an uprising an intuitive and unifying explanation for the patterns of destruction, the accounts of Roman historians and the reactionary imperatives behind the over-engineering of Hadrian's Wall, without recourse to complicated or contrived explanations. To ignore this mounting body of evidence may represent a lost opportunity to shed light on a significant gap in our history.

It has been fashionable in the last few decades for scholars to interpret these signs of turbulence from a more relaxed Romanocentric point of view – postulating less challenging scenarios of ritual deposition, mishap or site maintenance rather than forced abandonment or violent confrontation. The net effect is to see Rome still firmly in control. It could be argued that this is based not on archaeological evidence but on an unquestioning faith in the supremacy of the Roman army. This analysis is supported by some of the language employed: 'it is inconceivable that the Romans should have been driven from Scotland by superior force' (Frere 1999); 'thus no positive evidence can be adduced that the Caledonians were particularly warlike, nor indeed that they were ever successful in their wars with Rome'; 'the two serious attempts to complete the conquest of Britain, under Agricola and Severus, failed, not because of a defeat of the Roman Army on the island, but because of problems elsewhere' (Breeze 1988); 'Indeed, whenever the Caledonians met Rome in battle, from the time of Agricola onwards, they seem to have been beaten and so can have stood little chance of expelling the Romans by force' (Woolliscroft 2000).

If we approach the issue from the primary evidence, by comparing the 'control group' of carefully abandoned northern forts like Inchtuthil, Cardean and Stracathro, with the trail of destruction in southern Scotland, it opens up a radically different reading of events. It is not a great leap of deduction to suggest that an oppressed indigenous population, like those in Judea a few decades earlier, energised and given unintentional encouragement by Trajan's withdrawal of troops, took a golden opportunity and the inevitable happened. An uprising, catalysed by military disinvestment by an emperor who had his eyes firmly fixed on a more lucrative prize in the East. It could also be argued that a new warrior elite had emerged, two generations after the first punishing incursions of Agricola, which had adapted its tactics to counter the empire's numerical and technological advantages.

OPPOSITE. 42. A wide range of abandoned weaponry was found piled in pits and wells of the fort at Newstead (Trimontium). Note the deliberately bent sword complete with handle.

Recent history demonstrates that this is not such a fanciful scenario throwing up several analogies that have been studied in detail. The work of Sullivan (2007) has shown, that since the Second World War, over one-third of conflicts between 'superpowers and much weaker nations did not go as one might expect and resulted in stalemate or defeat for the larger polity'. The reasons are multifactorial including extreme cultural asymmetry, a traditionally bellicose indigenous population, geography, terrain, long supply lines and poor political investment in the war by the dominant state. Sullivan shows that although force of arms may produce early victories, if the ultimate outcome is dependent on the defeated party's ongoing compliance, the situation almost invariably goes bad for the superpower.

We should therefore not reject so readily the idea of success for the weaker protagonist in asymmetric warfare. Powerful states do lose wars and it is naïve to think that rapid communication, mobility, and concerted action by the Iron Age warrior class of North Britain could not be learned responses to previous contact. One need look no further for an analogy than the successes of the Jacobite army in 1745. During a period of just five months an under-resourced and relatively primitive force swept 400 miles from Glenfinnan to Derby destroying everything in its path. And they achieved this on foot and on horseback just as their Caledonian forebears may have done, employing a combination of surprise, courage and pent-up resentment. The Jacobean scenario offers other potential parallels too: a better-trained and better-equipped government army to the south, suddenly caught off guard – a depleted garrison, with the majority of its forces focused abroad, and leadership absent or complacent.

It is perhaps then not so difficult to envisage a major rebellion, beginning as a local insurrection, possibly led by the Selgovae, to have generated a short-lived juggernaut that consumed the outpost forts in the Lowlands and then the Stanegate territory. This would then provide a single solution to account for a number of observations in the historical and archaeological record: the British War, mentioned by Spartianus and Fronto which probably took place in the closing period of Trajan's reign or early in Hadrian's; the artefacts in the Newstead pits; the gravestone of Titus Annius from Vindolanda; the burning and desertion of many of the borderland forts; the scatter of early second-century Roman equipment across non-Roman sites in the Lowlands; and the catalyst for the building of the first of the great Roman walls. Without further excavation specifically focused on determining more precise dating and the fate of sites in this territory, it is probably not possible to take this hypothesis further at this time.

And so, after decades of scholarship and the ebb and flow of opinion, something of an enigmatic black hole remains in the fabric of this historical period, a hole through which, as we shall now consider, the unlucky IXth Legion may have fallen to its doom.

CHAPTER EIGHT

Exit the IXth

The story of the disappearance of the IXth Hispanic Legion from the records of the Roman Empire has features in common with other great mysteries like what happened to the *Mary Celeste* and who assassinated JFK. In each case, a terminal event undoubtedly occurred but with enough gaps in key evidence to leave everyone guessing.

The legion's fate, however, is too important to consign to conspiracy theory: it is inextricably bound up with a wider narrative of how Scotland's history is shaped and perceived. Did a whole legion really meet its match in the mists of Caledonia in the early second century? Was it crushed by a confederacy of northern tribes, as Sutcliff suggested? Alternatively, did Roman central command decide the legion was surplus to requirements, and allowed it to fizzle out after a transfer to mainland Europe? Or, as more hawkish Romanists suggest, was it annihilated at the hands of a more worthy opponent in the eastern empire in an unrecorded conflict? Whatever the answer, the disappearance of the legion is a case study in the portrayal of Rome's interaction with Scotland.

The facts are sparse, but a brief review of what evidence is available helps piece together a sketch of the legion and some of its movements before considering its ultimate fate. The original IXth Legion, one of the oldest in the Roman army, fought alongside Caesar in Gaul during the first century BC. It was disbanded soon after his campaigns ended but then reconstituted by his heir, Augustus. He sent it to Spain where it fought with distinction and gained the honorific title Hispana (the Spanish Legion) which it was to bear until its disappearance. Fatefully, it was selected as one of the four legions (with the IInd Augusta, the XXth Valeria Victrix and the XIVth Gemina) that successfully invaded Britain on the orders of the Emperor Claudius in 43. It is thought that from the late 40s it was based at the substantial fortress of Longthorpe near Peterborough, as indicated by stamped roof tiles of the IXth from the site.

It was possibly from here that the legion's one-time commander, Quintus Petillius Cerialis, Vespasian's brother-in-law, launched his ill-fated attempt to block the onslaught of the warrior queen Boudicca during her near-

43. Artist's impression of the IXth Legion's final battle. Based on currently available evidence, there is a reasonable likelihood this disaster took place in North Britain.

successful revolt in 60. After initial victories, which had included the complete devastation of the Roman colony of Colchester, Boudicca's forces turned on London and the south. Tacitus tells us in *The Annals* that Cerialis led the men of the IXth, who were greatly outnumbered, into a pitched battle that saw the slaughter of virtually all of the Roman infantry. Cerialis retreated with the remnants of his cavalry to the shelter of their camp and the badly mauled legion took no further part in the action. By the time the rebellion was successfully quelled by the imperial governor, Suetonius Paulinus, the unit required 2,000 reinforcements drawn from regiments on the Rhine. Since a legion of the early empire consisted of approximately 5,000 infantry, it is possible that it was under-strength when Cerialis faced Boudicca. A similar manpower issue would haunt the IXth in its later campaign in Scotland.

In the decade after the rebellion, the legion was based at Lincoln before

44. A selection of terracotta roof tile and brick fragments stamped with the logo of the IXth Legion (represented as either IX or VIIII).

moving its headquarters further north to York sometime in the 70s, a sequence of events attested by several stone inscriptions and more roof tile stamps. It was then from York that elements of the legion supported Cerialis when he had been promoted governor in finally crushing the Brigantes, the largest and most powerful tribe in the north. When Agricola became governor in 77, the IXth, together with detachments of the other British legions, executed the new regime's plans for the conquest of Scotland.

It is a remarkable coincidence, then, that the near loss of the legion at the hands of Boudicca in 60 was repeated during Agricola's Scottish expedition two decades later. The site of that attack is unknown but probably took place somewhere north of the Tay. In his description of the event, Tacitus reveals that Agricola's forces were separately encamped and that the *Hispana* was the weakest unit, prompting scholars to speculate that sections had been drawn off to reinforce troops on the Continent. After

45. A large segment of an
inscription from one of the
fortress gateways at York
confirming the presence of the
legion there in 108. Note how
the number nine is represented
on the bottom line – VIIII
rather than IX.

this setback the legion probably saw action at the battle of Mons Graupius
in 83 and when the campaign was over, returned to its base in York.

The last reliable evidence for the whereabouts of the IXth Hispana, is
an inscription from York, found near the south-east gateway of the fortress.
It records its involvement in building work during the reign of Trajan in
his '12th year of tribunician power', which firmly places the legion at the
fortress in 108. There are no further dateable inscriptions recording the
unit anywhere in the Roman world and it is unequivocally absent from the
list of legions inscribed on two commemorative pillars in Rome in the 160s
during the reign of Marcus Aurelius.

In terms of artefacts definitely attributable to the legion, a single roof
tile from the Roman tilery at Scalesceugh, just south of Carlisle, and two
others from Carlisle itself, represent the most northerly, and probably the
latest, physical evidence in Britain. Beyond this point, the trail goes cold,
and speculation begins.

Two principal theories have emerged of what befell the IXth: complete
or partial destruction in Britain in the early years of Hadrian's reign, or
transfer to the Continent and later loss or disbandment in the East. For a
century, approximately from the 1870s until the 1970s, the legion's destruction in Britannia was the dominant hypothesis. This model was famously
supported by Mommsen, who in 1885 suggested that: 'Under Hadrian,
there was a terrible catastrophe here, apparently an attack on the fortress
at Eburacum [York] and the annihilation of the legion stationed there, the
very same IXth that had fought so unluckily in the Boudiccan revolt.' In
short, the eminent German historian proposed that the legion had been
destroyed soon after the date of the York inscription, in 108.

The foundations of this hypothesis were soon shaken by the publication
of inscriptions that suggested a few senior officers of the IXth must have
served in the legion significantly after the 108 date. As a consequence,
another German scholar, Emil Ritterling, modified Mommsen's theory

when he published his 1925 treatise of the Roman legions in the multi-volume Pauly–Wissowa Encyclopaedia. Ritterling observed there were indications of major warfare in Britain at the beginning of Hadrian's reign and that the IXth may have perished during this crisis, and not in the earlier period suggested by Mommsen.

As if to seal the IXth's fate, two other British writers elaborated the final movements of the legion in print. Sir Ian Richmond, the Oxford don and archaeologist, acknowledged the prosopographical problems presented by the new inscriptions, and gave his own assessment in his major work *Roman Britain* (1955):

> Trouble in Britain is to be connected with the issue of victory coins in 119 and the fact that by 122 the IXth Legion was replaced at York by the VIth and disappeared from the army list thereafter. That the legion was cashiered, there is no doubt, and it seems evident that this fate, at the hands of the disciplinarian Hadrian, followed an ignominious defeat. But the unit was not annihilated. Some of its officers at least survived and nothing whatever is reported of the circumstances or place of the trouble.

46. Rosemary Sutcliff, author of *The Eagle of the Ninth*, at home in her study.

Even more inflammatory to those who were unhappy about the suggested loss of the IXth to northern barbarians, was the publication in 1954 of the phenomenally successful *The Eagle of the Ninth*. Sutcliff, who as a child had been seriously affected by Still's disease, a crippling form of juvenile rheumatoid arthritis, never married and despite the extent of her disability, energetically devoted her life to writing. Although initially known as a children's author, she soon created a genre of historical fiction that had wide appeal across the generations.

Sutcliff's plot for *The Eagle of the Ninth* had been partly inspired by the discovery of a bronze eagle in the ruins of the basilica of the Roman town of Silchester during an excavation in 1866. She cleverly wove the bird into her novel as the legion's lost standard, which in turn became the focus of atonement for Marcus Aquila, the son of the dead legate of the IXth. Since the book's publication scholars have suggested that the Silchester eagle (minus wings) was part of a less exciting although still impressive sculptural group and not a Roman legionary standard at all. This revelation did not alter Sutcliff's primary plot, which was summed up in the foreword to her book: 'Sometime about the year 117, the IXth Legion, which was stationed at Eburacum where York now stands, marched north to deal with a rising among the Caledonian tribes and was never heard of again . . . no-one knows what happened to the IXth Legion after it marched into the northern mists.'

Added to what had already been published by the respected German

47. The bronze eagle, minus wings, found in the ruins of the basilica at Silchester.

academics Mommsen and Ritterling, and supported by the writings of the establishment figure of Sir Ian Richmond, this seemed a perfectly acceptable storyline into which she could insert fictional characters and dramatic narrative. And so, the tale of the 'Lost Legion' entered popular culture where it remains today as Sutcliff's legacy. Its enduring appeal is evidenced by the continued interest of the public and commercial filmmakers alike with *Centurion* (2010), and *The Eagle* (2011), having grossed a total of $45 million.

But simple versions of history rarely remain unchallenged and by the late 1940s, a decade before Sutcliff's book was written, a broadside of criticism of the theory shared by Mommsen and Richmond, had been fired in the form of a paper by the redoubtable scholar Eric Birley. His first serious challenge came in a 1948 lecture entitled 'The End of the Ninth Legion'. It should be emphasised that this was no lightweight rebuttal, for Birley, as we shall see, spent a substantial portion of his academic life immersed in the prosopography of the leading Roman military personnel in Britannia. With a razor-sharp intellect, so acquainted was he with the detailed movements of Roman officials, that it was said of him in his 1995 obituary: 'Eric Birley could reconstruct history from a pair of used railway tickets.' He believed that the evidence of the CVs of at least three senatorial tribunes and a former legate of the IXth proved that it was still in existence during the reign of Hadrian and possibly later still, and could not reasonably have been wiped out just as the new emperor came to power in 117.

Birley's research into Roman officers' career pathways and his conviction that the legion could not have been destroyed in a British war, culminated in the publication of a weightier treatise, 'The Fate of the Ninth', in
R.M. Butler's *Soldier and Civilian in Roman Yorkshire* (1971). In this
article, he concluded that the legion was either transferred out of Britain
for Trajan's Parthian conflict before the VIth Victrix arrived, or stayed on
to help them build Hadrian's Wall, being subsequently shunted eastwards
to perish in Hadrian's Jewish War in the 130s.

This apparent rescue of the IXth from the demeaning clutches of popular
literature, not to mention northern barbarians, would not rest on the obser-
vance of average career trajectories alone. It was soon to be backed up by
what might be called the 'Nijmegen Connection'. In the late 1950s, a team
of Dutch archaeologists led by Jules Bogaers, excavating at the legionary
fortress on the Kops Plateau, at Nijmegen in eastern Holland, found a roof
tile apparently stamped by a VIIIIth legion (the other way of expressing
the Roman numeral IX), suggesting the presence of at least part of the
Hispana. Nijmegen, which is situated on the River Waal, a branch of the
Rhine, was previously home to the Xth Gemina that had been transferred
further east in 101 by Trajan to support his first Dacian campaign. This
resulted in a vacant fortress, the strategic vacuum of which was filled by a
major detachment of British troops. We know this because the next most
common tile stamps found at the fortress of Nijmegen, after the Xth
Gemina, is *Vex Brit* meaning 'the detachment from Britain', suggesting that
for a while after the Xth's departure, the fortress was manned by a compos-
ite garrison. The solitary VIIIIth roof tile, appeared to be supported by the
finding of a mortarium fragment (a type of Roman mixing bowl common
on military sites) also stamped by the VIIIIth Hispana, from the site of a
nearby pottery. Two other pieces of evidence then emerged: a Roman horse
harness pendant stamped 'IXth *Hisp*' was identified nearby and an altar
to Apollo dedicated by a *Praefectus Castrorum* of IXth Hispana, a camp
commandant, cropped up at Aachen which lies approximately 100 miles
to the south of Nijmegen. These objects, taken in conjunction with Birley's
biographical expertise, were more than enough to convince some academics
eager to place the legion's demise much further to the east, that the IXth
Hispana did not come to an ignominious end in northern Britannia. And
this is where the weight of academic opinion still rests today, as evidenced
by conclusions on the fate of the IXth found in many publications on
Roman Britain from the last decade – an almost universal rejection of the
previous positions of Mommsen, Ritterling and Richmond, and a dismissive
repudiation of Sutcliff's work as pure fantasy.

However, the demise of the IXth Hispana, one of history's great mysteries, merits closer examination of the essential data and consideration of
some alternative interpretations. Not surprisingly on further inspection the

facts are nowhere near as clear-cut as many would suggest and the devil
may be in the detail:

- The IXth, unequivocally stationed at York, was the most northerly
  of the four original British legions and after the withdrawal of the
  IInd Adiutrix in 87, was the most exposed of the now reduced British
  garrison. One may reasonably ask if Trajan, one of the most able of
  Roman generals, was foolhardy enough to relocate the whole legion
  to eastern Europe, thereby reducing the garrison of a 'dangerous
  province' like Britannia to only two legions for a full decade, before
  the arrival of the VIth Victrix in 122?
- If the IXth was still operating in Britain after the commencement of
  the construction of Hadrian's Wall in 122, it did not leave a single
  building inscription among the many other legionary inscriptions
  from the Wall.
- There is definite ceramic evidence of the IXth being in the vicinity
  of Carlisle at some point, in sufficient strength to require the production of official roof tiles. In the decade before the building of
  Hadrian's Wall (110–20), had it been moved northwards to a new
  fortress in Carlisle? A fortress positioned to face a developing threat
  from the south-west of Scotland, an area which is currently acknowledged to have been one of the main sources of trouble at the start
  of Hadrian's reign.
- The single VIIIIth tile from Nijmegen (a second tile was subsequently
  found) was unstratified, i.e. its date is uncertain and could easily be
  due to an earlier (before 100) presence of a vexillation of the legion.
- Nijmegen was the temporary base of several legions that left significantly greater material residue than that suggested for the IXth
  confirming how briefly it must have been in residence.
- The mortarium from near Nijmegen may also reflect an earlier movement of a *vexillation* of the IXth which, it has been suggested, took
  place as early as the 80s.
- The horse brass was found in an antique shop and was therefore
  not contextualised.
- The Aachen altar does not differentiate if the dedicator was retired
  from active service. There are many altars dedicated by men who
  record themselves as high-ranking officers but are far from their
  units at the time of setting up an inscription.
- Birley's prosopographic evidence relies on average career trajectories
  and does not allow for careers retarded by military failure or
  disgrace. It also does not take account of the problems caused by
  Roman dynasties giving the same name to a succession of male
  descendants.

- In a culture and a period obsessed with recording data, there is, to date, not a single inscription of the IXth in any theatre of war other than those mentioned above and certainly no evidence whatsoever of the legion being physically present in the eastern empire. The suggestion that the legion was lost in a Parthian, Armenian or Jewish war is, on purely evidential grounds, more whimsical than Richmond or Sutcliff's propositions.

To sum up, convincing evidence for the legion's move to the East and subsequent annihilation at the hands of the Parthians or Jews simply does not exist. However, the kernel of cognitive bias that lies at the heart of this issue merits some examination – could the desire to see the legion safely transferred out of Britannia owe something to a fixed Roman military supremacy viewpoint? It is interesting to note that the considerable evidence of major warfare in the north of Britain, in approximately the same time period as the IXth's disappearance, derived from Roman literary sources and from the archaeological record, has had little influence on the destruction-in-the-East theorists and is surprisingly rarely taken into consideration when discussing the fate of the legion. The result is a preference to view the concomitant building of Hadrian's Wall as a relaxed, unrelated event that was part of a wider Hadrianic strategy divorced from any suggestion that local circumstances warranted the vast barrier. If the disappearance of the IXth could be viewed in the context of a modern murder investigation, much greater store might be put on where was the deceased last seen alive and who was the last known contact?

So what is the evidence for warfare in Britain contemporaneous with the IXth's disappearance?:

- In the *Augustan Histories*, Spartianus lists several revolts across the empire at the start of Hadrian's reign and comments that '. . . the Britons could not be held under Roman control'.
- Cornelius Fronto, grammarian and confidante of Marcus Aurelius, when writing to Marcus to comfort him about losses in his Parthian war, suggested it would be helpful for Marcus to remember that '. . . in the reign of your grandfather Hadrian, what great numbers of soldiers were slain by the Jews, what great numbers by the Britons'. This is probably one of the more important fragments of literary evidence since Fronto, a precise man of letters, was suggesting that the British War was of a similar magnitude to the Second Jewish Revolt – an attested catastrophe for Hadrian's forces in Judea.
- The gravestone from Vindolanda of centurion Titus Annius, 'slain in the British War' and dated by Tony Birley to the late 110s. The

OPPOSITE. 48. A bronze
diploma of a time-expired
auxiliary soldier, Gaius
Gemellus, granting him the
privileges of Roman
citizenship. It also records the
discharge in Britannia of an
inordinately large number of
auxiliaries in July 122.

inscription employs the Latin word *bellum* for war – this is significant as its use is rare and implies a major conflict.

- Commemorative coins of Hadrian showing victory in Britain dated to the late 110s or possibly early 120s.
- Transfer of the VIth Victrix Legion from the Rhine in 122 to occupy the most northerly Roman fortress of York, which had recently been the home of the IXth.
- Hadrian's visit to Britain in 122, which signalled the initiation of the Wall. This was probably the same *expeditio* referred to below. An *expeditio* was the Latin term used to describe active campaigning by an emperor in a theatre of war.
- An *expeditio Britannica* is mentioned in the career inscriptions of two high-ranking military personnel, Maenius Agrippa and Pontius Sabinus. The latter is recorded as being directed by Hadrian to bring 3,000 legionary reinforcements with him to Britain, drawn from three legions on the Continent, the VIIth from Spain and the VIIIth and XXIInd from Germany.
- Burning and abandonment of several forts in the south of Scotland and the north of England dated to approximately this period.

So much for these existing observations that support the IXth's possible loss in Britannia, but are there any new ideas that can be brought to the table? Two other areas of potential evidence, which hitherto have received little attention, may throw further light on the last days of the IXth.

Firstly, because of the tendency of the Roman military to fastidiously record virtually everything, over a thousand bronze military diplomas, in effect the discharge papers of time-served auxiliary soldiers, have been found scattered throughout the empire. Although this sounds like a spectacular number of surviving inscriptions, it is still much less than 1 per cent of all those likely to have been awarded. These *diplomata* (Greek *di* = two, *ploma* = leaves) are notarised documents inscribed on two sheets of durable bronze plate, wired together, which confirm that the owner had been granted full Roman citizenship as a reward for twenty-five years of army service. The diplomas helpfully record: the exact date of writing; details of the individual being discharged; other eligible units; and the governor of the province in question.

One of these documents, belonging to a cavalryman, was found in very good condition in western Hungary in the 1920s. It records the discharge of one Gemellus, son of Breucus, a Pannonian (Pannonia includes parts of modern-day Hungary and Austria) who had been a trooper in the First *Tampian* Wing of Pannonian cavalry. His rank was *sesquiplicarius*, a trooper who received one and a half times basic pay. His place of demobilisation was Britannia and he, like many of his fellow veterans, had appar-

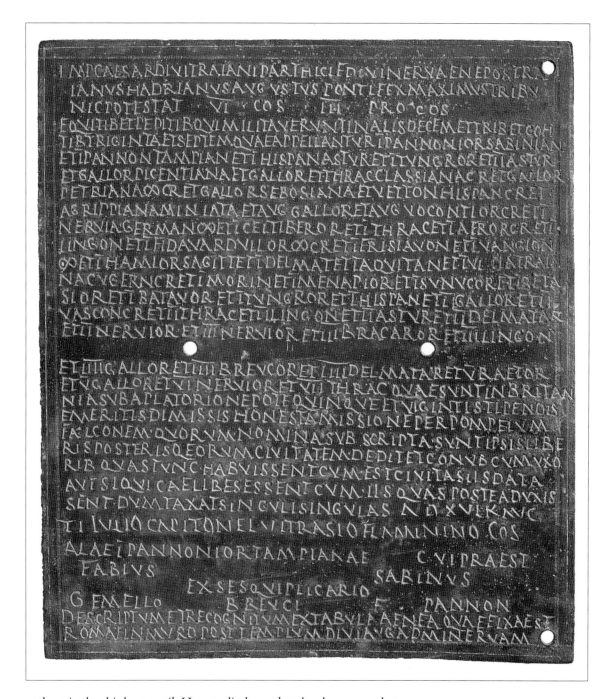

ently retired to his home soil. He was discharged at the changeover between
the outgoing governor of Britain, Quintus Pompeius Falco, and the new
incumbent, Hadrian's kinsman Aulus Platorius Nepos. These facts are interesting enough in themselves for filling gaps in our knowledge of this

49. Legionaries march across a bridge of boats as they embark on Trajan's Dacian campaign. Slung over his shoulder, each soldier carries a *sarcina*, a marching pack, in which *paterae* feature prominently.

shadowy period, but the exact date of Gemellus' diploma is even more fascinating: 17 July 122. This appears to be right in the middle of Hadrian's *expeditio* to Britain. What makes this diploma truly unique, however, is the huge number of other units named on the same document. Veterans from no less than thirteen cavalry and thirty-seven infantry regiments were listed as eligible for discharge in Britannia at the same time as Gemellus. Taking an average maturity rate of twenty men per 1,000-man unit per year, this represents approximately 1,000 men being released from duty simultaneously, the largest such listing recorded at any time on any diploma throughout the whole empire. Other bulk demobilisations are known, thought to be due to periodic high conscription rates quarter of a century previously, and are considered attributable to warfare. It has been argued, however, that large numbers of soldiers may be retained until a period of major crisis has passed and then be released from service without threatening the local security arrangements. It is tempting to speculate that this large group of veterans was held back until exactly when Hadrian could personally discharge them and thank them for holding, or regaining, the north of the province. This diploma then, is helpful in adding to the evidence of the high stress nature of the early 120s but does not in itself shed light directly on the cause of the activity.

Greater suspicion may be placed on the discovery of something that on the face of it appears rather mundane – Roman bronze mess tins. Part of every legionary's campaign kit, which included bedding, an entrenching tool, axe and water bottle, was a small bronze pan, about 15cm in diameter, used for cooking and drinking. We can deduce from the absence of pottery on large-scale excavations of campaign camps, such as that at Kintore in Aberdeenshire, that troops on the move sensibly did not take much in the way of breakable crockery with them and so bronzeware must have been crucial. These pans, known to British archaeologists as *paterae* or *trullae*, are such a characteristic part of Roman military impedimenta that several representations of them appear on Trajan's Column.

What is special about these bronze pans? Firstly, they are not cheap tin pots punched out en masse for the troops – they are mostly relatively high-status items of personal kit, many of which, from the evidence of their manufacturing stamps, originated in the bronze foundries of Campania, the region around Naples. Several of these exact types of pans were excavated in the ruins of Pompeii and Herculaneum and can be seen in the Museum of Naples today. It could reasonably be argued therefore, that a soldier would have been unlikely to readily part with what would have been an essential item of equipment, especially not a soldier on campaign. Secondly, although a few may be of a later period, an assessment of the date of manufacture of the majority of the pans identified in North Britain links them to the late first century and the earliest years of the second century.

So why might this be important? What renders this group of culinary equipment so interesting is that they turn up in disproportionate numbers in places unassociated with the Roman army in the south of Scotland. If the number of pans found in a native context is compared with examples excavated on Roman military sites, the ratio is approximately five to one. Finds of these pans are not new and their sporadic discovery has been noted in the Scottish archaeological record for over a century and still they are being found. For example, this near-perfect specimen (fig. 50) was found recently in the burnt-out remains of the Lowland broch of Castle Craig near Stirling. The currently mooted explanation for these anomalous finds is 'selective trade' between the Roman military and the native tribes.

This rationale depends on exactly how one envisages this trade taking place. Which raises the whole question of what sort of Roman-native interaction was really going on in the late first and early second century during what Tacitus unashamedly describes as Agricola's 'campaign of terror' in the Lowlands of Scotland? Even more improbably, it necessitates enough infantrymen and troopers willing to relinquish their principal utensil of sustenance at a time of major conflict. The largest and finest *patera* from

50. A late first-century *patera* emerges from the wreckage of a burnt-out broch excavated near Stirling. Note the relatively modern appearance of the heat dissipating rings on the pan's base.

51a. (Right) The large and
excellently preserved *patera*
found in the mud near a
crannog in Dowalton Loch,
Dumfries and Galloway. Like
many other Roman *paterae*
from Scotland, the vessel can
be dated to the late first or
early second century.

b. (Below) Roman military
ironwork hoard recovered
from Carlingwark Loch. Note
the deliberately fractured
sword tips.

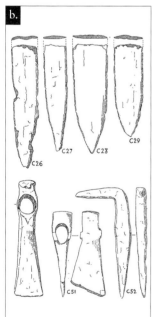

Lowland Scotland is the one found concealed next to a crannog in Dowal-ton Loch in the Machars of Galloway. This beauty, which has a decorated boss, was almost certainly not parted easily from the hand of its former high-ranking owner.

The 'lost *paterae*' are not the only examples of unusual Roman material from the period of the IXth's disappearance cropping up in non-Roman contexts north of the Tyne–Solway isthmus. A marble head from a Trajanic period statue, a larger than life-size leg from a bronze equestrian statue (complete with a hole in the heel for a lost spur) and at least three ironwork hoards all with significant components of Roman military equipment have been stumbled upon during agricultural activity across the south of Scot-land.

One of the most sinister and fascinating of these hoards comes from Carlingwark Loch in Dumfriesshire. Dredged from the bottom of the loch by fishermen in 1866 and contained within a large bronze cauldron of a type more common in the south of England, was a collection of predom-inantly Roman military ironwork. This included blacksmith's tools, regu-lation military cooking stands, fragments of chain-mail armour and, most significantly, the terminal portions of at least six ritually snapped swords. These swords may all have originally belonged to Roman military person-nel, possibly auxiliaries. In addition to these discoveries, most of the Roman

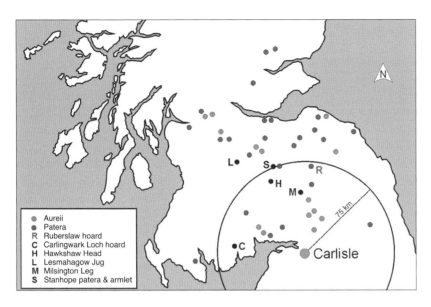

52. A distribution map of unusual Roman finds from non-Roman sites in the south of Scotland. Most of the finds can be ascribed to loss in the early second century.

gold coins (*aureii*) – which the Romans did not use for simple trade or even bribery – found scattered among non-Roman sites in the south of Scotland, date from before 120.

These items, spread over a wide area of Lowland Scotland would indicate a very atypical pattern of 'trade' which just happened to take place at the same time as the IXth reputedly departed for the Continent with no record of ever having reached its destination.

So much for popular culture and novel observations, but do the 'Eastern Connection' proponents have it all their own way in academic circles? In the recent past, three scholars of note have rejected the currently accepted view of the eastward drift of the IXth. The first, Professor Lawrence Keppie, Emeritus Professor of Roman Archaeology at Glasgow University, and author of one of the most respected books about the foundation of the Roman army, has challenged the prosopographical arguments outlined above (1989 and 2000). An expert on Latin texts and an authority on Roman inscriptional stylistics, Keppie has questioned the adherence to 'average' career pathways and 'probable' consular dates to counter the implied continued survival of the IXth Hispana late into Hadrian's reign. He has also highlighted that it was not without precedent for embarrassingly defeated legions to be written out of history by the Romans themselves, or for parts of legions with their attendant officers to survive the slaughter of the main body of the legion. Tacitus' descriptions of what almost happened to the IXth twice before in its earlier history, during the Boudiccan revolt and the later Agricolan campaign, provide convincing evidence of this latter phenomenon.

The second academic to challenge the 'Eastern Exit' hypothesis is Miles

Russell, senior lecturer in Prehistoric and Roman Archaeology at
Bournemouth University (2011). Russell is co-author of 'UnRoman Britain'
that puts forward an alternative view of the nature of 400 years of Roman
domination. He has specifically highlighted the illogicality of the suggestion
that Trajan moved his most northerly legion eastwards, unnecessarily
exposing the most troubled flank of Britannia. He has also emphasised the
complete absence of physical evidence of the proposed move east of
Nijmegen, to Judea or Parthia.

The third and most recent publication in support of reinstating the
legion's British demise is by the Hadrian's Wall scholar, Nick Hodgson. His
2021 publication in the journal *Britannia* forensically examines the prosopographic and archaeological evidence of the last days of the legion. Failing
to find any convincing proof at all for a move eastward, he concludes that
the balance of evidence tips significantly in favour of destruction in North
Britain probably in or around 122.

Finally, a brief review of the Varus Disaster mentioned earlier (see chapter
6), may be helpful when considering the possibility of the IXth's near-oblit-
eration in Scotland. In this Augustan period debacle, the unfortunate Roman
governor of the province of Germania, Publius Quinctilius Varus led three
legions and a similar number of auxiliaries and camp followers into oblivion
in an ambush in the Teutoburg forest in Germany. At least 30,000 personnel
and their pack animals perished in the ensuing running battle. It was not
only people who disappeared but also hundreds of tons of military equipment that vanished into thin air. For centuries, historians and enthusiasts
searched in vain for the physical remains of this great slaughter, known to
modern Germans as the Varusschlacht. However, it was not until the 1980s
that the metal-detecting exploits of a British army officer-turned-amateur-
archaeologist, Major Tony Clunn, then based in Dortmund, discovered the
first telltale finds of the great destruction about 100km further north than
previously suspected. Not a single trace of the battle had been discovered
in the previous 2,000 years. Based on this well-documented precedent, it is
therefore entirely conceivable that the physical remains of carnage on a
much smaller scale (perhaps 5,000–8,000 men and their equipment) could
still await discovery in the borderlands of Scotland.

Conclusions about the exit of the IXth

Allowing for the intrinsic uncertainties of prosopography (non-average
career pathways, fathers and sons with the same name, transcription errors,
etc.) and based on current archaeological evidence, and irrespective of the
exact order of events, the case for the IXth being lost, or at least terminally
mauled in North Britain far outweighs any evidence of it being whisked
away to the East. The hypothesis is simple: the legion, which as we have

noted may have already been depleted by Trajan's troop movements, was moved north-westwards whole or in part from York to a new fortress at Carlisle sometime in the 110s to counter a growing threat from the south-west of Scotland. Then, at a date probably around 120, an uprising began in the Lowlands that gathered momentum and engulfed Trimontium at Newstead and the other forts further south along two corridors, one down Dere Street to the Corbridge area and the other veering south-west towards Carlisle. At some point, probably early in the rebellion, the IXth, accompanied by a large auxiliary force (scholars rarely mention that some auxiliary units from Britain are also unaccounted for after the 120s), emerged to engage a native force of superior numbers.

Where? Judging by the scatter of 'stress' material, probably within a radius of 50–70km of Carlisle. Mayhem probably ensued for a period during which several, but almost certainly not all, forts in the extreme north of England were also attacked or abandoned. The Lowland tribes were perhaps in confederacy with a northern branch of the Brigantes, which may account for the southward-facing conundrum of the Vallum which will be considered in the next chapter on Hadrian's Wall. It would take Quintus Pompeius Falco, the governor, approximately eighteen months to bring things under control, using forces drawn from the southerly based XXth and IInd legions. At the same time, units will have distinguished themselves, accounting for the discharges noted on the Gemellus diploma and honorifics suddenly appearing in some unit titles. His successful rescue would earn him his next posting, the sinecure of the governorship of Asia, considered one of the major rewards for successful soldier-diplomats. It was left to Hadrian, the imperial tourist, to come to Britannia in 122 with the VIth Victrix – if it had not been transferred earlier – at the head of a punitive *expeditio* which included the personalities of two senior commanders, Sabinus and Agrippa (as recorded on inscriptions) with their legionary detachments from the VIIth, VIIIth and XXIInd drawn from Spain and Germany. Hadrian, after inserting his kinsman Nepos as governor, and billeting the VIth at York, took his place as head of the army at a great passing-out parade. He then initiated the Wall, or at least gave his blessing to work already underway, that carries his name to the present day.

This scenario appears to fit the evidence and acknowledges the uncertainties and biases of prosopography (on which alternative theories are built) and results in no forced necessity for the legion to be mysteriously moved eastwards. However, it would be good to have more material evidence to confirm the Borderlands as the epicentre of the unpleasantness. Only time and the future assiduous efforts of another legion, this time of metal detectorists, are likely to tell us if the forlorn artefacts strewn across the moorlands of Lowland Scotland represent the last echoes of the unlucky IXth *Hispana*.

CHAPTER NINE

The Wall

When the IXth Legion slipped unrecorded from the stage of history the next major, and possibly consequential event in the Roman occupation of North Britain, was the creation of the vast edifice we know today as Hadrian's Wall. Commencing construction sometime around 122, this enduring bastion, reputedly the largest single Roman structure in the world, snakes 80 Roman miles across the Tyne–Solway isthmus. Although the Wall itself lies entirely south of the current political border, and the name is often used as a metaphor by modern commentators and media to signify the 'frontier' between modern Scotland and England, it plays much more than a symbolic part in the history of early Scotland.

Often referred to simply as 'the Wall', it is not just a stone curtain but a complex cordon of integrated military installations. Some authorities suggest it shares much in common with other preclusive walls we can see

53. Scout looks north from a section of Hadrian's Wall near Housesteads fort.

springing up around the world today from Turkey to North America. More considered inspection, however, reveals that these more modern barriers are a very heterogeneous group and definitely not all similar to the Roman Wall. Occasionally referred to somewhat diminutively as: a 'political boundary marker', as for example the Berlin Wall; or a 'customs and immigration frontier', such as Trump's Mexican Border Wall; or an 'anti-terrorist barrier', like the Israeli Security Wall; our Roman leviathan seems to have much more in common with the definitively military architecture of the Maginot Line. And like the grand defensive/offensive structure named after André Maginot, the French Minister of War in the 1930s, Hadrian's Wall was possibly over-engineered for a similar reason – as an exaggerated response to a prior cataclysmic conflict. In the case of the Maginot Line the carnage of the Great War, and in the case of the Roman Wall the episode of major warfare in the north referred to in the previous chapter.

The term over-engineered is not used casually. It is impossible to escape the perceptual and emotional impact of the stark functionality of Hadrian's Wall, which appears to project a self-evident truth about its original purpose and function. Whether the onlooker is a chance visitor, a conflict archaeologist or the author of *Game of Thrones*, the visual cues declare a series of simple messages: that it was a very large barrier built of stone, bristling with strong points, manned lavishly by well-prepared troops, and that for three centuries it appeared to be expecting serious trouble from the north. When compared with the simple wooden fence of the German *limes*, also built by the same emperor, which links the two great riverine barriers of

54. The Maginot Line at Casemate d'Esch. The combination of heavily engineered linear barrier and strongpoint has features in common with the Roman frontier arrangements in North Britain.

the Danube and the Rhine, or the ditch and mound of the Fossatum Africae in North Africa, Hadrian's North British construction is a formidable integrated package of passive defence coupled with equally fearsome offensive capability. But despite the gestalt and the sensory overload when one experiences the Wall, diminutive explanations are still occasionally sought for its creation. In so doing, a fascinating variety of explanations for its construction have been synthesised, some less convincing than others.

Why a wall at all?

It has been argued that because of the Roman army's ruthless efficiency a curtain wall would never be required as a primarily defensive structure. While it may be true that the Roman planners never envisaged troops fighting hand-to-hand from the wall top, its basic architecture (the wall width and the finding of superstructural elements) would suggest that it was crowned by a fighting platform. The necessity for a running barrier (rather than a chain of watchtowers) has also been questioned but this perhaps overlooks a fundamental tactical purpose of such an obstacle. The clue here lies with the great natural barriers utilised by the Romans to insulate themselves elsewhere from the barbarian north: the Rhine and the Danube. These great rivers were used successfully for centuries, not to act as

Non-conflict hypotheses to explain the building of the Wall:

- Boundary marker: the suggestion that the Romans were required to define the empire with a physical marker goes back some way in modern historiography and has resonance with the demarcation of state boundaries today. It is not an unreasonable concept given Hadrian's declared desire to limit the empire. However, the argument that this was the primary reason for such a barrier fails to explain why markers of comparable magnitude are not found elsewhere in the empire.
- Customs barrier: this is an allusion to the excise function of a modern frontier and would imply that there was some commerce to tax. However, 100 years of excavation on native sites north of the Wall – save Traprain Law – has produced very little Roman material suggesting that 'trade' was an unlikely primary driver. Another flaw in this argument is that for a customs barrier, the architecture is even more over-engineered than would be required for fiscal purposes.
- Anti-immigration obstacle: this argument presupposes there was a burning desire for those outside the empire to adopt Roman culture

but is militated against by the same absence of Roman material culture in the indigenous archaeology to the north. Again, over-engineering is an obvious objection. This concept is perhaps unduly influenced by the current zeitgeist of xenophobia.

- Anti-bandit barrier: to guard against petty theft and cattle rustling, a simple patrolled palisade as in Germany would have sufficed since cows cannot scale a ditch and climb a large wooden fence. The Wall's heavily manned strongpoints would also be unnecessary.

- Hadrian the megalomaniac builder: Hadrian is celebrated not just as the fabulously wealthy tourist but also for his grand designs. A visit to his villa at Tivoli, the Pantheon or the Temple of Venus in Rome will confirm the sort of building projects he was capable of initiating. The overall design emphasis of the Wall is clearly military but there are architectural niceties that go beyond the functional, such as the relatively elaborate rustication of the masonry of many of the gateways. This feature however is not specific to Britain and is found in the detailing of forts of the Hadrianic period in Germany and probably reflects what automatically happened when projects received dedicated imperial funding. The 'grand designs' explanation is also unconvincing when one attempts to apply it to his other frontiers, such as the much more basic *Limes Germanicus*.

- A displacement activity: history teaches that idle armies are a recipe for simmering mutiny. On the basis that the Roman army was, among other things, an engineering phenomenon, this suggestion appears to have some merit. However, the same concept applies to all Roman frontiers and consequently fails to explain the unique features highlighted above. Also, from the contemporary accounts of serious trouble in the province, the army had quite enough to do without creating non-essential construction work for itself.

- A vanity project: this suggestion is in many ways analogous to the 'megalomaniac builder' idea but is possibly the weakest of all the hypotheses. With so many frontiers closer to the centre of power which received Hadrian's attention at approximately the same time, it seems improbable that he should choose the backwater of north Britannia to construct this barrier as an imperial ego booster. In so doing, it would have been at great cost to the imperial treasury and would have been projected at a population whose opinion was of no significance to the man who ruled the known world. But probably the greatest objection to this suggestion is the almost complete absence of flattering iconography and honorific inscriptions to identify Hadrian as the builder, which is in direct contrast to the situation on the Antonine Wall.

55a. Dr Axel Posluschny admires the section of reconstructed wooden frontier (German Limes) at the Saalburg near Frankfurt.

b. Section of reconstructed Wall and turret at Vindolanda (Erica Reid for scale).

c. Map of Hadrian's Wall showing some of the major installations and the distribution of hinterland and screening forts.

insurmountable obstacles (since both could be crossed with a little planning and effort) but to act as retardants that would slow down and funnel any onslaught into certain areas where the rivers could be crossed more easily. This gave Roman forces time to concentrate troops at pressure points to mount proportionate counter-attacks. If the frontier had been solely provided by disconnected forts, these could have been enveloped and neutralised by a sudden wave of large numbers of enemy troops.

If we develop the concept further, the massive obstacles of the great frontal ditches and mural curtains of the Walls of Hadrian and Antoninus, could be seen to emulate the channels and steep banks of 'artificial rivers'. Rivers which in themselves are not impermeable but act by slowing down and diverting large numbers of assailants to specific points where the Romans may benefit from numerical or tactical superiority. So, an important implication is that while lesser walls or chains of watchtowers operate well in detecting and blocking small raiding and cattle-rustling parties in times of peace, the structural elements of the great barriers facing into Scotland achieve their key design advantage by retarding large forces in time of war.

The personal hand of Hadrian?

'And so . . . he set out for Britain, and there he corrected many problems and was the first to construct a wall, 80 miles in length, which separated the barbarians from the Romans.' This brief statement by Spartianus, contributor of Hadrian's biography to the collective *Augustan Histories*, is the only passage in ancient literature that hints at Hadrian's personal involvement and why the barrier was constructed. Although the quality of the *Histories* is considered by scholars to be generally patchy, a closer reading of Spartianus provides some interesting insights.

Firstly, the original Latin reads '*qui barbaros Romanosque divideret*' – '. . . that separated the barbarians from the Romans'. As Guy de la Bédoyère has pointed out, the verb *dividere* is often translated as 'separate', but it usually has a much stronger meaning (1998). He suggests that in this context a better reading would be 'rend asunder', a more violent act than simple partition.

Secondly, despite his poor reputation for factual accuracy, Spartianus described the length of the Wall accurately, 80 Roman miles, so we can be reasonably confident that his work is not a complete fabrication.

Thirdly, the opening sentence above was followed by twenty-five lines of palace intrigue, such as the suggested impropriety between the Empress Sabina and her courtiers, which was totally irrelevant to matters in Britain. Consequently, this section may represent journalistic padding because of the meagre contextual information Spartianus had to work with. In essence,

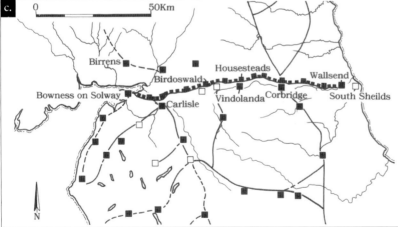

because of a lack of intelligence rather than artifice, he created a literary smokescreen that may conceal just about any activity at the time of the emperor's visit.

Fourthly, he stated that in Britain, in contrast to other provinces where

natural obstacles like rivers acted as frontiers, Hadrian 'held back the
barbarians by artificial barriers, by means of high stakes planted deep in
the ground and fastened together in the manner of a palisade'. Thus reflecting exactly the type of 'fence' erected in those sections bounding free
Germany that are not delineated by the Rhine or the Danube.

Finally, Spartianus made much of Hadrian's capriciousness even with
those close to him. This instability appears to have become more marked
towards the end of his life. Despite Dio's record of a vengeful backlash to
yet another major rebellion in Judea (the Second Jewish War, often referred
to as the Bar Kokhba revolt) in 132–6, Spartianus records 'there were no
campaigns of importance during his reign, and the wars that he did wage
were brought to a close almost without arousing comment'. These observations of Hadrian's view of the world, may go some way to explaining
the apparent absence of details concerning a war with barbarians in Britain.
As we have seen, there was undoubtedly a bitter conflict in Judea and the
inscriptional evidence would suggest that there was also a major campaign,
an *expeditio* to Britain in response to a prior bloodbath.

Before considering further the arguments for and against the emperor's
personal design brief for the Wall, Spartianus' bland opening statement
should be seen against the backdrop of Hadrian's global policy to demarcate
the empire early in his reign, presumably to limit military and financial
risk. It is often said the empire was at its greatest under the leadership of
his predecessor, the beloved Trajan, the implication being that Hadrian's
complex persona did not have the same vision or appetite for limitless
conquest. However, this is probably a slight on Hadrian's talents as a leader
and a visionary. His personal military experience and reputation as a pragmatic administrator perhaps helped him see the writing on the walls of the
Roman world of forthcoming barbarian turbulence. From Egypt to Iran,
from Britain to North Africa, the imperial expansionist juggernaut that he
had inherited from Trajan was about to run out of steam – problems apparent at the start of his tenure of power that may have been generated by a
military envelope stretched too thin by his forefather. It seems reasonable
to postulate that the urbane and cultured Hadrian recognised that his taste
for tourism, hunting, Eastern culture and all manner of fine things, would
not be satisfied if he was coordinating costly expeditions against multiple
insurrections. It was therefore likely that a frontier of some sort was planned
for Britannia much as it was for the rest of the Roman world. But when
the Romans required a boundary marker, that is usually what they built –
Hadrian went much further when he addressed the problems of North
Britain (plates 6 and 7).

So did Hadrian have a personal hand in the Wall's design? It is hard to
be sure. The splendid uniformity of the primary concept would suggest so.
It also seems logical that since his visit to Britain in 122 coincided with

approximately when the Wall was commenced that he should have some input into the design brief. We also know from dendrochronology that the date of the timbers of the considerably less impressive German fence was also contemporary with his grand tour, which first visited Germania in 121.

The Wall's longevity?

If Hadrian's personal input is difficult to judge, it is even more difficult to find consensus for the reason behind the persistence of the Wall, so it may be useful to take a general view of the mural complex. David Breeze, in the preview of his reworking of Collingwood's guide to the Wall, crystallised it in a single sentence: 'it is a massive stone wall not found anywhere else on the border of the Empire, with a density of structures again unparalleled'. By any modern standards, let alone those of Iron Age Britain, the Wall would be construed as overkill and therein perhaps lies a clue to its enduring purpose. This mighty barrier of masonry, with its impressive north-facing defensive ditch (which in places is cut through solid rock), its hundreds of turrets, dozens of milecastles, sixteen wall-hugging forts and huge revenue costs, lasted for 300 years because it faced a persistent challenge. Unlike flimsier modern examples, such as the Berlin Wall whose purpose was time served after its brief ideological epoch (thirty years), it was a structure that was to be maintained, manned and patrolled for the remainder of the Roman occupation of Britannia, well beyond the limit necessary to serve a single emperor's vanity. What continuing events could have precipitated an investment of so much manpower and material in an apparent back-water? And as excavation has recently shown, why was most of the northern aspect furnished with mantraps and spikes? A primarily defensive purpose of the Wall, which fits broadly into the epigraphic and archaeological evidence, seems to provide sufficient explanation for those who wish to apply Occam's razor to simplify some of the overly complex and less intuitive reasons advanced in recent years for the planning and construction of the Wall. However, to accept this explanation requires a significant shift in thinking of what the Caledonians were capable of when suitably provoked.

A credible enemy?

All of the above, therefore, indicate that a prime function of the Wall was to provide security for the province, which in turn invites the question instinctively posed by George R.R. Martin, creator of *Game of Thrones*, when he experienced it for the first time – security from what? What lurked beyond this impressive structure to necessitate such a response?

Could the Caledonians or their Pictish successors repeatedly mount significant military challenges to the supremacy of the Roman army for nearly 300 years? If the answer is no, then one is right to seek less militaristic explanations for the eye-watering magnitude of the enterprise: a displacement exercise for idle soldiers; a customs barrier; a symbol of power; a vanity project; a population control zone; a cultural outpost or any combination of the above. If the answer is yes, then one has a single explanation for why the Wall necessitated a massive and sustained presence in the landscape.

The belief that northern tribesmen represented skirmishing nuisances more suited to cattle rustling than warfare, is one that pervades current interpretations of Britain's Roman frontiers. However, until the 1940s it had been thought that the northern tribes, whenever circumstances arose, were an effective opposition to Rome and this understanding provided a reasonable explanation for the density of fortifications in the north, the loss of the IXth Legion and the initiation of the Wall. Over the last few decades however, this view has become unfashionable and there has been considerable historical revision in response to the zeitgeist. One of the latest theories, for example, suggests the 'Wallzone' was maintained to provide a parking lot for surplus troops with nowhere else to go, which leads to an absurd circular argument that the presence of the empire's best generals was a consequence of having a large army on the Wall.

It is probably reasonable to restate the well-attested example set by the 1745 Jacobite uprising that showed convincingly that the northern tribes could coalesce into a belligerent juggernaut at very short notice and carry wide-ranging mayhem far to the south.

This eighteenth-century analogy also provides an illustration of the form an imperial backlash may take: a major investment in the military infrastructure of the occupying power, including roads, forts and ports; punitive expeditions; famine; and ultimately rural depopulation. Recent excavations of indigenous homesteads on the Northumberland Coastal Plain by Hodgson and colleagues (2012), have shown significant abandonment of the network of farms north of the Wall, with terminal radiocarbon dates approximating to shortly after the time the Wall was built. Their conclusion is pretty clear: 'the Wall had a destructive effect on traditional society to the north and protected a developing provincial society immediately to the south'.

Hadrian's personality

In an attempt to understand the complexity of the Wall and its impact on the peoples it bisected, it is instructive to consider briefly the character of the progenitor of the project. Hadrian has long been counted among the

'Five Great Emperors' with other notable figures such as Trajan and Marcus Aurelius. Although the group was selected and the term coined by Machiavelli, which may ring some alarm bells, Hadrian's twenty-year reign was undoubtedly a period of prosperity for most people within the boundaries of the empire. He is credited with limiting expansionist policies and setting, and touring, the boundaries of the Roman world, although there is some evidence that Trajan before him was already beginning to demarcate borders such as the Danube frontier and the Stanegate.

Hadrian is often thought of as an imaginative builder. However, his reputation as hobby architect has probably been overplayed since other emperors' personal projects, such as the Domus Aurea of Nero, the Colosseum of Vespasian, the aqueduct of Claudius, the Palatine palace of Severus and the Basilica of Maxentius were equally spectacular. Although popularly regarded in the modern West as a cultured, sensitive polymath, Hadrian was also a man not to be crossed. In his later years, as Spartianus highlighted, his sociopathic behaviour became progressively more erratic sparking contemporary comparisons with the reviled Domitian. Indeed, his successor Antoninus Pius only just managed to have him elevated to a god after his death (several emperors of this period were deified) by threatening the Senate with his own resignation. If Cassius Dio is to be believed, Hadrian's vindictive persona was truly revealed towards the end of his life by the scale of the genocide he sanctioned in the wake of the Bar Kokhba revolt. His massacre of hundreds of thousands of Jews and his attempt to expunge the cultural fabric of Judaism should give every Hadrianophile pause for thought.

We may then ask what would have been this emperor's response if the latest generation of angry young warriors from the north had inspired a confederacy of the Brigantes, Selgovae and Novantae to sweep through imperial installations in the borderlands? Forts whose garrisons would have been partially depleted by Trajan's divestment to resource his eastern expeditions. Could this have been the *bellum* of the early years of his reign hinted at in his biography and the great loss of Hadrianic troops in Britain reported by Fronto to the young Marcus Aurelius? The same conflict witnessed on the gravestone of Titus Annius at Vindolanda and in the ashes of the fort at Birrens? If it was, it would not be difficult, considering his extreme response to the Bar Kokhba affair, to suggest that torching the lands of the isthmus and building a fearsome wall would be well within his scope. The monumental Hanoverian fortifications in Scotland after the 1745 rebellion are good surviving examples of imperial overreaction to insurrection.

How was the Wall constructed?

56. The massive 'star' fort of Fort George near Inverness. Built in response to the 1745 Uprising, the fortress was completed in 1769 – it has been continuously garrisoned by the British Army ever since.

According to numerous small inscriptions incorporated into the fabric of the Wall, the construction work, or at least its oversight, was carried out by detachments of the three legions stationed in Britain at that time: the IInd, the VIth and the XXth. As mentioned previously, the IXth is conspicuous by its complete absence from the list. Depictions from Trajan's Column illustrate the engineering capability of Roman troops by showing legionaries hard at work cutting stone and wood and carrying baskets of mortar to create permanent fortifications. It is hard however to ignore the fact that Rome was probably the greatest consumer of slave labour in the ancient world and to turn a deaf ear to the comments placed by Tacitus into the mouth of Calgacus, the Caledonian leader: 'Under lash and abuse, our very hands and bodies are worn down by the labour of clearing forests and bogs.' So, there is more than a marginal possibility that enslavement of the regional population, particularly those to the north, underpinned the building skills of the legionaries.

Plate 1. (*Left*) Detail from the spectacular processional frieze at the National Portrait Gallery, Edinburgh, painted by William Brassey Hole (1846–1917). Agricola glares at Calgacus as Tacitus looks on.

Plate 2. (*Below*) Dun Carloway broch on the west coast of the Isle of Lewis. Note the complex double wall construction with galleries and stairs. These structures are unique to Iron Age Scotland.

Plate 3. (*Right*) Iron Age gold torcs of native and continental manufacture found by David Booth, a metal detectorist, near Blair Drummond, Perthshire.

Plate 4. (*Below left*) A group of *dolabra*, Roman pick-axes, found in one of the wells at Trimontium – modern Newstead – near Melrose. Some of the iron shows almost no corrosion because of the anaerobic conditions.

Plate 5. (*Below right*) Two horse skulls from a pit at Newstead. Several cavalry horses had been slaughtered by the Romans, possibly to prevent them falling into native hands.

Plate 6. Housesteads Roman fort at dawn. The civilian settlements (*vici*) around the forts on Hadrian's Wall became quite large but remained unfortified – unlike the *vici* on the Antonine Wall. Note the field systems.

Plate 7. The enigmatic Vallum, the complex earthwork to the south of Hadrian's Wall, heads eastwards in a straight line. The Wall and Milecastle 42 can be seen to the north on the edge of the ridge formed by the Whin Sill.

Plate 8. Burnswark Hill in Dumfriesshire – the summit is encompassed by a 17-acre hillfort. Note the prominent ramparts of the extraordinarily-elongated North Roman siege camp in the foreground.

Plate 9. (*Above left*)
A young volunteer helps excavate the hoard of Roman lead sling bullets, dumped behind the rampart of the North Roman Camp at Burnswark Hill.

Plate 10. (*Above right*)
The remnants of Bow Castle broch overlooking Gala Water. The peculiar tumble of the broch's masonry was noted by James Curle in 1892. He suggested that Roman forces had destroyed this and the neighbouring broch at Torwoodlee.

Plate 11. (*Right*)
The double ditches of Rough Castle Roman fort and the huge ditch of the Antonine Wall running off to the west are conspicuous in the low winter sun. The defensive pits known as *lilia* lie to the right.

Plate 12. The capital of the Sol altar from Inveresk showing the elegant carving of the four seasons. Dedicated by a centurion called Gaius Cassius Flavianus, it displayed almost no wear when it was deliberately buried in the fort's *Mithraeum*.

Plate 13. A modern sculpture emulating an Antonine Wall distance stone now stands in Cow Wynd, Falkirk. This stone celebrates a less Romanocentric story than the originals. Note the broch, carnyx and defeated Roman soldier.

Plate 14. The rock-cut ditch of the Antonine wall on Croy Hill snakes westward along the edge of the ridge that traverses the highest points of the Forth–Clyde isthmus.

Plate 15. The columns and capitals that once graced the forecourt of the *principia* of the Antonine Wall fort on Bar Hill now stand in the Hunterian Museum in Glasgow University. The columns were excavated from the fort's well.

Plate 16. (*Left*) The red jasper intaglio of Caracalla found by Walter Elliot while field-walking at Newstead. It dates to the early third century.

Plate 17. (*Below*) The great hillfort of Traprain Law, seen from the south-west, basks in the evening sun. Archaeological survey of the fertile agricultural hinterland has shown a dense patchwork of indigenous settlement – Roman military installations are strikingly absent. The Firth of Forth, North Berwick Law and the Bass Rock can be seen in the distance.

Plate 18. Probably concealed in the early fifth century, the Traprain Treasure remains the largest hoard of hacksilver found outside the boundaries of the Roman Empire. Some of the vessels bear early Christian symbols.

Plate 19. Dumbarton Rock, a volcanic plug on the north shore of the Clyde Estuary, was surmounted by an Iron Age fort known as Alt Clut, which ultimately became the centre of an Early Medieval Brittonic kingdom.

57. The ditch and Vallum of Hadrian's Wall near Limestone Corner. Note the blocks of roughly cut stone removed from the ditch and dumped on the northern lip. The Wall itself lies below the modern road (B6318) – which like Fort George was built in response to the Jacobite uprising.

In design terms, Hadrian's Wall is an almost unique construction among the frontiers with which Rome encircled its empire. Almost unique because the slightly later Antonine Wall across the Forth–Clyde isthmus has a broadly similar plan in which all the major elements are interlinked. On other frontiers, such as the Rhine and the Danube, the linear barrier, forts and supporting structures are less cohesive.

The ditch and berm

The first element of the Wall, as encountered from the north, is an approx-imately 8m-wide V-shaped ditch, excavated with such resolve that the only significant breaks in its 118km length are where the Wall sits atop a sheer cliff face in the central sector or it fronts onto the Solway Firth. It was clearly an imperative in the initial design, since in places significant stretches were cut through solid rock, a feature particularly well displayed at Lime-stone Corner. The latter place name though is misleading for the rock here is not limestone but quartz-dolerite whinstone – a rock so hard that the

58a. Excavations at Byker in Newcastle revealed a series of pits lying between the wall base and the ditch (the dark band parallel to the pavement). These are orientated to be maximally obstructive.

b. The Wall in winter, looking eastwards to Housesteads.

Roman mason's futile cutting and lifting slots remain clearly visible today in the huge unbreakable blocks that litter the ditch and its margin.

The upcast from the ditch was generally thrown to the north creating a counterscarp, but immediately to the south, between the ditch and the Wall, was a ribbon of flat land known as the berm. Of variable width, this strip looks at first sight to be relatively nondescript. However, following landmark discoveries on the Antonine Wall, closer inspection by excavation revealed that long sections were covered in mantraps – essentially steep-sided pits – arrayed in methodically staggered alignments (Bidwell 2005). These obstacles probably contained sharpened branches or even stakes to add to their inherent qualities as entanglements.

The Wall

The next component is the Wall itself. To the surprise of many modern visitors, the long stretch of barrier from Bowness on the Solway to the Irthing Gap was not initially made from stone at all but from stacked turf with wooden fittings. The reason behind this anomaly was previously ascribed to poor availability of stone and lime in the western sector. This idea has been reassessed by scholars such as Graafstal (2012) and Hodgson (2017) and it is now generally thought that the use of a less durable earthen

b.

rampart was due to the speed with which these accessible materials could provide a serviceable barrier. Graafstal titled his seminal publication on this subject 'Hadrian's Haste' to highlight his belief that orders were likely given to expedite the Wall in this sector as a response to continued threat from the peoples of south-west Scotland. Hodgson has suggested that this section could have been built in less than a year with the full intention of replacing it in stone later. From the available archaeology, it seems that the stone curtain in the western sector was indeed in the process of completion towards the end of Hadrian's lifetime.

The stone Wall was initially planned to be 10 Roman feet thick, and a significant section of the eastern sector was completed to this specification. The width of the remainder of the Wall heading westward varied between 8 and 6 Roman feet, suggesting that there may have been a significant temporal or cost saving alteration in plan somewhere about Wall mile 27. The causes for this and the so-called 'fort decision' discussed below, are speculative but may have been exacerbated by further trouble in the province. The height of the Wall has been estimated to have been approximately 3.5–4.5m at the Wall walk level and even higher at the top of the crenellation. The presence of embrasures has been suggested by the architecture of Roman walls elsewhere and by the crenellated decoration evident on two of a small series of three Roman enamelled bronze cups and pans which were probable Roman souvenirs from the Wall itself. All three of these cups display around their rims, in sequence, names of forts on the Wall. The height of the Wall was in part dictated by what was practical for the purpose of deterring assailants but also because of limitations set by the construction technique. This consisted of facing stones of worked limestone or sandstone with a substantial core of rubble set in mortar or puddled clay. Through time, this matrix could become unstable and, probably aided by the region's wet weather, wall collapses and subsequent repairs seem to have been relatively common.

The planning and building sequence of the curtain wall have been debated for years but now thanks to the work of a modern-day antiquarian and amateur surveyor, John Poulter (2009), we seem to have a good idea of how it was planned at least. It would appear that the Roman surveyors laid out the eastern and western sectors using long-distance sightlines with local adjustments. Poulter has also persuasively argued that planning was from both ends and directed towards the irregular central section of the Crags, rather than the long-accepted east–west direction of travel.

Milecastles and turrets

The original design for the Wall called for a small fortlet set at a spacing of every Roman mile (1.48km) with two observation turrets in the interval. These milecastles had north and south gates and a couple of small barrack buildings designed to hold no more than ten to fifteen men. Some turrets, which were likely to have been two storeys high, do seem to have provided overnight shelter, judging by the presence of hearths, for two or three soldiers who, with the milecastle garrison, would have provided surveillance for that sector.

The original intention appears to have been for the main garrison of the Wall to be housed in a handful of widely spaced installations placed a mile or two to the rear of the curtain, like the fort at Vindolanda. It seems reasonable to suppose the men on the linear barrier were responsible for raising the alarm to which the hinterland forts would respond in force. It has been convincingly argued from geography and sightlines that some turrets on the Wall gave equally good visibility to the north and south thereby facilitating observation and emergency signalling for reinforcements.

It has been known for a long time that the original blueprint of curtain wall and milecastles was soon supplemented by the so-called 'Fort Decision'. This new development established sixteen large forts attached to, and in some cases straddling, the Wall itself – a decision which most now think was precipitated by further warfare in the north. The archetypal fort of this design is at Chesters, where the Wall crosses the North Tyne. Here

59. Milecastle 39 seen from the north – Sycamore Gap lies immediately to the east. Note the remains of two rows of internal buildings and the redundancy of the north gate that opens onto a steep slope.

Wall walk?

One would think that there could be little argument that a wall walk (fighting/patrolling platform) had been planned from the beginning to surmount a wall which had been designed at the outset to be 3m broad, a thickness which would seem perfectly adequate for two people to pass. But the presence or absence of this feature has itself become a bone of contention between those who think that the Wall was designed to have a significant defensive function and those who claim the Roman army would never be troubled to fight from a wall, preferring to deal with any threat by assertive action north of the barrier. If one is curious to experience a section of Wall and imagine how it might function, the portion of Wall and turret recreated at Vindolanda graphically shows the magnitude of the construction. To demonstrate that the Romans could and did build thin section stone walls, without a wall walk, examples can be found in areas of the German frontier where it is known as the *Teufelsmauer*, or Devil's Wall.

60. The Military Way can be seen as a clearly defined mound snaking along just south of the line of the Wall. Interestingly, the road is said to have been an afterthought with the original east–west access being provided by the Stanegate.

the plan resulted in the placement of three of the fort's double gates to the north of the barrier, and only one to the south implying that rapid deployment of troops was even more important than the physical strength of the defences.

Military Way and the Vallum

A road or Military Way, interestingly not part of the primary plan, was eventually constructed to lie behind the Wall and linked the cordon of defences. Flanked occasionally by its aggregate extraction pits, it can still be followed in long sections, particularly in the central sector.

The final and not insignificant element of the Wall complex was the huge structure we now call the Vallum that ran behind the Wall almost for its full length (plate 7). This comprised an intricate arrangement of a 3m-wide, 3m-deep, flat-bottomed ditch paralleled by two high mounds. As originally designed, there were limited crossing points of this significant obstacle at some milecastles, guarded by masonry portals. The Vallum is a real curiosity among Roman frontier works, not duplicated anywhere else but obviously considered of such importance when it was initiated, to be dug, like the frontal ditch, through solid rock where necessary. For many

years controversy has surrounded the purpose of this structure, originally thought to be an earlier barrier (hence the name Vallum – which simply means 'wall') and not associated with the masonry wall to the north. More recent investigations have confirmed that it was commenced under Hadrian, not long after the main curtain, and then partially slighted at approximately the time of the Antonine advance into Scotland about twenty years after it was dug. Explanations of its function once more depend on how 'hard' or 'soft' one views the opposition to the occupation and how much superfluous engineering one thinks the Romans may have indulged in.

A softer view portrays the Vallum as a rearward-facing frontier customs barrier, or demarcation line delineating a 'military zone'. A slightly more hawkish scenario has it as an anti-cattle-rustling barrier analogous to the frontal ditch. Finally, and probably more realistically in view of its imposing size, it represents a preclusive barrier or rampart protecting Wall troops from some, as yet unknown, major threat from the south. This possible threat may have been precipitated by the very disruptive nature of the Wall that will have cut through territory of the Northern Brigantes, creating foes behind and in front of the barrier. Whatever the southern threat was, archaeology suggests it had receded by the time of the Antonine invasion as the infilled sections of this massive structure were never re-dug.

61. The fossa of the Vallum is an impressive obstacle in its own right, seen here cut through very hard rock at Limestone Corner. The quarried blocks are likely to lie where the Roman sappers left them.

Wall policy and legacy

The Wall may well have been an over-engineered reaction to a previous catastrophe, but mural responses to military or political instabilities are normally relatively short-lived. So it is striking that Hadrian's Wall was resourced, resupplied, reconstructed and reinforced for nearly three centuries, only coming to an effective end at the same time as official Roman support for the province was withdrawn in the first few years of the fifth century. We do know that 'a wall' was breached at least once in a major uprising in the 180s and there are plenty of other references to trouble in the province that likely involved the Wall area. But it did endure, and so must have been relatively successful in delivering on its defensive promise.

Ferguson and Whitehead in 'The Violent Edge of Empire' (1992) have perhaps summarised the phenomenon of Hadrian's Wall best: 'States may opt for a hardened perimeter defence at the point they lose effective superiority, sometimes leaving walls as the high-water mark of their control.' Hadrian's Wall may simply be that, an admission that the forward surge could not be sustained and that total conquest was not possible.

The creation of a hard boundary is never good for social justice in any period, and results in those 'others' beyond the frontier being considered as unworthy of humane treatment. Walls are also guaranteed to create and stoke future enmity, if it wasn't already there, and are a recipe for long-running border warfare. There is no doubt that whatever the primary reasons were for initiating the Wall, similar problems would dog the defenders for many generations.

However, within a few years of the Wall's construction a new emperor was on the Roman throne and this new leader required a rapid victory to consolidate his power. And so, with the mortar barely dry, the Roman military machine turned its attention northwards again, leaving the Wall of Hadrian, temporarily at least, a strategy of the past.

CHAPTER TEN

Burnswark:
dark deeds in Dumfriesshire

A husband-and-wife team seemingly glide along the steep slope in the driving rain, like choreographed dancers. They have clearly done this before. Oblivious to the downpour, each lost in the auditory world of their head-phones, they sweep the surface of the hill, missing nothing, skimming the grass with even strokes. He, being ex-military, has forearms like a stevedore and has a monster machine. Her diminutive figure is complemented by a lighter but equally sensitive model. On their belts they carry quivers full of small flags of assorted colours on short bamboo canes. They are not alone, for in the grey light, six other volunteers follow in formation, scanning their allotted patches. In their wake, is a growing field of predominantly red markers, each one making its own small contribution to the story of what happened here on Burnswark Hill.

62. A member of the detectorist group Beyond the Beep completes a sweep of her sector in the South Roman Camp at Burnswark.

63. Burnswark Hill near
Ecclefechan in Dumfriesshire.
A 17-acre hillfort occupies the
summit of the hill that is
straddled by two Roman siege
camps. The South Roman
Camp (left) has three circular
ballista platforms and an
accentuated rampart facing the
hilltop.

A hundred paces away, two drenched archaeologists look on from the
relative shelter of an awning that rattles and flaps on the breezy hillside.
They know from the shipping forecast that a storm is coming in overnight
and structural damage to their equipment shelters is likely. Although it is
just past midsummer, at 1,000ft above the Dumfriesshire coast, with
nothing between them and the Atlantic, what could they expect? But neither
is dismayed. For they both know that after two years of preparation and
planning, the enlarging forest of crimson flags has exceeded their most
optimistic predictions. For red means lead.

But let us not get ahead of ourselves, for, like the black hole of post-
Agricolan Scotland, the years immediately following the construction of
Hadrian's Wall are also blank on the pages of Caledonia's history. We must
look once more to archaeology to assemble from military detritus and
domestic rubbish the bare bones of everyday events that are normally below
the purview of ancient historians. However, even major actions can pass
unrecorded into the mists of time leaving only gossamer traces. One such
episode which may have taken place during the Antonine period was the
cataclysmic event that occurred at Burnswark Hill in eastern Dumfriesshire
(plate 8).

The glowering eminence of this most striking hill broods over Annan-
dale like a sentinel. It is easily visible from as far away as Carlisle and the
whole western sector of Hadrian's Wall. On its flat-topped summit are the
remains of a 17-acre hillfort, the largest in the county and almost certainly
the *oppidum* of an unnamed local tribe. This is remarkable enough but

what makes Burnswark Hill unique is that it is clamped in the vice-like grip of two Roman assault camps. This singular complex of aggressively positioned Roman earthworks and native hillfort, which has no parallel in Britain and for that matter anywhere else in Europe, has attracted the attention of archaeologists and historians for centuries. Although there are buried traces of many Roman sieges across the continent, one has to travel to the superlative site of Masada in Israel to find another place where upstanding siegeworks tell the story of Rome's use of overwhelming force.

Here, at Burnswark Hill, one may also find a proxy for some of the archaeological trends in Romano-Caledonian studies of the last century. Evidence once thought to have been indicative of major conflict, was transmogrified in the 1960s into a pacified scene of Roman 'training camps and firing range'. This novel concept, unknown anywhere else in the empire, developed in step with the belief that the Roman army was essentially invincible.

Earlier writers, historians and archaeologists were however more accepting of hostile contact as an explanation for the extraordinary earthworks. For example, one of the first written references to this site was made in 1792 by an anonymous contributor to the first edition of what was to be the forerunner to the *Proceedings of the Society of Antiquaries of Scotland*. He wrote: 'The whole suggested to me the idea of a siege. The natives, from the plains, had conveyed their cattle and effects to the top of the hill, and increased their natural defence by walls.' The bellicose posture of the Roman installations, with the South Camp pushed up the slope to within 150m of the hillfort ramparts, and the abnormally elongated North Camp blockading the inhabitants' northern exit, were seen as evidence of intimidation. It represented a prelude to assault that was supported by the finding in the late nineteenth century of dozens of Roman missiles from the surface of the hillfort ramparts and from within the two Roman camps.

Edwardian archaeologists, however, refused to accept everything at face value, and vigorously debated several elements, particularly the presence or absence of a circumvallation – an encircling wall put up by Roman besiegers like the famous structure at Masada. Duncan Campbell has subsequently pointed out in his 2003 publication about the site, that the Romans preferred to attack defended settlements by a direct frontal assault, and he has calculated that less than 30 per cent of attested Roman sieges utilised a complete circumvallation.

Attempts to gain further information resulted in two archaeological campaigns of note, the first in 1898 by James Barbour on behalf of the Society of Antiquaries of Scotland and the second in the 1960s by the respected field archaeologist George Jobey. Other investigators and commentators of the site read like a list of the great and the good in Roman archaeology in Britain, including Roy, Haverfield, Schulten, Macdonald,

64. Plan of the Burnswark site showing the abnormally elongated North Roman Camp that blockades the north gate of the hillfort. The South Camp is orientated to the easiest gradient for assault.

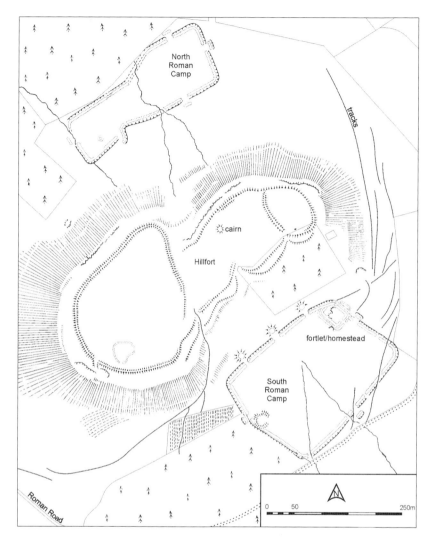

Collingwood, Birley, St Joseph, Richmond, Steer, Jobey, Keppie and Breeze. The main divergence in interpretation of the site, however, began in a muted fashion in the 1960s as an almost throwaway statement by Kenneth Steer, the then secretary to the Royal Commission on the Ancient and Historical Monuments of Scotland, in a publication about John Horsley, the eighteenth-century antiquarian. In his paper (1963), Steer suggested that the site might not have been one of actual battle but of a 'training camp'. This may seem counterintuitive today, but Steer's opinion carried significant weight: not only did he have a particular interest in the Roman army in North Britain, having done fieldwork under Eric Birley and Ian Richmond, but he had also been a real-life 'Monuments Man' in wartime British Intelligence. He further developed his theory that the camps were a training

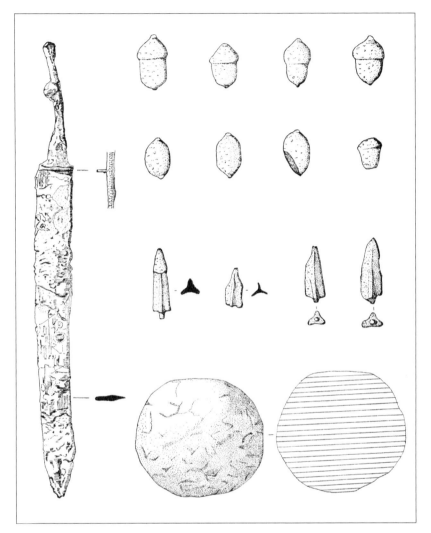

65. Missiles including lead sling bullets (top 2 rows), iron 'Syrian' trilobate arrowheads, and carved stone ballista balls found during George Jobey's 1960s excavations. He even uncovered a Roman short sword abandoned on the hillfort rampart (left).

facility, in essence an elaborate firing range for Roman troops to practise their artillery and other ballistic weapons. Steer saw this to be in accord with his own military experience and the apparently slighted nature of the old hillfort rampart. It was also seen as an explanation for the unusual profusion of *in situ* missiles discovered in the hillfort by Barbour in the 1890s. The publication of Jobey's subsequent excavations (1978) appeared to support Steer's theory by identifying numbers of leaden slingshot within the gateways, which he suggested were the position of temporary Roman 'targets' for such a firing range. The hypothesis took root, fostered by the belief in Roman supremacy, and over the next fifty years it eventually became accepted fact.

Steer's postulate, however, did not go completely unchallenged, and in the last few decades three more recent observers, Campbell (2003), Keppie (2009) and Hodgson (2009), have separately reinterpreted the site as one of actual conflict. The reliable data from previous excavations was however sufficiently limited and ambiguous for it to be read either way, so much so that a recent comprehensive review by Breeze (2011) painted a finely balanced picture.

It was against this inconclusive background that the Trimontium Trust proposed a new assessment of the site. A forensic approach was adopted to determine the pattern of ballistic material using techniques borrowed from conflict archaeology, including large-area metal detecting and experimental archaeology. Initial aerial reconnaissance of the site under favourable lighting conditions had enhanced the nuances of the earthworks and one immediate observation was the exaggerated profile of the hillfort-facing ramparts of both Roman camps. This asymmetric rampart construction seemed to be unique in Roman Britain and suggested that the builders had shored-up their frontal ramparts in anticipation of an action of some significance.

Aerial survey was followed by geophysics of the south Roman camp to assess the previous assertion that there had been substantial buildings there, something that would tend to support prolonged use and lean towards a 'training' scenario. The results were instructive – no trace of permanent buildings could be identified, which suggested that the occupation had been short-lived and more in keeping with a brief military intervention.

A systematic metal-detection survey was then performed encompassing the hillfort, both camps and a considerable portion of the surrounding area. Once the detectors, which can discriminate between different metals, had been calibrated against lead shot from the 1960s excavations, it was possible to non-invasively characterise, from the myriad of signals, over 650 objects that were highly likely to represent lead sling bullets. It soon became clear that the spatial distribution of the Roman missiles, in essence an unbroken blizzard across the south-facing rampart of the hillfort, was not compatible with fixed targets at the two gateways as had been suggested by Steer and Jobey.

Further revelations were to follow in the limited excavations the team had been given permission to undertake to 'ground truth' the detector finds. Two carved stone balls and a carved stone slingshot found in the same stratum as the lead shot confirmed suspected ballista activity. These discoveries were augmented by the find of a square profile iron bolt head in the same area, indicating that together with the iron arrowheads from previous excavations, all forms of Roman ballistic weapons had been in simultaneous operation at the site.

The last significant discovery of the first season came with the conclusion of slinging experiments on reproductions of the different types of lead sling-

66a. An array of lead sling bullets (*glandes*) excavated from both Roman camps and the ramparts of the hillfort, during Trimontium Trust's Burnswark Project 2015/16.

b. The distribution of lead slingshot points to a suppressive barrage by Roman troops, principally aimed at the south-facing rampart of the hillfort – a likely prelude to a storming assault.

c. These small lead bullets all have a 4mm hole which caused them to whistle in flight.

shot recovered from the site. Although most of the excavated bullets were of the expected types, a group of smaller, lemon-shaped missiles was identified, where each had a single 4mm round hole drilled into one flank.

Experiments confirmed that these small bullets could be shot in multiples, producing a scattergun effect and even more curiously, they were noted to be aerophonic – that is their holes made a whistling noise in flight.

The following season's work established where the 'firing lines' of slingers were positioned in the South Camp and that slingshot had been deployed in both North and South Camps. What had initially been identified as a single large lead signal was revealed as a hoard of unused bullets dumped behind the north camp rampart. All told there were more than 400 bullets in what at this time appears to be one of the largest caches of lead bullets in the empire (plate 9).

The profusion and, more particularly, the pattern of spread of Roman missiles across the most vulnerable face of the hillfort suggested that a major assault on the summit was by far the most likely scenario. The size of the camps indicated a Roman force of between 4,000 and 6,000 soldiers and the presence of screaming bullets is indicative that their 'targets' on the hilltop were likely to have been human.

When and why?

The distribution, characteristics and historical context of the Burnswark bullets, which have metallurgical signatures identical to securely dated missiles at the nearby Roman fort of Birrens, would suggest their use in an assault by the Roman army sometime during the Antonine occupation. The cause for this attack is unrecorded but may have been anything from a local tax rebellion to armed resistance against a perceived land grab. The *casus belli* however may be even more facile. The overkill nature of the event and the use of 'exemplary force' may be compatible with an emperor seeking legitimacy as a military leader, since Antoninus, who had rarely left Rome, was an able but civilian successor to Hadrian. But what did the term 'exemplary force' mean for the people of Burnswark Hill? The answer can be found in Duncan Campbell's comprehensive work on ancient siege-craft (2006). In the section covering Roman siege warfare in Judea he states: 'Typically, once the defences were scaled, all males of sword-bearing age were slaughtered, and the legionaries were given free rein to plunder and destroy.' He makes it clear that the women and children might only be spared to be sold into slavery.

As a poignant postscript to the project, Sharon, one half of the detecting duo of 'Beyond the Beep', discovered a group of signals that scattered from the northern gateway of the hillfort. It is possible this pattern marks the final resting place of a group of hillfort settlers who tried to escape the siege and make a run for it. The ferocity of the assault, with yet another blizzard of missiles, suggests that all the inhabitants may have paid the ulti-mate price for Antoninus Pius' only acclamation as *Imperator*.

CHAPTER ELEVEN

Hail *Imperator*: the Antonine invasion

Flavius Betto, once proud centurion of the XXth Valeria Victrix, looked down from the wooden breastwork of his fort, at the squad of auxiliaries digging the series of new defensive pits on the north side of the massive ditch. Pits that he hoped would give at least some advanced warning of the sort of attack that had almost overwhelmed the small garrison the previous evening. He shouted encouragement to his men to get the job done before nightfall, while under his breath he cursed the name of the emperor whose ambition had ensured that he would spend the last few years of his career stationed on the isthmus of Caledonia. But who was this new emperor and why was Betto here?

Historically, the brief but almost certainly troubled period, which saw this cohort of Belgian auxiliaries stationed just outside modern-day Falkirk, is important to the story of Scotland. The Antonine era takes its name from Titus Aelius Hadrianus Antoninus Augustus Pius, the venerable senator, aristocrat and unexpected heir to Hadrian. By the time of his accession, he was by contemporary standards an elder statesman, and Antoninus himself could not have predicted his own rise to power. Only a sequence of mishaps and misfortunes to Hadrian's other chosen successors propelled him towards the throne in 138. These events placed the fifty-one-year-old bureaucrat, who had only previously governed a non-military province, at the helm of what was in essence a military dictatorship, and his need to gain swift and credible military prestige was to result in grave consequences for a portion of the population of Scotland, as presaged by the events at Burnswark.

Some time soon after his accession, probably in or around 139, Antoninus ordered a mass invasion of southern Scotland. It is not entirely clear if his original intention was to complete the conquest of North Britain, started over sixty years before, or simply to move the frontier northwards by 100 miles to the Forth–Clyde isthmus. The emperor reinvested in a string of outpost forts, passing north-eastwards beyond his new linear barrier towards Angus, making Fife an extension once more of the province. Although military glory from an attempt at complete conquest may have

67. Altar dedicated to Victory by Flavius Betto, the centurion in charge of the auxiliary detachment at Rough Castle fort.

been the principal reason for the advance, other suggestions are plausible. Occupying the Lowlands of Scotland may have been designed to neutralise or buffer the threat from rebellious tribes further north. Alternatively, it may have been to offer 'protection' to friendly tribes in this area from northern aggressors, although the scarcity of Roman material culture from the indigenous settlements in the region (excepting Traprain Law) renders this less likely.

What did the Romans themselves tell us was Antoninus' plan for Scotland? Again the historical sources are sparse, with only brief references to the incursion by ancient authors. Pausanias (?110–?180), the second-century Hellenistic travel writer, better known for his travelogue about places like Corinth, Athens and Sparta, provided a passing mention: 'Antoninus deprived the Brigantes in Britain of most of their land as they had invaded the territory of the Genounians who are subjects of the Romans.' At first sight, this appears to be the typical Roman ploy of manufacturing an excuse to expand territorial control, but if it was, the rationale behind it is not clear. Pausanias' account has occasionally been portrayed as garbled (no Genounian district is known in Britain – although that does not mean it did not exist) and has suggested to some commentators that once more an ancient writer got things wrong, and he was actually referring to a different tribe of Brigantes in a different part of Europe. However, there seems to be a growing consensus that Pausanias was indeed referring to the initial Antonine sweep into southern Scotland in the late 130s.

A further brief allusion to the conflict in Caledonia is made by Fronto in a speech delivered to honour Pius in which he characterised the emperor as a 'helmsman who was able to steer the course of the war from Rome'. The *Augustan Histories* provides us with little more detail but does link the governorship of Lollius Urbicus with the building of the northern wall: 'For he [Antoninus Pius] conquered the Britons through his governor Lollius Urbicus, and after driving back the barbarians, he built a second wall, this time of turf.'

It may be useful here to supplement these literary references with a summary of the main physical evidence of survey and excavation of the Antonine reinvasion:

- The Roman frontier was moved forward by 100 miles to incorporate the Lowlands of Scotland and the Fife 'peninsula'.
- The Antonine Wall and southern Scotland remained heavily militarised zones for at least a generation.
- The Wall itself, although made of turf, constituted a major physical barrier and had exceptional passive-defensive features.
- No large fortresses like Inchtuthil – built and abandoned sixty years before – are known to have been initiated in the Antonine period with the purpose of supporting a prolonged occupation in the area south of the Wall.
- No villas or extensive civilian settlements (other than small fort *vici*) have been detected in the hinterland.
- Strikingly little Roman material culture or luxury goods drifted into native hands during a quarter century of occupation.
- There appears to have been selective destruction of some indigenous strongholds (the Lowland brochs for example) sometime during the Antonine occupation.

68a. Vertical image of the fort at Newstead (Trimontium) taken during the drought of 2018. Cropmarks show the walls and roadways of the fort (pale lines), and ditches of the fort and adjacent annexes (dark lines).

b. Quintus Lollius Urbicus' name on an Antonine period inscription from Corbridge.

Often portrayed as a petulant flash in the pan, Antoninus' advance into Caledonia was clearly not a trivial undertaking, requiring considerable financial investment and the dislocation of a large part of the Roman army in Britain for a significant time. From the archaeological traces, Antonine Scotland has the appearance of a conflict-ridden landscape with minimal attempt at infrastructural development to win the hearts and minds of the local population, including those of the Roman troops themselves if the limited amenities of the Antonine frontier were anything to go by. When *vici* are identified adjacent to Antonine forts in Scotland, they are usually quite small (Inveresk is a notable exception – see below) and heavily defended by ditches and palisades. Sebastian Sommer, an expert on the Raetian Frontier in Germany has highlighted this as one of the defining features of the Scottish frontier and suggests that this arrangement probably reflected a degree of local insecurity (2006).

So why did Antoninus have the frontier moved a mere 100 miles further north and not complete the conquest of the island? There seem to be three possibilities:

1. The Romans attempted to reconquer the northern tribes after a further uprising but failed due to a combination of determined resistance and the nature of the terrain. They consequently drew the frontier across the most cost-effective and defensible part of Scotland while retaining some prime Lowland territory.
2. It represented a modest incremental move of the frontier like the

one seen in Germany – also in the reign of Antoninus – where the *limes* was moved by only a few miles. This was presumably to take in new territory that required defence of a friendly local populace (perhaps the pro-Roman Votadini in East Lothian were threatened by other native groupings) or to extinguish resistance and create a buffer zone. With regard to Scotland, some scholars have argued that it was to move Roman bases closer to the source of northern trouble.

3. To make best use of a perceived threat from northern tribes as a justification to advance just enough to ensure the necessary victories to earn the emperor the acclamation of *Imperator* (the Scottish campaign was the only occasion Antoninus ever received the title in warfare).

It is possible that the situation was a combination of all three with the last factor being the most dominant given Antoninus' political status.

Lollius Urbicus

The emperor's Caledonian invasion was entrusted to a man well known to the hierarchy of the time, Quintus Lollius Urbicus. Promoted by Antoninus to the post of Imperial Governor at a relatively young age, he is known from inscriptions at Corbridge to already be active within North Britain by 139.

69. The Urbicus family mausoleum near modern day Tiddis in Algeria.

Urbicus was, however, no run-of-the-mill staff officer eased into a provincial army posting as a sinecure. A family inscription from North Africa indicates that although he originated from a relatively obscure colonial background in Tiddis in Algeria, he had metropolitan patronage, and moved rapidly up the *cursus honorum* to become a legate, a commander of a legion, under Hadrian during the Bar Kokhba revolt.

A notable observation is worthy of comment here. Three senior military personnel are specifically named, either by Roman historians or contemporary inscriptions, to have taken part in this second, even more violent, Judean campaign. All three, Julius Severus, Lollius Urbicus and Marcus Statius Priscus either were, or would soon become, governors of the province of Britannia. This accords with the observation made by Roman authors and subsequent commentators that respect was paid to the skills of the empire's best generals by posting them to a *provincia ferox* – an exceptionally unruly province like Britain.

The bare facts indicate Urbicus' command commenced in 138 and may have concluded in 143 as witnessed by the release of 'victory coinage' with the head of Antoninus on one side and the goddess Victory with an inscription '*Britan*' on the reverse. A major outcome of the campaign, as we shall see in the next chapter, was the building of the Antonine Wall, across the same isthmus previously identified by Tacitus as 'a good resting place for the Roman army'.

No contemporary account survives of the conflict that engulfed the

Lowlands of Scotland and the brief mention in the *Augustan Histories* gives little detail. Indeed, the scanty ancient commentary has led some authors to mock the campaign as a 'walkover' even though the actions at Burnswark and the estimated three-year interval between the onset of the campaign and the issue of the coins would logically indicate otherwise.

Ethnic cleansing?

As previously noted, the emperor's biographer stated that 'the Barbarians were driven back, and a new wall was built, this time of turf'. Interpretation of this apparently simple passage has however led to some scholarly debate about the interpretation of the phrase 'driven back'. Collingwood, in his 1936 landmark book *Roman Britain and the English Settlements*, suggested the indigenous people were removed rather than repelled. That is, literally transported en masse together with their dependents, to be forcibly relocated to the Antonine frontier in Germany. He postulated that this would account for the apparent depopulation of Lowland Scotland, which he argued was a consequence of the Roman occupation. He highlighted that a group of inscriptions from the Odenwald sector of the German frontier (south of Frankfurt), which had been dated to the mid-second century, testified to the presence of detachments of conscripted Britons. These auxiliary soldiers formed battalions known as *numeri Brittones* and were stationed on the outer fringes of the Roman defences in Germany. Intriguingly, inscriptions occasionally provide an indication of who oversaw the unit, with at least one mention of a centurion of the XXII Primigenia; the same legion, based in Mainz, also attested in the vicinity of Burnswark on an Antonine-era building stone.

Collingwood's theory of deportation has however been rejected, notably by Gillam, quoting Baatz, based on the architectural observation that the small forts in Germany associated with these troops remained essentially unchanged for a period considerably longer than the reign of Pius. Whether a certain design of fort can be definitively linked to a group of irregulars or not, the notion that the Romans would have cleared or neutralised fortified settlements in Lowland Scotland is certainly not far-fetched. It seems to have been given some impetus by the findings of the series of recent excavations previously mentioned, on the Northumberland Plain, where several indigenous settlements were abandoned, or forcibly cleared, in the mid-second century.

A survey of the denuded nature of the stone-walled hill forts of Lowland Scotland (e.g. Hownam Law and Burnswark Hill) would also support the hypothesis of systematic reduction of fortifications in what had been a densely occupied region. A few sites in a dilapidated state may be accounted for by natural decay and poor maintenance. However, widespread disman-

The curious case of the Lowland brochs

Brochs were a characteristic architectural style of northern Scotland, but an enigmatic group of these monumental stone towers can be found much further south, clustered mainly in Stirlingshire and the Central Borders. Archaeological evidence suggests that although structurally similar, they were a much shorter-lived phenomenon than their northern counterparts, flourishing briefly sometime after the first Roman invasion. It has been suggested that incomers from the north who had migrated southwards to fill a post-Roman invasion power vacuum constructed them. However, the absence of the characteristic small finds associated with northerners suggests brochs were more likely an adoption of a favoured building style probably by local elites. A few have some evidence of Roman material goods such as samian pottery or jewellery, which could be indicative of their status as power centres but it is uncertain whether these artefacts were attained by trade, scavenging or raiding. What is clear is that the southern brochs almost universally shared a similar fate of sudden and violent destruction – a finding re-emphasised by the excavations at Castle Craig in Stirlingshire (James 2011). The archaeological evidence of catastrophic burning, deliberate demolition of walls and hasty abandonment of valuables points to a date sometime in the mid-second century. The discoveries made by Piggott at Torwoodlee in the 1950s (1953), and by MacKie at Leckie in the 1970s (1982 and 2016) were specifically linked by their excavators to actions of the Roman army. Although MacKie's attribution of a heat-cracked ballista ball and an iron ballista bolt to a Roman siege has been questioned, there now seems to be sufficient circumstantial evidence from multiple other sites to suggest he may have been correct and to point a finger at the Antonine reinvasion as a potential cause for this unusual destruction horizon (plate 10).

tling to the basal courses, which appeared to have taken place over a relatively short timescale, might raise some suspicion that the occupying forces were not in a happy symbiosis with local warlords who would otherwise have been allowed to maintain their fortifications intact. It could be reasonably argued that the Roman military would order ramparts to be taken down and fortifications slighted – again a situation emphasised by Josephus in his *Jewish War* – but leaving the indigenous population in place. This would allow for continued supply to the Roman army of at least some of its considerable logistical needs.

Of course, there are more brutally efficient strategies that could explain

70a. Artist's impression of an attack on Leckie broch sometime during the Antonine period. A slinger attempts to set the roof thatch alight with heated clay sling bullets.

b. A heat-cracked stone found within Leckie broch on show in the Hunterian Museum. Could this have been an incendiary *ballista* ball?

the sudden displacement of a cultural group. The insertion of army-controlled or officially licensed settlers into a forcibly cleared landscape could serve the Roman army's voracious requirements just as easily and without the complications of a resentful population fomenting rebellion in the occupied territories.

Other more disturbing scenarios have been recorded in recent centuries in the dealings between occupying powers and local populations such as: the 'Harrying of the North' by the Normans, the near annihilation of the Great Sioux Nation, British Imperial interactions with the First Nations of Australia and New Zealand, and the treatment of the indigenous Chinese during the Sino-Japanese War. Forced famine, genocide, dispossession and translocation were techniques just as likely to have been employed in the first few centuries AD as they have been in the epochs since.

Other than the exceptional site of Traprain Law in East Lothian, or the relatively artefact-rich power centres of the handful of Lowland brochs highlighted above, few indigenous settlements within the occupied territories have been excavated to any great extent, but when they have, the results are illuminating. Boonies in Dumfriesshire, Hownam Rings in Roxburghshire and even Broxmouth, which is relatively close to Traprain, have produced exceptionally little in the way of Roman artefacts. The total corpus of Roman material culture from these three sites, bearing in mind that Broxmouth was excavated almost in its entirety (Armit and MacKenzie 2013), could be placed in a single sandwich box. Furthermore, only two of the six indigenous sites, which lie close to the Roman fort at Trimontium, investigated during the 1990s Newstead Environs Project, produced small amounts of Roman material, mainly concentrated at Lilliesleaf North. Here, the architecture appears to change, with the levelling of a roundhouse and the construction of a rectangular building. This phenomenon had been previously interpreted as a local adoption of Roman culture, akin to Haverfield's now outdated concept of 'Romanisation'. However, in current postcolonial thinking, the idea of the improving nature of *Romanitas* on the barbarian margin of the empire has been met with greater scepticism. Examples from other ethnographic studies such as the well-documented events in the Western United States alluded to above, raise the possibility that these perceived adoptions of Roman culture and architectural practices were in fact due to the locals being replaced by settlers and carpetbaggers sheltering in the lee of the invading army.

CHAPTER TWELVE

A Wall too far?

On the eastern fringes of the great metropolis of Glasgow, where a wedge of green land is buttressed by two sprawling suburbs, lies a small farm called Balmuildy. There, beneath the Friesian-dotted pasture between the River Kelvin and a landfill site, lies the stone foundation of a large Roman fort. Built in the second century by legionaries of the IInd *Augusta*, it would ultimately house a garrison of 500 Roman auxiliaries. Complete with two hypocausted bathhouses and a bridge across the adjacent river, this bastion of the empire has delivered up two stone inscriptions that proclaim it was constructed under the special direction of none other than Quintus Lollius Urbicus. The same Urbicus who only a few years before personally received the Golden Crown and the Silver Spear from Hadrian for exploits in Judea – military honours of the highest order for services rendered in one of the bloodiest campaigns in the annals of the empire. It was he, barely in his fourth decade and in the full flush of recent success, who was given the task of implementing the new emperor's invasion plan of Scotland. The culmination of this incursion saw construction of Balmuildy as part of a

71. A map of the Antonine Wall highlighting some of the forts mentioned in the text.

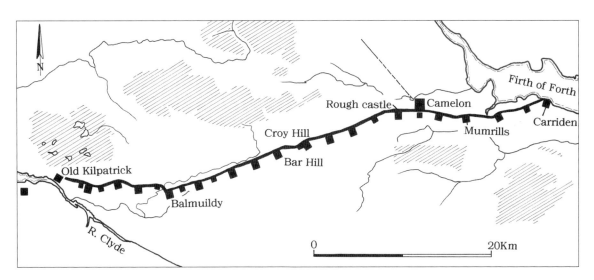

new frontier system that would ultimately bear the name of its founder –
the Antonine Wall.

Unlike its better-known counterpart 100 miles to the south, this Wall
gives an initial impression of being jerry built. Constructed mainly of perishable materials, turf, clay and wood (only two forts had perimeter walls of
stone – Balmuildy was one of them) and passing through the heart of industrial Scotland, unsurprisingly little of Urbicus' handiwork remains. First
impressions are deceptive though, for the 40-Roman-mile-long barrier that
extends from Old Kilpatrick on the Clyde to Bo'ness on the Forth, is still
a major engineering feat with surviving sections so impressive, that it finds
itself inscribed as a UNESCO World Heritage site (plate 11).

The Wall of Antoninus has several features in common with that of
Hadrian. It transects an isthmus and consists of a continuous barrier with
integrated forts. It has outposts and hinterland strongpoints, a military
road running along behind and, in many places, it has obstacles on the
berm. In other respects, it is very different. The northern Wall more closely
follows the defensively advantageous contours of the terrain and is rarely
straight. There are many more small forts, placed at intervals of only 2
miles compared with the 7 miles of Hadrian's Wall, resulting in one of the
most densely garrisoned sectors of the empire. The apparent absence of
watchtowers may be due to the tight spacing or perishable wooden super-
structures. Behind the Wall, there appeared to have been no need for a
Vallum.

The ditch

To help appreciate this shift in tactics and construction, it is worth considering some of the aspects of the northernmost frontier in detail. To the
modern visitor its most striking attribute is the huge frontal ditch, which
in places, such as Watling Lodge, is almost 12m wide and up to 4m deep.
It dwarfs some sections of its counterpart in Germany and in many places
it overshadows the fossa of the Tyne–Solway Wall. This feature may be
due to the relatively deep soft soils of the isthmus allowing the ditch diggers
to exaggerate the trough to rampart ratio with relative ease. If one compares
with fortifications in arid and rocky parts of the empire such as Spain or
Israel for example, defensive barriers often have to be built up from the
level surface in terms of piled stones rather than created by deep ditches.
The soil conditions, however, can only partially explain the magnitude of
the main ditch, for like Limestone Corner on Hadrian's Wall, significant
sections of the Antonine ditch are cut through rock. It may also be possible
that Antoninus personally dictated superlative specifications for this aspect
of the design to reflect his own investment in the project.

Finally, it could be that the resistance faced from north of the Wall was

sufficiently problematic to spur the Roman engineers to create a greater physical deterrent, with the intent of maximising the passive defensiveness of the structure. Even with today's advanced weapons systems, wherever occupying forces find themselves posted to particularly hostile territory, robust defences provide not just a physical barrier but also a welcome psychological support for the garrison.

The Antonine Wall ditch compares favourably with the largest military ditches anywhere in the empire, so how good was this ubiquitous system of defence? V-profile ditches successfully break up the physical momentum upon which frontal assaults rely and are even more effective when they are arranged in multiple layers. If further enhanced by a variety of unpleasant obstacles such as sharpened stakes or thorn bushes, ditches become the Iron Age equivalent of barbed wire.

Next in order of defence were obstacles on the berm in the form of numerous pits like their counterparts on Hadrian's Wall. It was originally thought that these defensive pits were limited to areas of locally-heightened security, but subsequent investigations by Bailey (2003) at Falkirk, showed that pits were present at multiple areas along the Wall, if not on all suitable sectors. It would appear that where there may have been specific landscape features calling for them, these obstacles even lay north of the main ditch, as in the so-called *lilia* at Rough Castle. A rare finding for Britain that caused something of a minor sensation when first excavated, the Latin term refers to the fanciful similarity of these pits, which may have had central spikes, to water lilies.

The rampart

The Wall itself was built on a 4m-wide stone foundation faced with dressed kerbstones and liberally punctuated by culverts to facilitate drainage. The

72a. The ditch at Croy Hill on the Antonine Wall and b. The ditch of the German Limes at Saalburg – Don (left) and Axel (right) for scale.

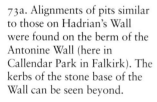

73a. Alignments of pits similar to those on Hadrian's Wall were found on the berm of the Antonine Wall (here in Callendar Park in Falkirk). The kerbs of the stone base of the Wall can be seen beyond.

b. The so-called *lilia* at Rough Castle fort – an array of pits lying to the north of the Wall ditch.

latter feature had not been employed in the initial design of the Tyne–Solway barrier and so the porous Antonine foundations were possibly a response to damage wrought on Hadrian's Wall by water ingress due to the northern climate.

When extrapolated from the width of the base, the rampart is estimated to have been approximately 3m high and was created from stacked turves of a regulated size. These were 'battered' inwards towards the 2m-wide top to aid stability, and even today when archaeologists section a stump of the denuded wall, the blackened layers of decomposed vegetation can still be clearly seen. The suggestion that the core of the first 20km of the Wall was made of clay and earth – with turves used only for the facings – prompted the suggestion that pasture must have been in short supply in the eastern half of the isthmus, although the reason why has never been adequately explained. More recent work (Romankiewicz et al. 2020) has suggested that the apparent abundance of clay may be due to turves cut on predominantly clay subsoil.

The Wall was possibly surmounted by a boardwalk and wooden breast-work. However, a similar argument to the one already encountered in rela-tion to Hadrian's Wall continues to rumble on about the need or otherwise for an observation or fighting platform. It is hard to be certain about this point, for it has been reasonably suggested that the spacing of the manned installations was close enough to obviate the requirement for an elevated sentry-walk and that this may have been needed only for access specifically at forts and fortlets. The opposite argument, that the close spatial relation-ship of the ditch to the Wall only makes sense if there is a patrolled elevated walkway, is equally potent.

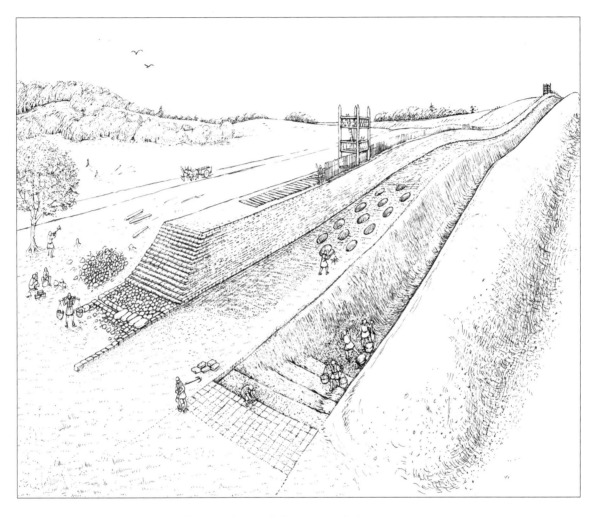

74. Artist's impression of the components that made up the Antonine Wall. The wooden watchtowers, sentry walk and breastwork remain speculative.

John Poulter (2018) has also emphasised the use made by Roman surveyors (*agrimensores*) of the topography to give added defensive and surveillance advantage by placing the line of the Wall on the forward craggy outcrops in the central sector. It is also noticeable that as a further frontal defensive feature, the surveyors sited sections of the barrier close to the southern lip of the strip of marshy land that runs across the Forth–Clyde isthmus.

Forts and fortlets

Like Hadrian's Wall, numerous integrated forts were also a feature of this frontier. The initial plan may have been for six primary forts with 'secondary' forts subsequently placed in between, perhaps in response to an increased level of threat, giving a total of seventeen in all – that is a

75. A section through the
Antonine Wall rampart at
Rough Castle reveals the layers
of turves outlined by the dark
stripes of long decayed grass.

garrison approximately every 2 Roman miles. Several small fortlets have
also been identified and the exact relationship of these to the primary forts
is still a matter of conjecture. The principal Antonine Wall forts were generally smaller than those on Hadrian's barrier averaging about two acres in
area inside the walls. Two of the larger forts, Castlecary and Balmuildy,
which like the forts on the Tyne–Solway frontier were stone-built, were
found to have architectural features designed to receive the curtain wall as
it approached from either side. This observation suggests these forts were
built early in the project and Urbicus' engineers may have originally
intended to build the Wall entirely from stone. None of the forts on the
Antonine Wall straddle the linear barrier as they do at some places on the
southern frontier.

Running behind the Wall and linking the forts was the Military Way, a
5m-wide engineered road surface that allowed for rapid movement of men
and supplies and, unlike its southern counterpart, this road was part of the
primary design rather than a later addition. A common misconception is
that Roman roads in Britain were paved. In fact, most, if not all, were
cambered gravelled surfaces on graded hardcore bottoming, sometimes
accompanied by lateral kerbing and drainage ditches. Often the only surface
trace that remains are the 'dimples' of the gravel extraction pits which run
parallel to the road surface. Examples of surviving lengths of road can be
found on Croy Hill and at Rough Castle.

76. Funerary sculpture showing three legionaries at ease, found at Croy Hill fort. The person being celebrated is probably the older bearded soldier in the centre. Note the suspension of their helmets for ease of carrying.

The Roman garrison of Scotland

The number of troops stationed on the Wall itself has been estimated at approximately 7,000, although this figure has been revised both upwards and downwards over the years. If we add the Wall garrison to the units stationed in the outlying forts, fortlets, supply bases and watchtowers, there may have been approximately 20,000 Roman troops based north of Hadrian's Wall at the height of the Antonine occupation, to support a frontier 60km long. It is difficult to gain a sense of what this concentration of military personnel must have been like, but we can compare it with the 21,000 British troops stationed in Ulster at the height of the 'Troubles', when the length of the border with the South was 500km. If we allow for extrapolations in population numbers over time and the relatively small landmass of the occupied sector, Roman Scotland must have been one of the most intensely policed regions of the empire.

Although the builders were likely to have been legionaries, with the IInd, the VIth and the XXth all attested, the garrison itself was thought to be mostly auxiliary. A few of these units, such as the Hamian archers originally from Syria, or the Tungrians from Belgium, were known to have been previously stationed on Hadrian's frontier before being moved northward. In some forts, the auxiliary troops were commanded by a legionary centurion, such as Flavius Betto at Rough Castle, and it has recently been suggested that a proportion of the regular troops were legionaries, such as those depicted on the small carving found at Croy Hill. The significance of this legionary presence is not clear at the moment but could suggest that indigenous resistance necessitated tighter control than had originally been planned.

A further interesting observation was made by the ceramicist Vivien Swan (1999), who highlighted the presence of fragments of pottery of North African type, a tagine-like casserole, from several forts on the Wall. These were linked to troop movements in relation to a contemporary war fought by Antoninus against a rebellion in Mauretania, modern-day Morocco. This pottery has suggested to some the presence of Mauritanian conscripts and to others a desire by Antonine troops to retain a cooking style they had recently enjoyed while on campaign.

Temporary abandonment of Hadrian's Wall?

An unresolved controversy surrounds the apparent desertion of Hadrian's Wall at the time of the Antonine advance – could both walls have been held simultaneously? Currently the dominant theory suggests that the southern Wall was temporarily 'mothballed' with partial dismantling to facilitate free passage across the lower frontier. The observations used to support this hypothesis may however be something of an over-interpretation for they appear to be based on the findings at a very small number of milecastle gateways which seem to have had their pivot posts replaced. This discovery has encouraged some to postulate that milecastle gates were totally removed creating unrestricted passage at multiple points along the Wall. This is said to be further supported by matching areas of slighting of the Vallum. The 'open' Wall model, however, makes little sense on a maintenance level and no allowance for the previous notion that a primary function of the Wall was to stop local cattle rustling. Perhaps there may be a compromise solution if we accept that Hadrian's Wall garrison numbers had been run down because of lowered threat levels in the Tyne–Solway corridor and if we suggest only a few milecastle gateways had been dismantled on regularly used routes to facilitate unsupervised traffic.

An alternative suggestion is that Hadrian's Wall forts continued to be maintained, with some troops rotating through the northern frontier, completing tours of duty from their 'home' bases. The latter argument has been made by Sommer, supported by his observations of military *vici* in

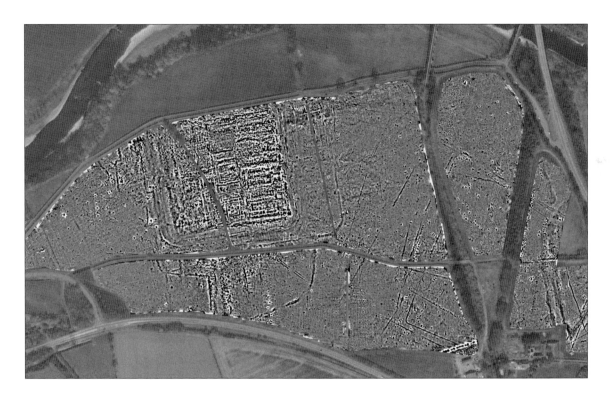

North Britain (2005). He has pointed out that the fort annexes on the Antonine Wall were significantly smaller than the *vici* to the south and could not have housed all the camp followers the troop numbers would have generated. He has argued that the forts further south were likely to have been maintained at some level and used as hinterland support for the northern garrison.

A more recent finding that casts further doubt on the theory of desertion of Hadrian's Wall during the Antonine push, has been the numismatic work of Brickstock on the coins from the two frontiers (2020). His technique, which estimates the wear on randomly dropped coins, suggests that there was no appreciable 'Antonine gap' in the profile of coins deposited in Hadrian's Wall forts during the period of the Antonine occupation. This in turn indicates that significant numbers of personnel remained in the Tyne-Solway area at the same time as the Forth–Clyde isthmus was held.

77. Magnetometry survey of Newstead Roman fort (Trimontium) outlining numerous internal buildings and multiple ditches of the fort and surrounding campaign camps. This technique is sensitive to traces of burning. The main extramural settlement (*vicus*) appears to lie in the defended annexe to the south.

Annexation of Fife and Angus?

In addition to his linear barrier, Pius sanctioned the building or refurbishment of a group of outpost forts that stretched in a dog-leg fashion from the isthmus north-eastwards towards the Tay. This impressive array of installations included notable examples of heavily defended forts such as

78. The multiple defensive ditches of Ardoch Roman fort in Perth and Kinross. The village of Braco in the background lends some scale to this pivotal fort.

Ardoch and Strageath. Ardoch, which at one time was home to a part-mounted Spanish cohort, particularly gives the impression of a garrison which took its safety very seriously indeed. But even here, where the astonishingly well-preserved ditch network is in places up to six rows deep – a rare finding on any of Rome's frontiers – there has been an energetic attempt to downplay resistance as a cause for the magnitude of defensive engineering. It has been suggested that the complex earthwork we see today is the result of the garrison 'shrinking' and not bothering to backfill its previous handiwork (Crawford 1949, Breeze 2014). This concept of the lazy shrivelling onion is novel and maintains the notion of desultory Roman military supremacy but is not particularly persuasive from a tactical perspective.

After reaching the fort of Strageath just outside modern Auchterarder, the Roman road heads towards Angus and links with the earlier Gask Ridge system of towers and fortlets before appearing to halt at the fort of Bertha on the Tay. This terminus is not completely certain, for although there are reputed to be no permanent Antonine installations beyond, recent detecting surveys have retrieved Antonine period coins from areas further to the north-east, a sector once thought to be only occupied in the Flavian era. This supports the reasonable suggestion that the whole of Angus as well as Fife was under military control in the mid-second century. Judging by the finds from northern forts of equine accessories, particularly horse brasses and 'melon' beads, it is highly likely that mounted troops played a major part in maintaining regular surveillance and policing of these reoccupied territories. The many cavalry-related artefacts from Newstead, including horse skeletons and a training gyrus, emphasise the general importance of mounted units in Scotland. The Iron Age equivalent of an air force, cavalry provided wide-ranging strike capability in a sub-Highland terrain that was otherwise poorly suited to the set-piece warfare of heavily armoured foot soldiers.

Command and control

Governance during Pius' reign was likely to have come from a headquarters centred at the eastern end of the Wall, at the military complex underlying Inveresk, on the outskirts of modern Musselburgh. This large fort, trenched by Richmond in 1946–7, lies at the tip of a natural ridge in a bend of the River Esk, and is flanked by an extensive defended settlement, complete with large field systems extending south and east into the fertile East

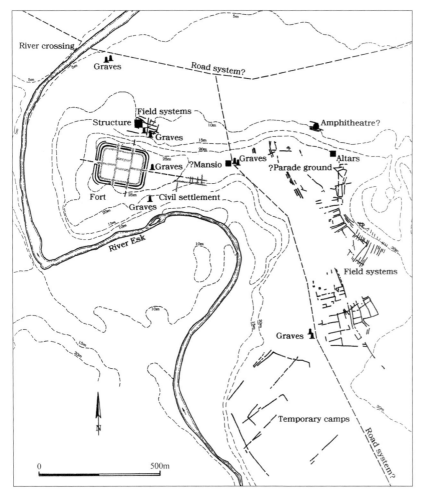

79. Plan of the Roman conurbation surrounding the Antonine period fort at Inveresk near Musselburgh. Inveresk hosted high-ranking Roman officials and Scotland's only known *Mithraeum*.

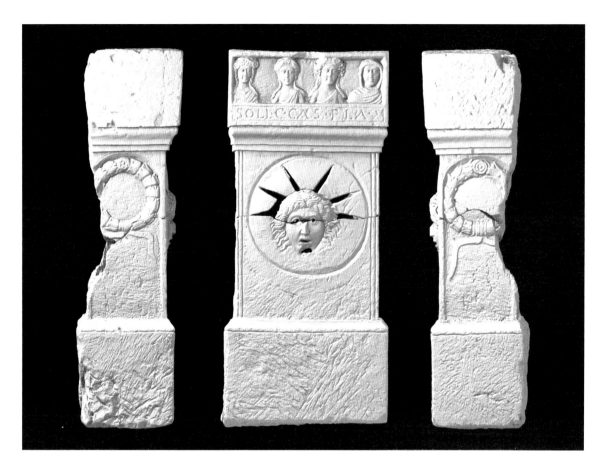

80. The sun god Sol's altar from Inveresk. Note the apertures to allow the god's corona to be backlit and the carving of the four seasons on the capital.

Lothian plain. The main road leading south from the conurbation is likely to be Dere Street, suggesting Inveresk may have been for a while the terminus of the trunk route. A left-hand fork of the southern exit road from the *vicus* not unexpectedly points towards the distant bulk of Traprain Law, which was the likely seat of the client kingdom of the Votadini.

To underscore its importance, Inveresk has yielded a funerary inscription of a member of the provincial governor's bodyguard and also, uniquely, two inscriptions set up by the imperial procurator. The latter discoveries have perhaps been rather underappreciated, since the procurator was in effect second-in-command of the whole province of Britannia. No other inscriptions of such high-ranking personnel have so far been found in North Britain, so Inveresk is likely to have been an important centre of control, however brief the period of occupation. Further to the procuratorial inscriptions and the extensive nature of the substantial buildings outside the fort, including a hypocausted structure and a possible wooden amphitheatre, the site has recently produced evidence of Scotland's only *Mithraeum*.

During renovation work at the local cricket pavilion, two stone altars

Mithras

Mithras the sun god, whose male-only mystery cult for a time rivalled Christianity, was exceptionally popular in the harsher environment of the Roman army from the first to the fourth centuries. As part of the symbolic lexicon, Sol the sun god plays a central role in the credo of light versus darkness. Thought to have had origins in eastern Zoroastrianism, the cult developed its own distinct iconography, including the famous bull-slaying scene, and a mysterious hierarchical system of initiation ceremonies where neophytes underwent ordeals to pass to the next level. Several *Mithraea* have been found in association with the Roman army particularly in the western empire, the most notable in North Britain being the well-preserved structure outside the fort of Carrawburgh on Hadrian's Wall.

in an extraordinary state of preservation were uncovered in the remains of a building thought to be a sanctuary. One has exceptionally high-quality carvings of the sun god Sol complete with recess for lighting effects in his corona and a well-executed frieze of the four seasons (plate 12).

Inveresk's littoral position on the Forth estuary supports its probable role as a port of resupply for the Wall, receiving shipments from bases further south like South Shields. There now seems to be enough evidence to suggest that the fort and wider settlement were well placed to become a key forward base like Corbridge. The presence of senior officials could suggest that there may have been an even greater plan in store for Inveresk if the Antonine occupation had been extended.

Distance sculptures

A unique feature, which sets the Antonine Wall apart from other Roman frontiers, was the erection of a series of large sculptural tablets, probably in duplicate pairs, at the junctions between the segments allotted to the work parties of the three legions. So far nineteen have been found, essentially by chance ploughing during the widespread land improvements introduced in the eighteenth and nineteenth centuries. These stones are much more than the perfunctory sector markers found on Hadrian's Wall. They are small masterpieces of Roman propaganda that illustrate the victorious Roman army venerating its gods or applauding Antoninus as Victory looks down upon bound naked barbarians who bow in subjugation. Most of these 'distance slabs', as they used to be known, are displayed in the Hunterian Museum in Glasgow, reflecting the higher find density in the west due

81. A modern copy of the large sculpture erected to commemorate the building of a section of the Antonine Wall by the IInd Augusta Legion. It stands in Harbour Road on the outskirts of Bo'ness near the find spot of the original.

to the shorter allotted building segments in that sector. It is also worth noting the enigmatic observation that distances in the western zone are given in 'feet' whereas measurements in the east are in 'paces'.

The National Museum in Edinburgh holds the largest sculpture, which is from the eastern terminus at Bridgeness on the Forth – there is also a remarkable plaster replica in the Hunterian. By British standards, this is a stunning piece of Roman dedicatory sculpture that features the *Suovetaurilia* in the right-hand panel. This sacrifice of bull, sheep and pig was associated with the initiation of grand projects and was usually a state-sponsored ceremony marking major building works or military campaigns. In the middle panel is a dedication to Pius recording a length of Wall built by the IInd Legion. The often-used motif of a cavalryman riding down a group of partially dismembered locals is reserved for the left-hand panel.

Recent work by Louisa Campbell (2020) has brought to life the original colour scheme that would have rendered these sculptures difficult to overlook. Their aesthetic is a little unrefined (blood red, faces bland, hands too big, etc.) and would jar if placed alongside classical sculpture of second-century date found in public spaces in Rome or the villas of the elite. However, they are of markedly higher quality than carvings found on most military sites and almost certainly suggests that if the state was not directly involved in financing these triumphalist masterpieces, then there was at least a central diktat to make Antoninus Pius look good. This contrasts with the scenario on the Tyne–Solway Wall, where mentions of Hadrian are so sparse that for many years it was thought to have been built by Severus – adding further support to the assertion that vanity project was not the primary purpose of the southern Wall.

Most of the Antonine panels are well preserved suggesting they were either exposed only briefly to the elements or displayed under cover in a structure of some kind – several have masonry fixing-clamp slots. They were sufficiently revered for some to be deliberately taken down at the time of the Roman withdrawal, presumably to prevent barbarian desecration such as the pulverised Antonine inscription found in the well at Birrens. Campbell has recently controversially suggested that the sculptures were in fact designed to be distance markers and placed by the side of the adjacent Military Way where they would be more frequently observed – rather like the Roman predisposition for elaborate roadside mausolea.

A further development in the story of these unique examples of Roman propaganda, has been the recreation, by the Antonine Wall Rediscovery Project, of four hand-carved copies of the original sculptures close to the line of the Wall. To redress some of the ethnographic imbalance, a further modern sculpture has been commissioned, also in the style of a distance sculpture, which makes a statement on behalf of the indigenous population. This sculpture, which is made of sandstone with natural red strands flowing through it, stands in Cow Wynd in Falkirk, and was designed in consultation with the local community (plate 13).

Final abandonment

The last uncertainty to be considered here for this most northerly frontier is a seemingly simple one but one which has been mired in as much controversy as all others mentioned above – the longevity of the Wall. In the first half of the twentieth century, during the successive regencies of the Scottish Roman experts, Macdonald and Robertson, the Wall was considered to have experienced at least two and possibly three periods of occupation. Interspersed with variable episodes of abandonment, it was suggested that the Wall was occupied well into the last half of the second century, at least until the 180s. Hodgson (1995) has reconsidered the evidence for the supposed multiphase occupation and has cast doubt on this interpretation, convincingly suggesting the apparent destruction levels of evacuation are in fact reconstruction or maintenance episodes during a continuous period of occupation.

But how long was that phase? From the 140s to the 180s as suggested by scholars of the earlier twentieth century, or a period essentially spanning marginally less than the reign of Pius – effectively twenty years until the late 150s or early 160s?

A major plank of evidence used to support a shorter timescale is a small inscription from Hadrian's Wall reputed to have been found in 1751 at about Mile 8 or 9, between the forts of Benwell and Rudchester, indicating building in the vicinity by the VIth Victrix Legion. Abbreviations supplying the names of two consuls date the stone to 158. This inscription and a companion stone from approximately the same area, indicate building or rebuilding of a structure. Unhelpfully, both are now lost, a frustrating but not unusual fate for inscriptions unearthed in the eighteenth and nineteenth centuries which were treated in a more casual fashion than they are today.

It has been suggested that the stones did not originate from within a fort, and the deduction has been made that a legionary work squad must have been allocated a repair job on the curtain wall. This in turn has been extrapolated to indicate that the army was resurrecting Hadrian's barrier to facilitate the closing down of the Antonine frontier at the same time. And so, 158 became the proposed date for the beginning of the end of the Antonine frontier.

There are, however, a couple of caveats. Firstly, the inscriptions may have originated from a minor structure in the vicinity, other than the curtain wall or a fort, such as a milecastle or turret that required maintenance – the stone was certainly not a grand inscription. Secondly, as we have already seen, both walls may have been held simultaneously and consequently serviced and repaired, even if not in imminent prospect of reactivation. This would be a reasonable thing for underemployed legionaries to be doing as numerous other small inscriptions suggest various sections of masonry were randomly falling down throughout the Wall's 300-year existence. So it is perhaps straining the meagre evidence to say that a little repair work – the very argument used to dispense with the three-phase Antonine Wall occupation – could characterise strategic policy for the northern Wall as a whole.

A second piece of evidence for early withdrawal from of the Antonine Wall is a building inscription ascribed to Julius Verus, which was found in the River Tyne at Newcastle during dredging at the Swing Bridge in 1903. This is an interesting stone for a number of reasons. Firstly, it can be confidently attributed to the period of around 158 when Verus was known to be in Britannia. He too had seen action as a junior officer in the Bar Kokhba revolt in Judea like his father (or uncle) Julius Severus. Secondly, the inscription has been interpreted that he was leading a group of reinforcements drawn from the 'Two Germanys' and were now bound for the three British legions, although no explanation is offered for why additional troops were required. Thirdly, these reinforcements, if that was what they were, were unlikely to be taking such a detour simply to return home to their bases of York, Caerleon and Chester. A faster and safer route from Germany would have taken them much further south. We shall never know the exact answers to these questions but the general tone and the presence of legionary reinforcements disembarking this far north indicate serious trouble in the vicinity requiring the three main battle groups to be bolstered under the command of an experienced general. For some, this is enough to suggest that the end of the 150s was sufficiently turbulent to persuade the Roman decision makers to pull out of southern Scotland and abandon the Wall when Pius died in 161.

The final factor to support the shorter occupation hypothesis was the detailed analysis of the pottery from the Antonine Wall by archaeologist Brian Hartley in his landmark publication of 1972. He found no convincing evidence of samian ware dating to later than the 160s from the northern Wall area. However, some doubt has now been cast on the ability of Hartley's observations to accurately differentiate pottery to within a span of twenty years. His own conclusion excludes the Wall being held later than 180 but he himself conceded that his pottery evidence didn't completely exclude occupation from 160–80. This would be supported by the coin and pottery evidence from Newstead, which strongly suggests the fort there was held at least until the early 180s. Based on logistics alone, would it be likely that Trimontium was left unshielded in hostile territory for a full generation before finally being abandoned? And what of the few later coin finds of Marcus and Commodus from the Antonine Wall forts of Castlecary, Old Kilpatrick and Mumrills? Perhaps the answer lies in these being the losses of occasional *exploratores* (scouts) reconnoitering forward positions and squatting in the ruins for temporary shelter, or perhaps a selected few forts were maintained to provide a residual forward policing function with Newstead in the hinterland.

It was also previously accepted that there had been a brief temporary abandonment of the Antonine Wall sometime in the 150s. This was attributed by some authors to a supposed revolt of the Brigantes – the one alluded to by Pausanias – resulting in troops being pulled back to deal with an enemy in the traditional Brigantian territory of what is now northern Yorkshire, but little weight is now given to this theory. Hodgson (2009) convincingly suggests that Pausanias' comments relate not to a Brigantian revolt in the Pennines, which he attributes to an invention by Haverfield, but to the Antonine invasion of Caledonia in 139.

Hodgson does however support the idea of a major revolt in 155–8. Centred in south-west Scotland, it could provide an explanation for the more extreme signs of stress such as the unusual troop movements alluded to above and also Antonine-period burning of a number of forts in the south and west, e.g. Birrens, Drumlanrig and Bishopton. He envisages a major rebellion (even though it was likely to have been successfully suppressed) as being a prime contributory factor to Rome rethinking the benefits of northerly occupation and ultimately leading to the complete withdrawal of Antonine forces from Scotland.

Recent Wall studies

There has been no large-scale excavation on the Wall in the last few decades with most of the smaller interventions being led by stalwarts of Antonine Wall studies – local archaeologists such as Walker and Bailey who have continued to explore and confirm significant findings like postulated forts and fortlets. Bailey (2003) was also first to discover the important obstacles on the berm, alerting colleagues on Hadrian's Wall to a similar phenomenon. Campbell's innovative work (2020) on distance sculptures alluded to above and the recent publications of previous excavations at Bearsden Bathhouse (Breeze 2016) and Croy Hill (Hanson 2021) are also to be applauded. However, most recent field investigations have relied on resurvey of upstanding remains, albeit with modern techniques such as LiDAR or photogrammetry.

The 2014–19 Antonine Wall World Heritage Site Management Plan focused on preservation, brand image and tourist appeal, and has given birth to a new research strategy. Antonine Wall studies are therefore not static and there has been a recent reappraisal of the construction sequence and function of the Wall. One of the most notable revelations has been an insight into the Roman surveyors' techniques used to lay out the Wall, as investigated by John Poulter, who, as we saw earlier, has contributed much to the understanding of the construction of Hadrian's barrier. Unlike Hadrian's Wall, the Antonine Wall was likely planned to facilitate the siting of the garrison and therefore the Wall itself mirrors the more defensible high ground leading to a markedly sinuous course with relatively few straight lines (plate 14). This is quite unlike the so-called Forward *Limes*, the Antonine-period extension to the Neckar–Odenwald German frontier which has at least one unbelievably linear stretch of over 80km that barely deviates from the true. There has also been a pendulum-like response to the thinking around Gillam's 1976 suggestion that the Wall had originally been planned with only six forts and interposed mile-fortlets (milecastle-equivalents) – in effect a mini Hadrian's Wall. Although a significant number of fortlets have been traced since the 1970s, in what has been termed 'the great fortlet hunt', this theory has been challenged once more and there is current support for the notion that all seventeen forts were in the original plan. But how to explain the proximity of some mile-fortlets to adjacent established forts? While much of this latter research is in itself fascinating and undoubtedly painstaking, there is a groundhog-day feel, suggesting there is perhaps an over-preoccupation with process and an avoidance of some of the thornier issues of insecure dating and the Wall's historical context. It is encouraging however to note an increasing interest in the collateral effects of prolonged occupation such as the work by Campbell (2016) on dispersal of Roman material to non-Roman sites, and the recent synthesis by Macinnes (2020) on the impact of the Wall on local Iron Age society.

The Wall now?

Still traceable in large sections through town and country alike, the narrowest isthmus of Scotland is transected by this impressive example of Roman engineering, which offers a striking contrast of ancient structure with the

surrounding post-industrial landscape. For example, one of the forts, Castle-cary, lies next to a bend of the M80 motorway and is bisected by the Glasgow–Edinburgh railway line, within a stone's throw of the modern attractions of the Falkirk Wheel and the Kelpies. The rock-cut ditch at Croy Hill remains a breath-taking testament to Roman single-mindedness and the whim of an emperor who, unlike his subordinates, barely experienced the landscape outside of Rome let alone the wilds of Caledonia.

Since its designation as a World Heritage Site, the popularity of the Antonine Wall as a tourist destination has risen and the signage and interpretation at the various sites have improved dramatically, particularly since the Rediscovery Project. The best Roman finds from the Wall can also be seen in concentrated form in the impressive gallery of the Hunterian Museum in Glasgow. However, after reviewing this remarkable testament to the military aspirations of a Roman emperor, one is left with the feeling that it could benefit from a dedicated interpretative facility on the Wall itself. Until this happens, it is likely that the important stories the Wall has to tell will remain muted, and it will fail to reach its rightful place in the popular imagination (plate 15).

82. The stone-built fort of Castlecary, which can be identified by its elevated platform (arrows), is now bisected by the Glasgow–Edinburgh railway line. The clump of trees occupies the central range of buildings.

CHAPTER THIRTEEN

Trouble up north: bribery and incursions

Walter Elliot's bucolic Friar Tuck demeanour is a front. A man of firmly independent views, his flat cap surmounts an exceptionally active brain that does not readily attune to accepted dogma, irrespective of the preacher's credentials or seniority. As his Border reiver surname suggests, authority holds no fears. In his six decades as an agricultural fencer he has also developed an intimate relationship with the history of the land of his birth. Walter's formidable local knowledge is revered, and he is a recognised expert on the area's past.

So it seemed natural that on a Friday night as he was about to sit down to dinner, Jim Middleton, an old acquaintance, knocked on his front door. Jim, a recent convert to metal detecting, was brandishing what looked like two turquoise buttons. Through the copper sulphate crust, Walter recognised the silvery face of Marcus Aurelius and smiled back at the two tarnished denarii. 'Well, well, where did you find these?' he asked. 'Synton, and there's more where these came from,' said Jim, also a laconic Borderer, as he opened a Tupperware box filled with dozens of coins.

And so, the story of the resurfacing of the Synton hoard unfolded over the next few days with the arrival of Fraser Hunter, at the head of a National Museum retrieval team, and Walter using his fencer's divining rods to investigate a nearby palisaded Iron Age enclosure. Now, ten years on, the 211 shining silver denarii present a stunning array in the Trimontium Museum.

Walter though was not hugely surprised to learn of the new discovery as he had been involved in another cache of denarii found by detectorists the year before only a few miles east of Synton. And that too was not his first encounter with a hoard from the area, for he had played a key part in rescuing a third, even larger, deposit of more than 300 denarii that had been uncovered next to a ploughed-out hillfort near Peebles. To Walter, these discoveries made sense when seen against the area's tumultuous history. But why were bags of Roman coins, some of which had never been in circulation since they left their Roman mint, being buried near native homesteads across southern Scotland?

A time of turbulence

84. A commemorative stone erected by the men of Calpurnius Agricola at Corbridge. Note that the honorand (Sol Invicto representing the reviled Commodus) has been effaced in an act of *damnatio memoriae*.

The period from the evacuation of the Antonine Wall, until the next documented Roman incursion early in the third century was, according to historical sources, not without considerable incident. The *Augustan Histories* tell us that war was threatening at the start of the reign of Marcus Aurelius (161–80) and that his able general, Sextus Calpurnius Agricola, had been dispatched to deal with British issues on the emperor's behalf, being appointed governor from about 161. As is typical of the *Historia*, detail is lacking and the nature of the strife he was sent to deal with is overshadowed by news of events in Parthia, Germany and a major flood of the Tiber that required disaster relief in Rome itself.

However, for all its shortcomings, it appears that the *Historia* was accurate about the arrival in Britain of Calpurnius Agricola who, like so many governors of Britain, had also overseen that other troubled province, Germania. His presence is confirmed on various inscriptions from forts across the north of the country. Two stones from Corbridge record detachments of two legions, the VIth *Victrix* and XXth *Valeria Victrix*, completing building work under his leadership sometime between 162–8. Construction activity also attributed to his period of office, at the forts of Hardknott, Carvoran and Ribchester, has been interpreted as preparation for the withdrawal of Roman forces from the Antonine Wall. Repair of war damage may also be a possible explanation as the presence of significant legionary detachments this far north would be supportive of a period of considerable unrest. However extensive the war was, he seemed to have quelled it successfully, at least in the short term.

The War of Commodus

As with many periods in history, outbreaks of warfare in North Britain at this time appear to have been generational. Characteristic intervals of approximately twenty years separate those conflicts, which are of a magnitude to merit comment by Roman historians. However, early in the 180s, there occurred one of the largest explosions of violence ever recorded in the north. An event which, given its likely magnitude, seems to be somewhat under-reported by contemporary Roman historians and modern commentators alike. The emperor on the throne was Commodus, the troubled son of Marcus Aurelius, and the recorder of the event was Cassius Dio. Dio is generally considered a reliable historian and, unlike the writers of the *Historia*, was an eyewitness to the events of the late second and early third centuries.

After briefly describing a concurrent war in Dacia, Dio recorded: 'His [Commodus] greatest struggle was the one with the Britons. When the tribes in that island, crossed the wall that separated them from the Roman legions, and did much damage cutting down a general together with his

Cassius Dio (155–235)

Dio was no backwater diarist – as a senator's son he was nurtured in the bosom of the empire and over his long life was elevated to the roles of senator, consul, proconsul and provincial governor. An intimate association with the levers of power of the Severan dynasty gave him significant insight into the politics and events of the late second- and early third-century Roman world. Born in Nicaea in Anatolia of mixed Greek and Roman heritage, he was also a historian of considerable merit, second only to Tacitus in terms of importance and quality of references to events in North Britain. These references form part of an extensive eighty-book history of Rome covering a span of 1,400 years.

Like Tacitus and many other ancient historians, Dio's writing tended to leave some of the detail of events rather thin by modern standards. As with Tacitus, however, there appears to be no good reason to reject the factual elements of his testimony, especially where these do not have a direct bearing on individual personalities.

troops, Commodus became alarmed and sent Ulpius Marcellus against them.' There then followed a much lengthier passage describing the rigid martial qualities of Marcellus and his particularly unpleasant nature. Dio concludes: 'and he [Marcellus] ruthlessly put down the barbarians of Britain' before the governor himself was subjected to a show trial and near-miss execution at the hands of the paranoid Commodus. These few lines of sparse prose merit expansion and possible correlation with some of the evidence from various sites across North Britain.

Firstly, there is considerable uncertainty about which wall Dio was refer-ring to and it has been assumed, at least latterly, that it was the Tyne–Solway barrier that featured in the prelude to the massacre of Roman troops. It is however just possible that it was the Antonine Wall, particularly if we are willing to entertain a later date of desertion for a few of the larger forts like Castlecary and Mumrills. This timescale may also prove a better fit with the abandonment of Newstead. Some light is further shed by Dio himself who provides a reference to the Maeatae who lived adjacent to 'the wall that divides the province'. The Maeatae are the same tribe who broke their treaty and ultimately sided with the Caledonians in the uprising. Modern scholars have suggested that it was they who gave their name to the hillforts of Dumyat and Myot Hill, which are both in mid-Stirlingshire and certainly not situated as far south as the Tyne. This suggests that the wall Dio associated with the Maeatae was the Antonine Wall.

A further clue arises from a closer reading of Dio's original Greek text. This states that 'the tribes crossed the wall that separated the barbarians from the Roman στρατόπεδα', which probably means 'camps' and not 'legions' as is often translated. These camps may be a reference to forts in the Scottish Lowlands on the line of Dere Street. There is ample evidence of burning at Newstead and Cappuck, which lie south of the Antonine Wall and both of which were ultimately to perish by fire.

Coins from Newstead dating to the late 170s would suggest this fort was firmly in the front line of any rebellion in the reign of Commodus. The later Antonine 'upper burned layer' seen everywhere in archaeological sections at Birrens may also be related to this event. As we have seen, when Robertson excavated this fort, which lies about 30km north of Carlisle, she was in no doubt about the characteristic signs of chaotic destruction that to her were axiomatic of at least two violent episodes. In future, a closer look at Antonine Wall forts using more modern techniques may add to this list of burned forts lending further clarification to which wall Dio was referring to.

A distinct carbonised destruction layer has long been recognised at the Roman town of Corbridge. The site lies just south of the Dere Street portal in Hadrian's Wall and close to two other Wall forts to the north and east of it, Halton Chesters and Rudchester, where destruction layers have also

been identified. With respect to Corbridge, there seems to be no dubiety about widespread destruction of a type that could be interpreted as the result of violence rather than rebuilding. However, pinning the date down exactly to the 180s has exposed all the difficulties of refining narrow time periods by archaeology and has necessitated some mind-bendingly complex interpretation. The data has been unpicked by Hodgson (2008), within the limitations of the piecemeal nature of the excavation and recording of the digs, and it now seems reasonable to accept this large site could have been damaged sometime between the 170s and early 180s by enemy action. This observation adds to the mounting evidence for a major episode of warfare that would be in accord with Dio's account. It has also been pointed out by Anthony Birley that the Greek word used by Dio for 'general', 'στρατηγος', was often employed to indicate a very high-ranking official and it has been argued that this was the imperial governor himself. If this was the case, it suggests that the Roman troops who were over-run by the northern tribes (who Dio refers to as *Britons*) may have included signifi-cant numbers of regulars and/or *singulares* (bodyguards). If the victims had

85. Aerial image of Newstead (Trimontium) fort immediately after ploughing. Note the carbon staining of the burned fort and adjacent bathhouse revealed in the wet plough soil.

been less noteworthy, it is unlikely that Dio would have described the affair as a war.

The magnitude of this episode graphically illustrates the destructive potential of the northern tribes and the relative vulnerability of Roman forces when the circumstances were right. It was also a harbinger of what was to face Roman troops in North Britain from a previously unrecorded confederation, whose military prowess had been honed by generations of conflict with Rome. A people who would now manifest themselves as one of Rome's most tenacious enemies – the Picts.

Ulpius Marcellus

Whatever the relationship between the rebellion of the 180s and the archaeological evidence of burned forts in the Scottish Lowlands, the fearsome general Ulpius Marcellus was sent to Britain by Commodus to deal with the rebellion. We know from exact dates provided by at least three diplomas that he was the imperial governor in the late 170s and the campaign to retrieve the situation was almost certainly brought to a close by 184. We can also be sure that his reprisals were ferocious, if Cassius Dio's descriptions of the man are anything to go by. Reputed to have schooled himself to go without food and sleep for long periods, Dio records that the new governor was a ruthless figure, messing with his men and even sending out fake orders to his subordinates in the middle of the night just to keep them sharp. An inscription by Junius Caelianus, the legate of the VIth Victrix, which has been tentatively dated to the period of Marcellus' governorship, was found a few kilometres north-west of Carlisle. It records Caelianus giving thanks 'ob res trans vallum prospere gestas', 'because of successful achievements beyond the Wall'.

Clearly, this was not a good time to be a native living in the territories within a few days' march north of Hadrian's Wall. The widespread desolation seen in the archaeological record, such as the prolonged desertion of the Northumberland Plain and the hillforts of the Cheviots, may be partly due to the vicious backlash that would have followed in the wake of the governor re-establishing Roman control. Dio himself records that Marcellus 'ruthlessly put down the barbarians of Britain'. The eyewitness account by Josephus of how relatively 'benign' Roman generals meted out retribution during the First Jewish War, suggests the consequences for the insurgents may have been particularly severe. The close of this bloody episode was to be commemorated by Commodus taking his seventh acclamation as *Imperator* and issuing victory coins dated to 184, on which he is described as *Britannicus Maximus*.

The record of the period after the Commodan War is a little confused but there seems to have been a threatened mutiny, once more by British

troops – possibly due to Marcellus' extremely harsh leadership – who tried to appoint their own legionary legate, a man called Junius Priscus, as emperor. He wisely turned them down, reputedly saying, 'I am no more emperor than you are soldiers.' Remarkably, Priscus survived the normally lethal outcome of attracting the attention of the increasingly deranged Commodus.

The strife hinted at by the written records and the archaeology of late second-century North Britain, took place upon a backdrop of a truly chaotic period of civil war for the rest of the empire. Pertinax, who previously served as a junior officer with the VIth Legion in York and had himself been governor of Britannia from 185–7, began a brief three-month reign as emperor at the start of 193. He acquired the position after the assassination of Commodus (in which he may have been complicit) on the last day of 192 and was then in turn murdered by his own praetorians. This internecine carnage was not atypical, for Romans slaughtering Romans was a recurrent theme of the empire whenever a succession was contested. The short period of civil war (by Roman standards), known by later historians as the 'Year of the Five Emperors', saw Pertinax, Didius Julianus, Pescennius Niger, Clodius Albinus and the ultimate victor Septimius Severus, battle it out in a series of punishing clashes across Europe and the Middle East.

Within four years of Severus emerging victorious from this existential struggle (finally despatching the last pretender Clodius Abinus, the erstwhile governor of Britain), Virius Lupus was sent to Britannia in 197 to become Severus' new imperial governor. According to Dio, Lupus was immediately

86. A *sestertius* of Commodus showing reclining Victory presenting a shield emblazoned with 'Victory in Britain' to a *tropaeum* – a commemorative agglomeration of weapons following a successful war.

forced to 'purchase peace' from the Maeatae, the same tribe he described 'living next to the cross-wall which divided Britain'.

As direct evidence of this form of Roman quick-fix diplomacy, several hoards of silver denarii such as the Synton hoard described at the beginning of this chapter (the latest coin is one of Commodus) have been discovered throughout Scotland. Chance finds of the last 250 years, denarii hoards are scattered from the Borders to the Moray Firth. It is highly likely that Dio was referencing these types of donatives and subsidies that had been employed throughout the reign of Commodus, and that are similarly unearthed in other trouble spots such as Dacia – modern-day Romania.

As far as North Britain was concerned, the final major actor in this pre-Severan drama was Lucius Alfenus Senecio, the last governor of all of Britain (the country was to be subdivided after the reign of Severus). He was appointed between 205 and 207 and it appears he fared at least as badly as Virius Lupus in contending with the incursions of the northern tribes. Despite large subsidies of silver denarii to Caledonian warlords, the historian Herodian tells us Senecio could not cope and finally resorted to the tactics of all struggling caretakers – beseeching the emperor himself to come and sort things out. And so, probably in the winter of 207, it is recorded that the governor conveyed a message to Rome hinting strongly that only the imperial presence would be able to deal effectively with the threat from the north. Once more, the testimonies of governors and historians confirm that the tribes were out of control and that a major revolt was again underway across the northern frontier.

CHAPTER FOURTEEN

The African emperor and his brats

The sky today is the colour of wet slate as low clouds scud in from the east coast – Scout's ears are back, and my hood is up against the blast, as we pick our way through the gloom in pursuit of a little-known remnant of the Roman war machine. The snow is beginning to drift against a field wall that surmounts a long, low earthwork looming out of the greyness. Awkwardly positioned to make the best of uneven terrain, and resulting in some unusually un-Roman angles, this is all that remains of a rampart that once measured over a kilometre in length. The massive Roman camp at Channelkirk, here at the head of the Leader Valley in the Scottish Borders, is almost 2,000 years old, and although virtually totally eroded, the ghost of the 160-acre enclosure leaves little doubt about the phenomenal reach of Roman retribution. But what precipitating event brought a host of Roman engineers and legionaries to a wind-scoured hillside in Caledonia? Like so much about Roman Scotland, the answers are controversial.

In the spring of 209, one of the largest forces ever assembled for conflict on British soil clattered its way northwards through the recently refurbished frontier of Hadrian's Wall. Estimated at more than 40,000 troops, with an unknown number in amphibious support, it dwarfed armies of later epochs. To set this horde in perspective, the combined number of Scottish and English soldiers at Bannockburn in 1314 was unlikely to have exceeded 25,000 and less than 20,000 combatants took part in the battle of Hastings. The third-century Roman invasion of Scotland was to be a punitive mission so vindictive that the normally restrained Dio placed the words of Homer's genocidal Agamemnon in Severus' mouth as he instructed his troops 'to spare no-one not even the unborn in its mother's womb and to leave no-one alive to memorialise the dead'. This was to be an intervention that was extreme even by Roman standards.

Who was the man who had commanded all of this? As we have seen, Lucius Septimius Severus (145–211) was the last man standing of the five contestants for the imperial purple in the final decade of the second century. But why did a man, who was to become one of the most celebrated emperors of the Roman Empire, consider it necessary to make a personal appear-

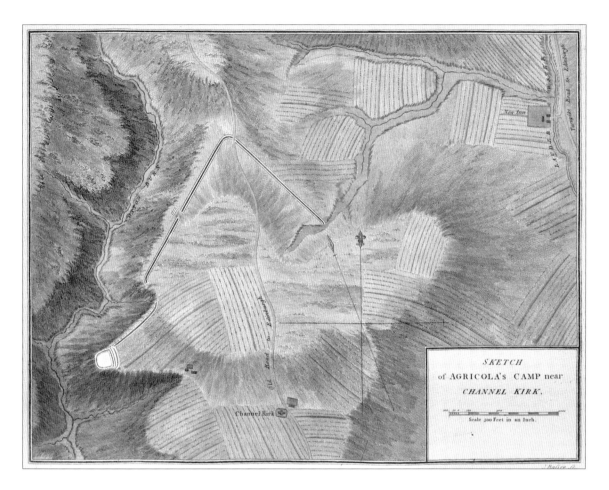

SKETCH
of AGRICOLA's CAMP near
CHANNEL KIRK.

Scale 300 Feet in an Inch.

87. The remnants of the huge (160-acre) Severan marching camp on the hill near Channelkirk. The fortification was becoming ploughed out even by the time of this map drawn by General Roy in the late 18th century. He attributed the earthworks to Agricola.

ance in Caledonia and to lead such an immense invasion force with overt murderous intent?

Severus was born in the heyday of the Antonine principate, in the affluent North African city of Leptis Magna. Leptis, originally a Phoenician settlement on the coast of modern-day Libya, was to become one of the major cities of Tripolitania particularly after it benefitted from generous imperial patronage. The son of an equestrian, he ascended the *cursus honorum* with apparent ease and went on to a distinguished military career, some of which has been outlined in the preceding chapter. However, it should be emphasised that he was no bureaucrat like Antoninus, who happened to be in the right place at the right time. It took considerable guile, self belief and military guts to be the sole survivor of the vicious warfare of the 'Year of the Five Emperors' (193) and its immediate aftermath.

He was clearly of a restless martial spirit, for less than five years after his emergence as victor he directed his energy to a disastrous foray into Parthia. There, in 197, his forces ground to a halt, suffering considerable losses at his ill-fated siege of Hatra, an ancient Parthian city which lay a couple of hundred kilometres north-west of Baghdad. The defences of Hatra were so secure that they had also repulsed the forces of Trajan 100 years before, proving that even the usually victorious Roman army could find some nuts just too hard to crack.

What then brought this battle-hardened emperor, accompanied by such a vast force, to the opposite end of the empire? Was the excitement of campaigning on the northern frontier enough to persuade a vainglorious and thrill-seeking emperor to take one last bow on the military stage as he felt old age closing in? It is recorded that soothsayers and assorted omens had informed him he would not return alive from the expedition, and he would die on campaign – in the end he proved them right. Or was it simply to extract his warring sons, Caracalla and Geta, from the fleshpots of Rome, toughen them up with a short sharp expedition to the empire's edge and at the same time give his soldiers something to do while resolving the problems of Britannia's floundering governor?

Classical texts offer all three reasons as possible explanations but there is archaeological evidence to support a fourth hypothesis: large quantities of silver coins had been poured into Scotland over the preceding decade as inducements to keep the northern tribes at bay. Could Severus' temper, for which he was renowned, have finally erupted in an act of spiteful retribution for this apparent breach of contract?

Whatever the exact reason, his campaign eventually assumed the proportions of a sledgehammer – after mustering troops on mainland Europe, Severus came to Britain in 208 accompanied by his family, *vexillations* of several legions, the Praetorian Guard and a cloud of attendants,

88. Bust of the Emperor Septimius Severus in the Capitoline Museum, Rome.

Herodian (170–240)

Herodian was another contemporary chronicler of the adventures of the Severan dynasty in Scotland, although modern commentators treat his writing with greater circumspection than the more austere Dio. A Graeco-Roman minor official, he produced a history of Rome spanning the half-century that commenced with the death of Marcus Aurelius. Herodian devoted considerable scroll-space to Severus' Caledonian invasion and padded out the bare factual details of the campaign with a little more spice than Cassius Dio. They both agreed, however, on the apparent idleness and debauched lifestyle of Severus' two sons. Herodian also tells us that the unstable Caracalla made an abortive attempt on his father's life while parlaying with Caledonian leaders.

Julia Domna and the wife of Argentocoxus

Surprisingly, it was the austere Dio rather than the indelicate Herodian who provided one of the more scurrilous reports of the Caledonian campaign. He tells us that in a lull after the first treaty had been agreed between the combatants, a meeting took place between the Empress Julia Domna and the unnamed wife of the Caledonian leader Argentocoxus. The Empress had quipped about the fluid morality of the reputedly polygamous native wives only to be told by the chieftain's wife that Scottish women had sex with the strongest men of the tribe, unlike Roman women who debased themselves with the weakest. Sadly Dio does not tell us how this riposte was received.

and we are also told by Dio, another large quantity of cash. We now know that even more bags of denarii, despite failing previously to have the desired effect, eventually found their way to northern power centres in a further doomed attempt to buy peace.

It may seem curious that this tumultuous period in Scottish history, which witnessed the bloody activities of a prominent Roman emperor and his sociopathic son, and was recorded in some detail by two renowned classical authors, has largely been ignored. Although two recent publications by Hodgson (2014) and Elliot (2018) reset a little of the balance by taking another look at this fascinating episode, it remains unrecognised by most contemporary Scots. But before considering why this should be, what confirmation do we have that any of the events alluded to by Dio or Herodian took place? Gratifyingly, the evidence is considerably more impressive than for many of the other Roman interventions in the north and comes not just from texts but also from archaeological, epigraphic and numismatic sources.

Archaeological discoveries that have shed light on Severus' *expeditio* have been made particularly at installations in the north-east of England and on coastal estuaries of eastern Scotland, supplemented by aerial photography of marching camps and bridgeheads extending northwards from an apparent mustering point in the Borders. Excavations at the two main sites in Scotland that have produced convincing Severan material, Cramond on the Forth and Carpow on the Tay, have been illuminating, but not without their own controversy.

Cramond

A Roman fortress has been recognised at Cramond, where the River Almond flows into the Forth estuary, since at least the seventeenth century.

89. The Cramond lioness devours the head of a bound captive. The funerary statue was found in the mud at the bottom of Cramond harbour.

The fort, which is approximately 5 acres in size, is situated on a knoll adjacent to the church overlooking the harbour of this attractive village which lies only 8km from the centre of Edinburgh. At the beginning of the eighteenth century, a Roman altar dedicated by the Second Cohort of Tungrians to the Mother Goddesses of the Parade Ground, was dug up in the village. This was the same unit of auxiliaries that had previously been stationed at South Shields, the supply fort on the Tyne. Cramond, which was also likely to have been a Roman port of some significance, has been excavated on several occasions since the 1950s. Coin and pottery evidence pointed almost immediately to a major Severan presence, in contrast to the striking absence of third-century material from almost every other permanent Roman fort in Scotland. Over the last two decades, further work has established that there was an unusually large defended annexe to the east of the main fortifications where more evidence of Severan and even later activity has come to light. This strongly suggests that Cramond acted as a forward supply base for Severan forces, possibly exclusively provisioned by sea, and had some sort of military afterlife extending into the third century, a span which did not end with Caracalla's return to Rome after his father's death. At present, the number of granaries is standard, although more may await discovery in the enigmatic eastern annexe.

Cramond harbour is also renowned for the serendipitous discovery in the winter of 1996, by the local ferryman, of a larger-than-life Roman sculpture of a lioness devouring the head of a male figure. The bearded man is naked, and has his hands bound behind his back forming the classical representation of a vanquished barbarian in a striking memento mori. The forepaws of the lioness are flanked by two snakes, symbolising the everlasting soul presumably of the honorand, and not the victim.

The bulging eyeballs and prominent musculature of both lioness and barbarian suggest a mid-second to third-century date for the sculpture. It is generally thought that the carving was being shipped into the fort precinct to form the crowning decoration of a high-ranking individual's tomb, possibly an officer, when it broke loose from lifting gear and plunged into the water of the harbour. The motif of a lion devouring its prey is relatively common in Roman art (see the smaller but slightly more genteel Corbridge lion, which is only eating a goat), but the clear message here at Cramond is domination and is a sculpture that is unique in Britannia. The sheer size of the tableau is something of an indication of the prominence of the fort and what awaits discovery in the neighbourhood.

Carpow

There was a tradition of a Roman fort on the south bank of the Tay near its confluence with the Earn, long before it was first excavated in earnest by Eric Birley in 1961. Until then, comments by Crawford and St Joseph, drawing on evidence from their aerial images, show they considered it to be no more than just another auxiliary fort with probable Flavian origins. This viewpoint changed radically in the 1960s with the discovery of a legionary-sized headquarters building, an impressive 50m long, with a range of other major structures including what was then thought to be a *praetorium* (commandant's house) but is now interpreted as a suite of baths. Birley's discovery of stratified coins of Caracalla, and his wife Plautilla, dated to 202, confirmed the Severan association and the finding of a significant number of legionary-stamped roof tiles identified the site as one of an unexpected legionary fortress. Interestingly, the tiles belong to the VIth Victrix based at York, which by that point had been awarded the previously unknown honorific suffix of *BPF*, which is shorthand for *Britannica Pia Fidelis* ('Britannica pious and dutiful'). A further find of an inscription, incomplete but ascribed to Caracalla, from the east gate appeared to confirm the 27-acre site as the forward base of the Severan invasion dating to 209. However, this panel, which carries the motifs of another legion, the capricorn and pegasus of the IInd Augusta from Caerleon, has itself given rise to controversy. The carving has recently been re-attributed to the earlier period of Commodus, mainly because of its zoomorphic griffon-headed *pelta* (the arcing shield motif), which is characteristic of an earlier Antonine period. However, a further assessment of the east gate by Keppie (2019) proposes a new arrangement of the surviving fragments and suggests a new reading is possible, which restores its original Severan dating.

90. Fragment of a dedicatory panel from the fortress of Carpow. The Pegasus and Capricorn were emblems of the IInd Augusta Legion and the gryphon headed *pelta* on the right border was common in the Antonine period.

Some commentators have suggested that Carpow had its origins in a prior Commodan-period incursion such as the previously mentioned punitive expedition of Ulpius Marcellus that took place after the uprising in the early 180s. However, the presence of a coin of 207 suggests that the fort was abandoned after the Severan restoration of Hadrian's Wall in 205–8. The Commodan hypothesis would imply that the fort was held as a remote installation over 100 miles north of any reinforcements on Hadrian's Wall for a period of approximately twenty years (185–205). Although such isolated Roman outposts are known (e.g. Apsaros on the Black Sea lies an almost equal distance beyond Rome's eastern frontier), it seems that to effectively maroon legionary troops here must have been part of a larger project for which there is no evidence at least until the Severan campaign.

91. Coin from the reign of Caracalla showing a pontoon bridge with the inscription *traiectus* below, meaning 'thrown over'.

Whatever the misgivings about the carvings on the gateway, it seems more intuitive to ascribe the foundation and relatively short-lived occupation of Carpow to the period immediately after the Severan campaigns of 209 and 210. Irrespective of the exact dating, it has long been suggested that the location of Carpow is in keeping with a bridgehead for a crossing of the Tay: the pontoon bridge depicted on bronze coinage of Caracalla of 209, a rare motif in itself, may point to his northern campaign.

South Shields

Much further south, at South Shields fort on the south bank of the Tyne where it flows into the North Sea, excavations have uncovered convincing evidence that the fort, founded in the Hadrianic period, was repurposed during Severan times as a supply base with most of its internal buildings replaced by a unique series of twenty-two granaries. The presence of a number of lead Severan bag seals suggest that a major logistics effort was in place to supply grain to troops in the north in the early third century. At the present time, it is not possible to be sure if these fort modifications were to create a coastal distribution depot for the recently refurbished Hadrian's Wall or to act as a forward supply base for the Scottish campaigns, or both.

The littoral position of all three sites (Carpow, Cramond and South Shields) supports the notion that resupply of the Scottish expedition by sea was paramount in the Severan period. The minimal evidence for reoccupation of most other forts away from the coast would indicate the short-lived intention of an amphibious incursion. However, it is worth noting some significant structural changes at Corbridge. Here, two outstandingly large granaries were constructed in the heart of the Roman town that lies on the line of Dere Street where it crosses the Tyne some 20 miles west of South Shields. Corbridge had already changed its role to a supply base in the decades before the Severan expedition. It is, however, telling that an altar was found adjacent to the granaries that was dedicated by an officer who we find was in charge of the facilities during an *expeditio felicissima Britannica* (most successful British campaign). As we have seen in relation to Hadrian's visit to Britain, the use of the term *expeditio* usually implies the personal involvement of an emperor, on this occasion most likely Severus.

Severan campaign camps

The discovery of previously unknown Roman sites in Scotland by aerial reconnaissance has a long tradition owing much to the personal enthusiasm of early pioneers such as O.G.S. Crawford and his associate Alexander Keiller (of the marmalade dynasty). However, it was the work of Kenneth St Joseph (1912–94), based at Cambridge University, which was synony-

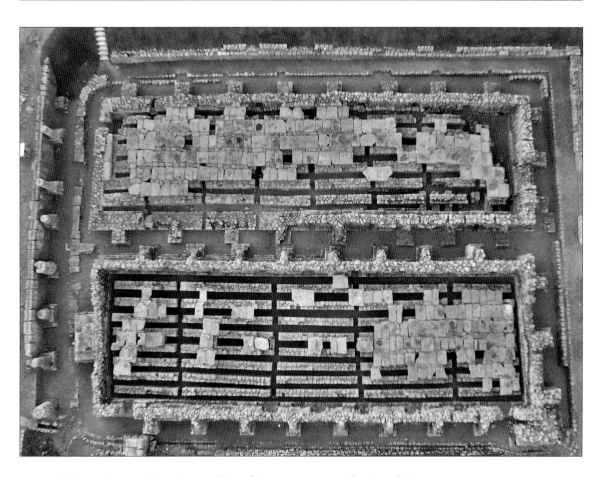

92. Vertical view of the large granaries at Corbridge. These cereal stores are immediately recognisable by their elevated floors and buttressed walls.

mous with our improved understanding of the movements of units of the Roman army in North Britain principally by identifying the cropmarks of the campaign camps for which the Roman army was renowned.

St Joseph constructed persuasive arguments based on camp surface area and inter-camp spacing (12–15 Roman miles – the distance a Roman force might march in a single day) that identified series of installations and attempted to relate these groupings to particular Roman campaigns. With respect to Severus, it was generally accepted that there were two series of temporary camps that could be characterised as installations related to his 208–10 intervention. These were the eleven 63-acre camps and eight 130-acre camps which extend diagonally north-east from Stirlingshire terminating just south of Stonehaven on the Aberdeenshire coast. However, following excavation which showed that an Antonine period road was laid on top of one of the 63-acre camps, it now seems probable that only the 130-acre group can be assigned to Severus and Caracalla. This group has also been shown to belong to the latest period from investigations at the site of Ardoch where there is a palimpsest of overlapping camps allowing

Campaign camps

Roman campaign or marching camps are vast but structurally ephemeral installations consisting usually of a single relatively shallow perimeter ditch (often only 2m wide by 1m deep) accompanied by a dump rampart punctuated by four, six or even eight gateways. It is thought that pointed wooden stakes carried by the soldiers in their packs supplemented the relatively slight ramparts. A few of these perimeters remain visible today (Pennymuir and Kirkbuddo for example) and some were drawn by Roy such as Dalginross, but for the most part, the earthworks have been eroded by weather or agricultural activity leaving cropmarks as their only trace. Most are playing card in shape with characteristic rounded corners, ranging in area from as small as 1 acre up to a massive 165 acres at St Leonard's Hill. Influenced by Josephus' description of virtually instant fortifications for overnight stops, it was thought until quite recently that these camps were for short-lived occupation only. However, wide-area excavation at Kintore in Aberdeenshire has shown that the original builders not only camped there for an extended period but the camp itself was reused by subsequent Roman forces passing along the same route years or even decades later.

93. The dark linear cropmark of the ditch of the south-west angle of the camp at Carnwath contrasts strongly with the paler ripening wheat. This 45-acre camp was discovered by Kenneth St Joseph in 1977.

Kenneth St Joseph (1912–94)

Known affectionately to some of his students as 'Holy Joe', St Joseph was the doyen of Roman aerial archaeology. During the Second World War, he was engaged as an aerial-photo analyst, developing a superlative eye for pattern recognition. Influenced at an early age by O.G.S. Crawford, the allegedly cantankerous but brilliant 'Flying Scotsman' (who also commenced his archaeological career with aerial reconnaissance in the First World War), St Joseph quickly recognised the potential of aerial photography for mapping the movements of ancient armies. Over his long career he discovered a considerable number of new Roman sites, reputedly more than 200, many of which were campaign camps. In 1973 he was awarded a personal chair of Aerial Photographic Studies at Cambridge University, and brought a new dimension to the field of aerial reconnaissance by meticulously confirming his photographic findings through trial excavation. His success in the field even persuaded Cambridge University to buy its own aircraft, which remained in service for almost four decades. His groundbreaking work in Scotland, which he published assiduously, has been built on by later proponents of the technique such as Maxwell, Hanson and Cowley.

the relative stratigraphy to be revealed. There has been more confidence in assigning the Borders series of four gargantuan 165-acre camps, which extend north along the line of Dere Street towards the Forth–Clyde isthmus, to the extraordinarily large Severan army. The camp at St Leonard's Hill, just south of Lauder, was discovered by St Joseph in 1948 and was, until relatively recently, the largest recorded camp in the Roman Empire. Large enough to accommodate 40,000 men, it is difficult to imagine this earthwork could belong to any other battlegroup than that of Severus.

Severus' progress

What details can be gleaned from Dio and Herodian of the first year of the campaign suggest that the conflict rapidly deteriorated into a guerrilla war with the indigenous peoples prudently melting into the hills to avoid pitched battle while carrying out hit-and-run attacks designed to undermine the morale of Roman troops. Arminius, the German resistance leader, employed a similar strategy as he engaged Quinctilius Varus' army of three legions in the battle of the Teutoburg Forest in AD 9.

From the distribution of the 130-acre camps, it would appear that the Severan battle force penetrated as far north as the Mounth, just south of Aberdeen where the Grampians meet the North Sea. Dio's description of Severus reaching the most northern point of Britain is possibly hyperbole as there is no evidence of a campaign camp of any size north of Inverness. It could therefore be a symbolic interpretation of the landform of the

Mounth, which Dio described as the extremity of the island. The series of five camps to the north-west of Aberdeen were, on the basis of C-14 data from Kintore, founded at a significantly earlier date and probably Flavian, and not related to Severus' expedition.

Massive Roman casualties?

Despite Severus' failure to bring native forces to a set-piece confrontation, Dio records that Roman losses stood at tens of thousands: 'for in fact the water caused great suffering to the Romans, and when they became scattered, they would be attacked. Then, unable to walk, they would be killed by their own men, to avoid capture, so that a full fifty thousand died.' This passage has been interpreted to mean that Roman casualties were, for whatever reason, grossly exaggerated and may have been due to difficulties with the elements and terrain rather than battle-related losses. Irrespective of how the casualties were sustained, this tally is impossibly high and could reflect Dio's fundamental antipathy towards the Severan dynasty, perhaps trying to create an allusion of a Varian-sized disaster. However, it does suggest that there were significant losses on the Roman side, and it is interesting to consider non-battle related causes. One that has received little

How far north?

For many years the upstanding rampart at Ythan Wells, 55km to the north-west of Aberdeen, was thought to be the most northerly extent of Roman penetration into northern Scotland. Captain Alexander Shand, an Aberdeenshire-born officer in the Royal Artillery, had first recorded this campaign camp in 1785. To St Joseph, working 150 years later, Ythan Wells seemed to be an abbreviated terminus for the series of Roman camps that appeared to be heading for the Moray Firth. His meticulous approach to aerial survey paid off when in 1949 he discovered cropmarks of a camp, with Flavian-style gateways, at Auchinhove, which lies a further 20km to the north-west. In 1959 he went on to discover a further, even larger, camp a few kilometres to the east at Muiryfold. However, the most likely (and possibly the most contentious) contender for the most northerly camp in the empire, lies at Bellie on the banks of the Spey, even further to the north-west and only 4km from the Moray coast. At least three earthworks cluster in the area, one of which has a rounded corner that would be compatible with Roman engineering. The tantalising nature of the cropmarks was insufficient, however, to persuade St Joseph and Crawford to confidently confirm the Roman origin of the site, and Jones (2011) still includes the camp in the 'probable' group. Despite decades of reconnaissance no further Roman installations have been discovered beyond these Morayshire sites. Although camps could yet be discovered north and west of Inverness, at this time it would appear that the 'extremity of Britannia' said to have been witnessed by the emperors Severus and Constantius, was something of a literary exaggeration.

attention, which may explain a high mortality rate, and Dio's description of general debilitation, is the possibility of an epidemic to which history has shown large bodies of soldiers are susceptible. The reference to water could just, therefore, relate to water-borne pathogens such as typhus, which may have terminally sapped the strength of the Roman troops. Spread to the indigenous population, a phenomenon graphically illustrated by the invader-introduced diseases that decimated the populations of the Americas, could also account for the non-violent desertion of native settlement in the Scottish Lowlands such as that confirmed by excavation at Broxmouth (Armit and McKenzie 2013). And if sustained, could account for the apparent quiescence of third-century Scotland until population numbers slowly recovered.

By the end of the first full season's campaigning in 209, Severus was reported to have accepted a nominal victory and had come to terms with the northern tribes, who apparently ceded 'a large part of their territory'. It was during this season that Herodian and Dio both record dark incidents which signalled Caracalla's malign intent towards his own family. Perhaps the most serious was his attempt to stab Severus in the back as he rode out with him to accept the initial surrender of the Caledonian leaders – the attempt was only narrowly averted by watchful attendants.

After the surrender – in reality a temporary cessation of hostilities – Severus headed south to overwinter 209/10 in York, awarding himself and Caracalla the honorific titles of *Britannicus Maximus*.

During 210 the emperor's chronic ill-health took a turn for the worse (he was reported to have been borne on a litter for the previous year's campaign) because Dio tells us Severus sent Caracalla alone as sole commander for a second season's campaign in response to the breakdown of the armistice signed the year before. It was at the beginning of this second invasion that Severus, using the infamous words borrowed from Homer, entreated Caracalla to slaughter the entire barbarian population. Hyperbole aside, it is likely that Caracalla's expedition did lay waste to the countryside, and given that the Roman army represented one of the few forces able to cataclysmically affect a large area in a short time frame, it may account for the apparent deliberate destruction of some of the contemporary souterrains in Angus. This destruction horizon had initially been recognised in the 1950s by the father of souterrain studies, F.T. Wainwright (1953), whose observations were based on his own excavations of the souterrains of Ardestie and Carlungie near Carnoustie. At these sites there seemed to be deliberate and systematic destruction of the earth houses, while the associated settlements above appeared to survive. Dating evidence suggested that these chambers had been dismantled during the late second or early third century.

Armit, in his review of the fate of souterrains in eastern Scotland (1999),

Souterrains

As the name suggests, these enigmatic structures are subterranean build-ings, often stone-lined (but occasionally roofed with wood and turf), frequently curvilinear in plan and often associated with overground roundhouse settlement. They appear to be largely a phenomenon of the Atlantic Iron Age fringe with variants in Ireland and Cornwall. However, the most notable souterrains in Britain are Scottish and are mainly found north of the Antonine frontier in the Fife and Angus areas. Their purpose has always been a matter of debate, but they do not seem to have served any defensive, ritual or funerary function. Use as a store for food surplus seems to be the most convincing explanation.

94. The souterrain at Carlungie near Carnoustie in Angus lies amid newly ploughed fields. The curving form, side chambers and drystone walls are characteristic. The structure would have originally been roofed with stone slabs.

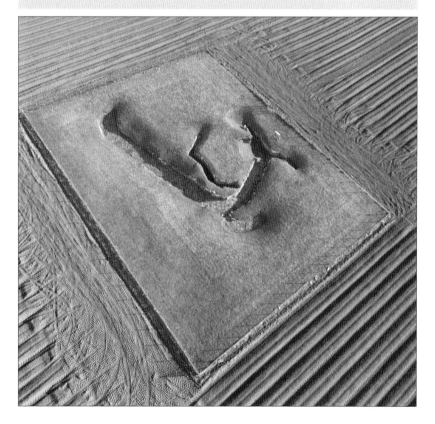

felt that 'the evidence would allow for a single episode of abandonment', a so-called 'souterrain abandonment horizon'. The distribution of these deliberately dismantled storage chambers does appear to correspond to the area likely to have been penetrated by Severan forces and it may be reason-able to attribute their destruction directly or indirectly to Roman troops.

Armit however suggested that demolition could have been due to events a couple of generations earlier. He proposed the cause might have been removal of the patronage of the Roman army at the time of the Antonine withdrawal and subsequent loss of business by Angus farmers who may have been supplying surplus foodstuffs to the Roman army. This sounds a plausible explanation, but it does presuppose a trading partnership that is not borne out by the finds from non-Roman sites which, by continental standards, are sparse. Indeed, from the small amounts of Roman material found in or around souterrain sites, it seems that if there was any trade, it was fairly one-sided and would in essence constitute tribute (in modern terms extortion or protection money). If we accept that there was a single souterrain abandonment event, then it is intuitive to assume that the souterrains were deliberately destroyed by Roman troops or possibly by the indigenous population themselves who were forced to infill them under duress or prior to desertion. For parallels, again see examples of indigenous peoples coerced to destroy their townships by the troops of Titus and Vespasian during the First Jewish War.

'Pay the army!'

In York, over the winter of 210–11, the emperor's condition continued to deteriorate (Herodian suggests this was assisted by Caracalla), and he succumbed in February, at the age of sixty-five after holding power for eighteen years. Dio records that on his deathbed Severus told Caracalla and his brother Geta to 'pay the army and scorn all others' and, even more narcissistically, he is reputed to have sized up his own funerary urn and commented that 'it will hold a man that the world could not contain'.

Severus was cremated with great pomp in York but even before his ashes were cold, both his sons appear to have planned to abandon the Caledonian expedition and hurry back to Rome to consolidate their power. Unfortunately for Geta, his older brother followed through on his plan to assassinate his sibling, and Caracalla became sole emperor the same year his father died. He was to rule, mainly chaotically, for another six years before being stabbed to death by one of his own soldiers while relieving himself at the side of the road.

Such was the ignominious end of the last Roman emperor to attempt the complete subjugation of North Britain. Although many future cross-border incursions were yet to unfold, one is left with the impression that Rome's final large-scale gambit had been played and that everything from this point forward was to be on a diminishing scale. The mailed fist of Rome had, for more than a century, punched against Caledonian ghosts – apparitions that were about to condense into a much more solid form that would slowly but surely shift the balance of power.

CHAPTER FIFTEEN

The post-Severan aftermath and the rise of the Picts

It has been a couple of hours since the rain stopped, and the sun is now dipping behind the trees. The soil is surprisingly sticky, and Walter Elliot has developed heavy halos of mud around his old walking boots that conspire to stop him plotting a straight line across the field – a field he has trudged exactly like this for at least five decades. His eyes have adjusted to the longer shadows and the deceptive allure of the small, rain-washed pebbles that keep attracting his attention, but the conditions are now just right for field walking even though his stomach tells him it's home time. The breast pocket of his jacket is comfortably bulging with a few sherds of samian, one with a nice fragment of a hunting scene and a couple of segments of black burnished ware. And then he sees it, fingernail-sized, perched red and bold on a tiny clod of mud. With a trembling hand – he still feels the thrill of first contact even though this is now his eighth Roman ring stone – he picks it up and gently rubs the surface clean, momentarily fearing that it may still be a piece of alluvial dross that has tricked his eyes. But no – there on the burnished jasper surface, as sharply defined as the day it was cut, is the youthful portrait of the mad, bad Caracalla (plate 16).

As with the Antonine abandonment, the date of extraction of Caracalla's forces is uncertain, but from archaeological evidence we know approximately when the coastal forts of Cramond and Carpow were deserted. The last coin from either site dates to no later than 209, which indicates they may have been given up soon after the young emperor bolted for Rome. A further pointer is provided by an inscription from Tyneside which shows that the Vth cohort of Gauls previously stationed at Cramond was rehoused back at South Shields, reconfigured to accommodate a larger force, by 220 at the latest.

The Severan withdrawal ushered in a further lacuna in Scotland's history of almost a hundred years, but on the Continent the third century was a period of extreme political and military turmoil. It may simply be that Roman historians had enough on their minds to be bothered by any British sideshow. Indeed, from the time of the murder of the fratricidal-patricidal Caracalla in 217 to the accession of Diocletian in 284, the Roman world saw the rise and fall of no less than twenty-five emperors. Most were destined to die violently, either on the battlefield in pernicious power play or as the result of assassination by their own troops. The longest reign of this motley band was thirteen years (Severus Alexander, the last of the Severan dynasty was murdered alongside his mother by his generals) and the shortest lasted only twenty-one days (Gordian II killed at the battle of Carthage). The rot was effectively stopped in the 280s by Diocletian's introduction of a completely new system of governance.

With regard to Scotland, the absence of recorded violence in the third century has been attributed to a period of Severan peace by some, and post-traumatic stress by others. Whichever is closer to the truth, it is interesting to note that some commentators appear unaffected by the recent shift to post-imperialist thought as they insinuate that brutalising an indigenous population into quiescence was an admirable act of rectification. Although geographically on the margins of a crisis-ridden empire, a lasting effect must have been felt in Caledonia both as a sequel to the gargantuan incursions of the Severan dynasty and the fallout from the continental conflict. So, is there any real evidence to indicate that the post-Severan period was one of tranquility or does this disguise a post-invasion wasteland such as Tacitus had described a hundred years before?

While it may be tempting to see Roman brutality as a direct cause for the country's apparent dormancy, diplomatic efforts to influence and control the northern tribes were still being made in third-century Scotland. Two silver coin hoards dating from this murky period, one from the Borders area and one from Falkirk, attest to Roman hegemony over a still func-

95. The great hoard of almost 2,000 silver *denarii* (more than ten years' pay for a legionary) from Falkirk. Probably hidden sometime in the mid-third century.

tioning native society. The former hoard of 290 coins (latest denarius dated to 222) was found by a detectorist at a ploughed-out hillfort at Edston, near Peebles in 1994. The much larger Falkirk hoard, a spectacular cache of over 1,900 denarii (latest coin dated to 230) was found in 1933 near the line of the abandoned Antonine Wall, suggesting that a local warlord may have taken control of an old Roman strongpoint.

Both hoards indicate that whoever the Roman governor was at the time (possibly in the reign of either Severus Alexander or Elagabalus) he was concerned enough about keeping northern power groups compliant, to send envoys bearing donatives of this size to even small tribal units in the Scottish Lowlands. So perhaps this style of 'silver diplomacy' once more replaced long-distance punitive incursions as a way of keeping the peace, even if temporarily, accounting for the relative paucity of reports of conflict – a silver carrot rather than an iron stick.

The Picts

Despite the archaeological and historical gaps in our knowledge, the latter part of the third century saw the appearance, for the first time in literature at least, of one of the most remarkable and dreaded of Rome's opponents – the people who came to be known as the Picts. The Latin title, Picti, the 'painted ones', was first recorded in a panegyric – a flattering poem – to Constantius Chlorus, the father of Constantine the Great, in the year 297.

Picts

At an etymological level, the name *Picti*, the 'painted ones' or the 'tattooed people', was probably akin to the nineteenth-century slang term of 'redskins' used by American soldiers and settlers to denigrate indigenous peoples. Some scholars have attempted to link the title to a separate Gaulish tribe, the *Pictavi*, but the frequent references made by Roman authors to the body art displayed by warriors on the fringes of north-west Europe would logically suggest this Latin word was the likely origin of the name – '*nec falso nomine Pictos*' wrote Claudian (370–404), which means 'the not inappropriately named Picts'.

It is unlikely that the Picts actually used this name when referring to themselves, but the term was understood sufficiently widely in the post-Roman Latin-speaking world to be frequently employed by Early Medieval writers such as Gildas and Bede for those living north of Hadrian's Wall.

However, it is likely that the grouping of people it was used to describe had been an entity for some considerable time before then. Commentators have suggested that tribal coalescence was an inevitable consequence of frequent Roman invasions over the 200-year period from the time of Agricola to Constantine.

It is equally likely that Picti does not refer to a single tribe but to a confederation of northern peoples who shared the characteristic of adorning themselves with tattoos or other less permanent skin motifs. This technique of self-expression was of course not unique to the Picts but only the peoples from North Britain seem to have merited the specific epithet *Picti* by Roman authors.

Tattoos and the Scythians

Body decoration by the indigenous population of Britain was first alluded to in Caesar's report that 'all the Britons cover themselves with woad which gives them a blue colour'. Now that tattooing has undergone its phenomenal resurgence as a fashion statement, Caesar's comments for once do not appear to be classical embellishment. Unfortunately, no depictions or detailed descriptions exist of the Picti and the conditions necessary for mummification or freezing, which have preserved tattoos on Egyptian ladies and Otzi the Ice Man, are absent from most of Scotland. The general comments we do have are furnished principally by Herodian: 'they tattoo their bodies with coloured designs and drawings of all kinds of animals; for this reason, they do not wear clothes, which would conceal the decorations on their bodies.' These descriptions have parallels close enough to the body art of another people, the Scythians of the Russian Steppes, to merit some comment.

A nomadic warrior people whose territory extended from Siberia to the Black Sea, the Scythians were well known to ancient authors, first receiving literary treatment by Herodotus (c.484–425 BC). They too had a reputation as fearsome fighters, and had similarly mastered the practice of tattooing, vividly revealed on the well-preserved cadavers from recently excavated Scythian tombs buried in the permafrost of modern Russia. Exotic animals and scroll motifs abound in well-executed pictograms often covering the chest and shoulders but also extending onto the legs and arms.

But this is not just a superficial ethnographic similarity, for a fascinating link occurs here, between Picts and Scythians, in a Pictish origin myth recorded by Bede. Writing in the Abbey of Monkwearmouth–Jarrow, Bede states (probably repeating an old Irish tradition) in his *Ecclesiastical History of the English People* (c.731) that the Picts were refugees from Scythia who had put to sea in a quest to find themselves a homeland. After arriving first in Ireland, they were redirected eastwards and landed in Scotland, where

96. Artist's impression of a Pictish warrior showing bronze armlet, neck torc and assorted body art.

he says they colonised the north. On the face of it, this appears to be a complete invention with no foundation whatsoever, but one might suggest that Bede had at least been aware of the warlike reputation and the body art habit of both groups, so for him, the Scythians could indeed be the progenitors of the Picts. However, according to modern science, no genetic link so far can be shown between the two ancient peoples.

Scholars are more confident that the Picts were autochthonous, that is, literally sprung from their own land, and probably represent an amalgamation of several of the many tribes listed on Ptolemy's map of North Britain. The concept of tribal coalescence is given further support by a comment made by Dio in his *History* when he says, 'there are two principal races of the Britons, the Caledonians and the Maeatae and the names of the others have been merged in these two'. We can now probably think of Picti as a catch-all term the Romans introduced to describe those tribes north of the Forth–Clyde isthmus (the Caledonians being just one of them) who had a propensity for body art. Over time the Caledonians and Maeatae also disappear from Roman usage to be replaced by Picts and Scots, the former from the north and east and the latter from the south and west.

As mentioned earlier, the people we call the Picts, like the Etruscans, left no literature of their own despite having a distinctive archaeological signature. While this enhances an air of mystery it does nothing to help balance any negative assessments made by external commentators. Other than biased Roman sources who portray the Picts as overtly warlike, we are largely dependent on early Christian writers such as Bede and Gildas who themselves were not particularly objective.

Pictish art and symbols

More impressive than any literary reference to the Picts, is their abundant surviving artwork, described as one of the great insular art forms and of international importance. Demonstrating a shared complex symbolism that transcends geographical boundaries, ultimately extending from the central isthmus to the Western and Northern Isles, the Picts were much more than a convenient grouping of tribes. Pictish art and symbols were applied to many surfaces, but their most enduring creations are undoubtedly the phenomenal carved symbol stones that remain one of the true wonders of the Scottish archaeological record.

In an attempt to lay the foundations of a systematic study of Pictish symbol stones, Allen and Anderson put forward a simple class system in 1903. Class I stones are almost certainly the earliest, arising in the fifth to seventh centuries (or even earlier) and occur on natural outcrops or unworked stones exemplified most notably in Aberlemno 1. Class II stones are usually worked and shaped slabs, most often one side displaying a

Christian cross while retaining superimposed Pictish symbols on at least one of the faces. These stones are thought to have been carved more recently, perhaps in the seventh to ninth centuries. Later stones often feature recognisable biblical stories and scenes from the gospels while mixing pagan symbolism and other motifs including warfare, hunting with hounds and even depictions of falconry.

There is some debate over what exactly constitutes a Pictish symbol, but most authors would agree that there are at least thirty to forty frequently used ideograms found throughout Pictland. The symbols show no significant Roman influence although some of the objects portrayed would be familiar to a soldier on the northern frontier. Symbols break down into two broad groups of a) zoomorphic pictograms that include animals such as snakes, eagles, stags, fish and wolves, and b) inanimate geometric figures such as conjoined double discs and more domestic items such as mirrors and combs. In the latter group, there appear to be abstract interpretations of unusual but natural phenomena, such as the 'pictish beast', which looks porpoise-like and the Z-rod, which suggests a stylised

ABOVE LEFT. 97. Aberlemno 1. A snake, Z-rod and double disc are still discernable motifs superimposed on this ancient standing stone.

ABOVE RIGHT. 98. Aberlemno 2. A Class II stone from Aberlemno churchyard. The carefully worked slab displays an infantry and cavalry engagement, probably a battle scene, surmounted by a Z-rod and other symbols. The opposite face shows a classic Celtic cross surrounded by interlaced fantastical beasts.

99a. Pictish animal symbols –
top left is the 'Pictish Beast' –
probably a porpoise.

b. Commonly used geometric
or inanimate objects.

lightning bolt. The symbols frequently occur in pairs and while they continue to defy interpretation, there is growing suspicion that they denote names of people or tribes. Although a few stones are associated with ogham inscriptions, and the late period Drosten stone has the eponymous Drosten's name inscribed in Latin, an equivalent of the Rosetta Stone for Pictish symbols has yet to be discovered. Some Class II stones have been identified as grave markers although only a small number have been associated with funerary remains. While carvings on many of the more elaborate stones are clearly much later than the Roman Iron Age, recent work by Aberdeen University at the promontory fort of Dunnicaer has suggested that the symbols were in use at a much earlier date than previously thought (Noble and Evans 2018). In an assessment of the possible date range Noble suggests that some symbols could be dated to the fourth century or earlier. Although the zenith of their culture and power was still to come, these early dates support the case for Rome being instrumental in Pictish genesis.

Among the few examples of surviving Pictish jewellery, the most impres-

sive are the massive silver neck chains. These are likely to have belonged to members of the elite and were possibly symbols of royalty. Ten of these ostentatious chokers survive with find-spots ranging from south-west Scotland to Aberdeenshire. Metallurgical analysis suggests that the silver was derived in the first instance from recycled Roman bullion. Most often plain, formed from simple heavy links, their Pictish association is confirmed by the occasional presence of symbols on their locking rings. Two other early hoards of silver, the Norrie's Law hoard from Fife and the Gaulcross hoard from Aberdeenshire also have Pictish connections.

Modern scholars envisage two main Pictish kingdoms, North and South Pictland with the Grampians and the Mounth that connects the Central Highlands to the North Sea, roughly dividing the two groups. In possession of some of the finest land north of the Forth–Clyde isthmus, the Picts were clearly a force to be reckoned with, so how were they viewed by the Iron Age's greatest superpower?

100a. Massive silver neck chains made largely from recycled Roman silver bullion. Unique to Scotland, at least ten have been found so far.

b. A couple of the chains have Pictish symbols on the locking link – here the Z-rod and double disc.

The warlike Pict?

Did the Picts deserve their reputation as fierce warriors, or should this be interpreted as Roman propaganda – in essence promoting the avatar of a worthy opponent? Were they in fact, as has been described by some modern scholars, really only 'arty farmers'? If we assume that Dio, Herodian and the later panegyrists, when referring to Caledonians and Maeatae, were

101. A *turricula* or dice shaker from Germany. The top two lines read PICTOS VICTOS, which means 'the Picts have been defeated'. The bottom lines say 'now you can play safely'.

describing the same people who would become the Picts, then they probably should be considered to have been pretty ferocious. Reputed by Dio to have a mainly pastoral way of life, possessing no walled towns, he emphasised their formidable qualities as fearless infantry and horsemen, able to tenaciously hold their ground and, as an example, to use psychological warfare by beating apple-shaped bronze spear butts (examples of which have been found) on their shields. Warriors were described as mainly unclothed, presumably to show off their splendid tattoos, although anyone who has visited Scotland will appreciate nudity could not have been their everyday state. Herodian similarly describes their nakedness to flaunt their tattoos and tells of their preference for iron jewellery, of which, perhaps because of Scotland's acidic soil conditions, little has survived. It is now thought that the classical emphasis on complete undress was likely to be something of a Roman trope and some form of armour, such as leather and chain mail would have been adopted, if only by the elite.

Although Roman and Early Medieval accounts concur that the Picts measured up to their fierce image, a few modern commentators continue to diminish this reputation. Some have demanded firmer evidence of Pictish belligerence, although it is not entirely clear how this could be produced. From an objective point of view, one might think that the high density of Roman forts and camps, two of the greatest frontier barriers to have survived from ancient times, one of which was maintained for 300 years, and several specific references to the Pict's martial skills by trustworthy classical authors, would speak for themselves. The Roman-Syrian historian Ammianus Marcellinus (330–400), for example, suggested that during the so-called 'Barbarian Conspiracy', Picts may have raided as far south as London until they were eventually repulsed by Theodosius' continental reinforcements.

As if to underscore the legendary nature of their warlike reputation, a *turricula*, a cheese grater-sized dice shaker, comprising a bronze tower with an opening at the bottom and a small flight of steps down which the dice would tumble, has been found in the remains of a Roman villa in Germany. This fascinating gaming device, now in the Landesmuseum in Bonn, is decorated on three sides with the aphorism: VTERE FELIX VIVAS, which means 'use me well and live life to the full'. The fourth side, the one with the steps, bears the unique declaration (in slightly distorted Latin to accommodate the dimensions of the metalwork): 'PICTOS VICTOS HOSTIS DELETA LUDITE SECURI', which means 'the Picts have been beaten, the enemy destroyed, play in safety'. This extraordinary find has a resonance with keepsakes of more modern soldiers that memorialise the names of their most potent foes.

'Pictish wars' certainly became a fairly regular feature of later Roman writing with events recorded in 305–6, 312, 342, 367, 382 and 400 all attributable to Pictish incursions, occasionally in concert with other barbarian allies. If further evidence is required beyond physical remains and the testimony of the Romans themselves, Early Medieval monks were outspoken about the warlike nature of the Picts. Gildas particularly displayed considerable invective in his *On the Ruin of Britain* about the cruelty inflicted on the British people by two foreign nations, 'the Scots from the northwest and the Picts from the north' after the departure of Roman troops. Gildas outlined how a Roman legion came to rescue the locals, with Roman forces driving the foe northwards and building a new wall of turf. He says that 'the Roman Legion had no sooner returned home (to mainland Europe), than the former foes, like ravening wolves . . . broke through the boundaries and spread slaughter on every side, and like mowers cutting down the ripe corn, they cut up, tread underfoot and overrun the whole country'.

Christian Picts

The Picts appear to have undergone something of a transformation in the sub-Roman period after their adoption of Christianity. This is illustrated by the increasing complexity of their artwork over the four centuries following the departure of Rome and the addition of a rich Christian symbolism particularly on their cross stones. It is open to debate, of course, if one should equate a refinement in artistic temperament with a major softening

102. The remains of Burghead promontory fort seen from the sea. A number of Pictish sculptures have come from the site, which has been largely destroyed by modern development.

of social behaviour. Central to their conversion were two early saints, St Ninian, said to have been missionary to the southern Picts, and St Columba, evangelist to the northern Picts.

Despite the adoption of Christian theology, there appeared to be reluctance on the part of the Picts to let go of more militaristic iconography, which as noted above was often admixed with stylised ecclesiastical and biblical scenes. Indeed, it would appear that some of the more chaotic early figurative representations of Pictish military exploits evolved into a regimented form on later sculpture. Military traditions have a long memory and perhaps the serried ranks of later Pictish warriors represent a faint memory of those early interactions with Rome.

In terms of architecture, only traces remain. An elongated house form has been discerned but the majority of dwellings appear to continue in the roundhouse style. It is noticeable that the hillfort tradition of more southerly Iron Age Scotland is largely absent from north Pictland with many open settlements like Birnie and Culduthel. This again suggests that the requirement for local defence was obviated by the presence of a strong regional overlordship that in effect 'policed' the kingdom. That is not to say that defence was not an issue for the Picts in some places and at some times. A few major coastal centres were heavily fortified though perhaps not to protect the inhabitants from other Picts but from seaborne invaders like the Vikings who harried northern power centres from the ninth century onwards. One of the most impressive and massive of these coastal strongholds is Burghead on the Elgin coast. Here a fine range of Pictish carvings have been unearthed but sadly much of the fort itself has been lost to later development.

Although domestic architecture may not be particularly remarkable, aerial archaeology in recent years has revealed a wealth of Pictish funerary structures, particularly the distinctive monumental square and round barrow cemeteries in the north and north-east (fig. 122).

The Picts today

Our understanding of the Picts is undergoing something of a renaissance after a long period of relative quiescence. Given the national and international importance of their artwork alone, it is hard to see why Pictish studies could have languished in scholarly circles (apart from a few notable exceptions) for a significant portion of the twentieth century. A cursory look at how the Picts are portrayed, or in some cases not portrayed, in Scottish museums confirms that their significance to Scottish identity has, until recent decades, been somewhat muted. But the evidence of the past is difficult to completely suppress by the fashions of the present, and new archaeological discoveries are again propelling Pictish studies into the modern consciousness. Far from being a mystery race, as previously portrayed by popular media, more is now known about them than many other peoples of this epoch. Considerable data has been assimilated by new ventures led or assisted by universities, such as Aberdeen's Northern Picts Project. Recent discoveries at multiple sites, including the ecclesiastical complex at Portmahomack (Carver 2008), the royal centre of Rhynie (Noble et al. 2013) and the hillfort of Tap o'Noth, have added to the increasingly solid base of knowledge for these people who for over half a millennium exerted their influence throughout mainland Scotland and the Isles with occasional forays much further south.

The Pict's nemesis may well have been a combination of Anglian pressure from the south, the Hibernian kingdom of Dál Riata pushing from the west and, ultimately, seaborne attacks by the Vikings from the north. But rather than mysteriously disappearing or being dramatically wiped out, they were probably gradually subsumed by a series of conflicts, treaties and coalitions. Evolving into the Early Medieval kingdom of Alba, this unique culture left behind its symbols in stone and silver as testaments to the centuries when the 'painted ones' came together to resist the might of Rome.

CHAPTER SIXTEEN

The man who changed the world: the coming of Constantine

If you take a stroll in the city of York of an evening, take time to meander to the front of the cathedral to meet the man who single-handedly altered the face of Europe. Lolling in a chair beside York Minster, idly twiddling his sword, reclines a bronze statue that appears oblivious to his menacing pose outside a place of worship.

Flavius Valerius Aurelius Constantinus Augustus, better known as Constantine the Great (274?–337) was, as far as Europe was concerned, one of the most influential figures who ever lived. Generally acknowledged to be the individual who in the early 300s wove the fraying fabric of the previously pagan Roman world into the unified force of the first Christian

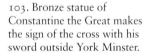

103. Bronze statue of Constantine the Great makes the sign of the cross with his sword outside York Minster.

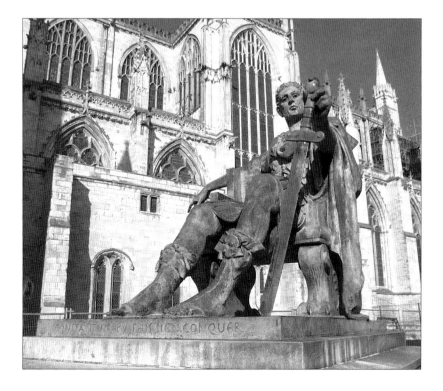

The division of Britain

The administrative structure of the country under-went radical change for the first time under Cara-calla who divided the province into two: Britannia Superior with its capital in London, and Britannia Inferior with its administrative centre in York. These territories were further subdivided during the Tetrarchy – that period when Diocletian had divided the whole empire into eastern and western portions each governed by its own senior *Augustus* and junior *Caesar*. By the time Constantine became sole ruler once more in 324, the province had been split into four – the *Dioceses* of Britain. The exact geography of these is unclear but a reasonable summary would be: *Maxima Caesariensis* – the south-east; *Britannia Prima* – Wales and the south-west; *Flavia Caesariensis* – the Midlands; and *Britannia Secunda* – the north. By this time, there was clearer separation between military and civilian powers (the latter being entrusted to civil administrators called vicars – *vicarii*). Eventually a fifth diocese, Valentia, was added in 369. This was originally considered by scholars to encompass the area of southern Scotland between the Walls but is now thought more likely to refer to Cumbria or North Wales.

empire, his ensuing dynasty was to have a profound effect on the trajectory of European history that resonates to the modern era.

What is less well known is that when he was a young Caesar, Constantine spent two of his formative years (probably 305–6) campaigning against the Picts in Scotland with his father, the co-emperor Constantius Chlorus. As with Hadrian, Commodus and Severus before them, there seems to have been a plea for the imperial presence from those in charge of the northern reaches of the province, to help face off yet another barbarian incursion. The literary references to this event are thin but there is a passing mention in the *Panegyrici Latini*, a set of laudatory poems to later Roman emperors by unknown Gallic Church fathers. So how did this set of circumstances arise?

Although the 200s are seen as a period of relative peace in Britain – perhaps too readily attributed to the successes of the Severan campaign – the province was involved in at least two major breakdowns of central government towards the end of the third century. Firstly, between 260 and 274, the north-western sector of the empire, effectively Gaul and Britannia, temporarily broke away and formed the so-called Gallic Empire. Four emperors were to reign over this separatist territory in quick succession. Then only twelve years later in 286, Britain and a segment of northern Gaul seceded under the leadership of Carausius, the commander of the British fleet. Even though a naval officer, Carausius appeared to command the respect of the British legions. With their help and a legion based in northern Gaul, he remained in power for a further seven years despite an attempt in 289 by Maximian, the legitimate emperor of the West, to have

him ousted. Of relatively modest origins, Carausius attempted to reach a
point of accommodation with his enemies, occasionally issuing series of
coins that proclaimed his unity with co-emperors Maximian and Diocletian.
In the end, Carausius was assassinated by Allectus, his second-in-command,
seven years after proclaiming himself emperor. Allectus in turn reigned for
only three years before he too was killed in 296 in a confrontation with
Constantius Chlorus, who had officially been appointed Caesar in the West
by the Emperor Diocletian and had been allotted the task of recovering the
province from the rebels. Although much of the written history of the end
of the third century is focused on this activity in the south of Britannia or
on the near Continent, it is highly likely the northern tribes found the
opportunity to cause trouble in the hinterland. A clue is provided by
Diocletian's assumption in 285 of the title *Britannicus Maximus*, although
it has been suggested that the title may have been won for him by the then
loyal Carausius against Saxon invaders.

'From where the earth ends'

When Constantius had successfully concluded his punitive campaign against
Allectus in 296, he presumably removed a significant number of rebel officials and made further changes to the administrative structure of the
province. It has also been suggested that he ordered some refurbishment
of the Wall (Birley 2005) before returning to mainland Europe to deal with
further uprisings. In 305, by which time Diocletian and Maximian had
retired and Constantius had been elevated to the status of Augustus, he
visited Britain one last time for a campaign against the Picts. His heir, the
young Constantine, had successfully freed himself from what was essentially
house arrest in Rome (imposed by the mistrust of the co-emperor Galerius)
to join his father in Britain for the northern expedition. We are provided
with little detail of this campaign other than Constantius being reported
to have been very impressed, as others had been before him, with the almost
perpetual daylight of the long summer nights of the far north. There is the
possibility that Constantius may have been glory hunting in Pictland
although his panegyrist specifically claims that he was not seeking British
trophies. Interestingly, the same writer suggests that Constantius, who had
been dogged by poor health for some time, did have an ulterior motive. It
is reported that he had sensed his impending death and wished to cast his
eyes on heaven in advance of his demise – the name Chlorus (an epithet
used only after his death) means the 'green' or 'pale one', sparking theories
among modern historians that he suffered from some form of chronic
anaemia. Seeing heaven was apparently something the Romans believed
might be achieved from northern Scotland because of the astronomical
advantages of high latitude. The writer concludes: 'the regions closer to

heaven are holier than those inland, and it is more fitting that an emperor is sent by the gods from where the earth ends [*ubi terra finitur*]'. Whatever spiritual connotation this Caledonian expedition may have had, Constantius considered that he had achieved some form of victory, for by January 306 he too had taken the title of *Britannicus Maximus*. In an uncanny parallel to Severus 100 years before, Chlorus returned to York at the end of the first campaign and died there in the following summer (306), during the second season of his Pictish war.

Archaeological evidence of early fourth-century contact?

The fact that the Pictish campaign had been scheduled for at least two years rather than one may indicate that the *expeditio* had not exactly been a walkover and necessitated major logistics. It is therefore a little surprising that no definite archaeology can be ascribed to this campaign or indeed any later movements of what must have been significant numbers of Roman troops. There are no campaign camps even tentatively dated to the incursions of later periods, which may be because armies of the later empire simply reused previous fortifications (Hanson 1980) – the palimpsests at Chew Green and Ardoch for example could easily obscure later encampments – or the smaller field armies of this time employed a different method of overnight defence that did not require ditch-digging. A few small bronze fourth-century coins have been found in caves on the Dumfriesshire coast and in the Springwood area of Kelso in the Scottish Borders but these have no known association with Roman military activity. Perhaps the increasingly frequent metal-detector finds of small denomination fourth-century coins, often attributed to 'modern' losses, come from the pouches of soldiers campaigning in mid and southern Scotland who were reusing the marching camp enclosures of earlier centuries.

More eye-catching but equally unprovenanced is the ornamented fourth-century gold crossbow brooch ploughed up on the shores of the Moray Firth in 1847. Now on display in the British Museum, it almost certainly belonged to some distinguished Roman of the time period in question, but the circumstances of its deposition remain a complete mystery.

Workmen digging peats in Dumfriesshire found a further piece of exotic gold jewellery, known as the Erickstanebrae brooch, in the eighteenth century. Having an intriguing lattice-style frame, the fibula has been perforated with the words IOVI AUG on one side, and VOT XX on the other with FORTU scratched on the underside. It has been suggested by Birley (2005) that it commemorates the *vicenalia* of Diocletian – the twentieth anniversary of his proclamation as emperor – and may have been lost by a high-ranking officer, Fortunatus, under the command of Constantius while on the Pictish campaign. This may seem a considerable leap of deduction, but the brooch

104a. Fourth-century gold crossbow brooch from the Moray Firth area.

104b. The golden
Erickstanebrae brooch found
in Dumfriesshire, has a lattice
inscription that is thought to
commemorate Diocletian's
vicennalia, the twentieth year
of his accession to the throne.

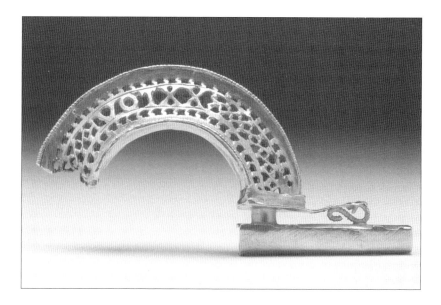

was clearly of special significance and it is difficult to otherwise explain
the presence of such a unique artefact in a remote area of southern Scotland.
It has also had a remarkable afterlife: found near the Roman road at
Moffat, it made its way via the William Randolph Hearst collection to its
current home in Los Angeles County Museum, and a gilt silver copy was
subsequently gifted to the National Museum of Scotland.

The accession of Constantine

When Constantius died in York in 306, Constantine was immediately
proclaimed *Augustus* by his troops – an unequivocal and provocative challenge to Diocletian's tetrarchic system. This method of power-sharing,
which consisted of two senior *Augusti*, each with his respective junior
Caesar, had been devised to spread the administrative load across the vast
empire that Diocletian had split into eastern and western halves. But more
than this, it was created to act as a check and balance to prevent a dangerous concentration of power in any one individual. Thus, with this clear
declar-ation of much greater intent, began Constantine's struggle to become
sole emperor, which as things turned out would take eighteen years of
complex and bloody civil war.

So what of his relationship with Britannia? From what we can discern
from the issue of *adventus* coins (special coins minted to commemorate
the visit of an emperor to a province) and the sparse literary sources,
Constantine made two further personal visits to Britain. The first in 312
was probably to oversee withdrawal of troops to supplement his continental
forces in his struggle against Maxentius in Italy. The second was possibly

in 314 when it appears he undertook a major campaign, once more against the Picts, which resulted in the assumption of the title of *Britannicus Maximus*, just like Commodus and Severus before him.

Interestingly, apart from fifteen rather functional, and mainly poorly executed, milestones scattered from Cornwall to Hadrian's Wall, there are no inscriptions from Britain marking the reign of Constantine or can be confidently ascribed to his actions. Clearly buildings were being built, gods honoured and military events taking place, but no inscriptions have so far been found which celebrate this great emperor – an absence likely to be due to atrophy of the habit of epigraphy. Perhaps this exemplifies a slow descent into illiteracy and a 'dumbing down' of society in general. Keppie, in *Understanding Roman Inscriptions* (1991), comments: 'The Roman inscriptions of the late empire seem less numerous than those of earlier centuries; often they are also more poorly executed. To us there seems an evident decline in standards.'

There is therefore the strong possibility that although much was probably happening on the northern frontier, it just wasn't being written down or recorded. It is also likely that roads, old marching camps, forts and the Wall itself were being recycled, with archaeological evidence indicating extensive reuse and refurbishment rather than *de novo* building, reflecting a gradual decline in the infrastructure of Roman society in general.

As highlighted above, small denomination fourth-century coins are occasionally encountered in Scotland, but these are treated with considerable caution, often being dismissed in archaeological reports, probably too readily, as modern losses. Apart from a couple of high-status objects like the brooch illustrated above, this period in Scotland is almost archaeologically blank in contrast to the rich villa culture that prevailed well to the south of the Wall. Hopefully, some future large-scale field survey, possibly by metal detection, will locate finds that are unequivocally fourth century in date, and identify the movements of Constantinian troops.

This scenario is perhaps optimistic but not impossible, as the finds from a German hillside have recently demonstrated. The site at Harzhorn, in Lower Saxony, was discovered by two detectorists searching for traces of a medieval fortification on what until then had been considered a relatively barren hill. Their first finds were rather inauspicious – heavily corroded iron masses – but fortuitously these were identified as hipposandals, the Roman equivalent of horseshoes for draft animals. There followed a succession of progressively impressive finds including widely scattered spearheads and ballista bolt tips, all of which indicated that the slopes of Harzhorn had been the scene of something special. German archaeologists, attuned to the features of battlefield debris, quickly recognised these objects pointed to a previously unsuspected field of conflict. Now after nearly twenty years of excavation and painstaking detection, the choreography of a battle

Metal detecting: laws and archaeological attitudes

Other than the universal rule that a detectorist must have prior landowner consent, the laws that govern metal detecting vary widely across the world. Even within Britain and Ireland, there is a spectrum of accessibility varying from no detecting at all in the Republic of Ireland to variable laws of Treasure Trove in the remaining nations. In England and Wales for example, the law dictates that only precious metals are worthy of claim for the state by coroner's enquiry, whereas in Scotland, every ancient artefact found is the potential possession of the Crown. Hence, the outcry within the heritage community when the fabulous, but bronze, Crosby Garret Roman helmet and cavalry face mask, a priceless find from the second century, was auctioned privately. It would be fair to say that the attitude of archaeologists in general has been one of grudging acceptance bordering on suspicion, partly driven by some misunderstanding of the limited depth capabilities of the technology – only the top few inches of ploughsoil is generally accessible despite manufacturers' claims.

The legal situation varies even more widely across Europe where there is a considerably greater degree of state restriction leading predictably to clandestine behaviour. Another negative effect of this legalism is the marked reduction in the incidence of declared finds of ancient metal artefacts on the Continent. The far-sighted development of the Treasure Act and constitution of the Portable Antiquities Scheme in England, with Finds Liaison Officers, have been revolutionary in developing a pragmatic approach to the issue and to harness the resource of thousands of well-intentioned detectorists who have a legitimate interest in their local history. The spectacular leaps made recently in numismatics and artefact typology in Britain are simply not matched in mainland Europe.

A final consideration of the benefits of detecting is the ability to cost-effectively sweep large areas of otherwise archaeologically barren ground to identify metal projectiles, particularly widely dispersed lead ammunition, and it is this which has revolutionised the specialism of battlefield archaeology.

between an unknown native tribe and Roman forces has been ascribed to a northerly campaign of troops of the Emperor Maximinus Thrax in 235/6. And so, in a single stroke, a previously uninteresting hillside has been confirmed as one of the most northerly Roman battle sites on mainland Europe.

Hopefully one day the trail of fourth-century Roman forces in Scotland will be revealed by the distribution of small denomination coins or even weaponry – but in the meantime, it is worth remembering that Constantine's attention lay elsewhere. Like so many emperors before him, he had a view to the spoils of the East, ultimately moving his capital from Rome to the Hellespont, the land bridge between Europe and Asia. Here he would build a fabulous new city, Constantinopolis (modern Istanbul), which would be the final resting place for this man whose world-shaping journey to become the first Christian emperor had begun on the northern frontier of Britain.

Stilicho and Traprain Law, the harpooned whale

On display among the many treasures of the dazzlingly ornate cathedral of St John the Baptist in Monza, is a beautiful ivory diptych showing a handsome family trio – a warrior father, complete with spear and shield, a bejewelled wife and a dutiful son at his mother's side. Although no inscription confirms who they may be, it is generally accepted that the three figures represent the Vandal – Roman general Stilicho – his wife Serena (niece and adoptive daughter of Emperor Theodosius I) and their son Eucherius.

Pointed footwear lapping over the bottom of the frame impart a modernistic air to the group whose expressionless faces stare out at the onlooker. This remarkable fourth-century survival provides rare detail not just of the style and opulence of the elite of the day (both man and boy have impressive *fibulae* at the shoulders, revealing how they would have been worn) but it also commemorates, as Edward Gibbon described him, 'the last of the great Roman generals'.

Flavius Stilicho (359–408) was the archetypal general of the late fourth century. From a military rather than an aristocratic family, like many of the key figures around him (his father was a Vandal cavalry officer), he rose through the ranks, firstly by virtue of his own military prowess and then by the patronage of his father-in-law, the Emperor Theodosius I. Ultimately, as regent of the boy-emperor Honorius (384–423), he became one of the most powerful generals of the Western Roman Empire. Renowned for his military successes against numerous barbarian tribes and other Roman foes, there is the strong likelihood he may also have led at least one campaign against the peoples of Caledonia.

But the tale of Stilicho's involvement in Pictish affairs is in itself an example of the difficulty experienced with the history of North Britain of this period – essentially a story pieced together from fragments of poems. These accounts present all the inherent problems of emotive language and imprecision common to poets such as Claudian, and the polemical outbursts of aggrieved clerics such as Gildas, writing with hindsight, invective or religious bias. Patchy as they are, they remain useful for filling some of the gaps in our knowledge of an otherwise shadowy fourth century. Britain

105. Fourth-century ivory diptych currently displayed in Monza Cathedral, thought to be of the Vandal general Stilicho, his wife Serena and their son Eucherius.

appears to have remained a breeding ground for rebellion, both internally within the Roman army and from foes on all sides. One of the most notable episodes to involve the northern tribes is known today as the Barbarian Conspiracy (367).

From an archaeological perspective, the situation in the north appeared to become progressively unstable from the time of the Conspiracy. Although there are firm indications that Hadrian's Wall remained functional, both manned and supplied, until the late fourth century, poorer quality material culture and the evidence of shoddy building maintenance suggest that infrastructural funding had become increasingly insecure. This is paralleled by a marked reduction in inscriptions from this period and the observation that coins of the late occupation become sparse, as small denomination bronzes replaced silver coinage of any quality. It would also appear that as central support for the province began to break down, the opportunities for northern forces to launch cross-frontier raids increased. References exist, for example, to a series of wars likely involving the Picts, spanning the period from Count Theodosius' successful expedition in the 360s until

Barbarian Conspiracy?

This term was coined to describe the rebellion against Roman forces in Britain, said to have taken place around 367. Our primary source is the soldier-historian Ammianus Marcellinus, in his *Res Gestae*, which chronicled the history of Rome from the early principate until the death of the Emperor Valens in 378. He tells us that defence of the province had been weakened once more by the withdrawal of troops, this time by Magnentius in an ill-fated attempt to maintain power (350–3). Picts, Scots and Attacotti (a previously unknown tribe) are alleged to have stormed the northern province while coordinated landings by Saxons took place in the south and east. Reputedly, there followed a year-long rampage in the south of Britain, although no definite archaeological evidence of the event has so far been found.

It has been suggested, however (Andrew 2022), that such widespread rebellion was unlikely to be due to a spontaneous barbarian uprising. It may have been precipitated by the fiscal exhaustion caused by Julian's short reign and disastrous campaign against the Sasanian Empire in the East, coupled with the xenophobic Emperor Valentinian's (321–75) intense dislike of barbarians. These resulted in a cessation of tribute payments (and consequently the pay of freelancers such as *areani* – the border scouts) resulting in massive frontier instability.

Whatever the cause of the conflict, it was reported that London was not retaken and order restored across the province until a major relief force had landed in Britannia the following year under the leadership of Flavius Theodosius (the father of Emperor Theodosius I). Flavius, an able general, was awarded the title of *comes rei militaris Britanniarum*, a designation created during times of crisis. He is often referred to by modern authors simply as Count Theodosius.

the province is finally cast adrift in the early fifth century.

Allusions to Stilicho's military intervention in the province in the 390s are gleaned from the works of the poet Claudian. Although the historical value of his poetry is attenuated by the constraints of the panegyric form, the poems provide some colour as they refer to the emperor 'taming the appropriately named Picts and his roaming sword pursuing the Scots', and Stilicho 'providing Britannia with forts – and taking such care that the province did not fear the Scots' javelins nor tremble at the Picts', and finally 'then came the legion, shield of the northern Britons, check of the grim Scot, whose men had seen life leave the tattoos of the dying Pict'. Taken in conjuction with vague references to carnage in Orkney and Thule (possibly Shetland), these vignettes all hint at major military expeditions far to the north.

The scientific understanding of the situation in fourth-century Scotland, however, is not helped by the almost complete absence of firm archaeological data from this period north of Hadrian's Wall, aside from the insight provided by the great hillfort of Traprain Law in East Lothian.

106. A selection of bronze third- and fourth-century coinage from Britain compared to a modern 5p piece. Note the progressive deterioration in quality and size from the top left (Constantius I) to bottom left.

Claudian

Claudius Claudianus (370–404) was an Alexandrian-born poet of some considerable merit whose works were so admired by contemporary Roman society and the Senate, that they earned him a statue in the forum. He wrote several works (panegyrics) praising the Emperor Honorius and Claudian's hero Stilicho, in which conflict with the Scots and Picts featured repeatedly.

Traprain Law

The trail of rich archaeological evidence from the hilltop fortress of Traprain stretches into the mists of the Bronze Age, so one may wonder why this point has been chosen to expand on one of Scotland's most important archaeological sites? The story of Roman period Traprain prior to the fourth century, broadly exemplifies much of what we already know of Rome's intervention in North Britain, mirrored in other Roman military sites north of Hadrian's Wall: occupation-period artefacts, including pottery, jewellery and coins, all of which reflect the halo of military imports arriving with successive waves of Roman troops into Scotland. Traprain really comes into its own, in terms of extraordinary archaeology, at the end of the third century when evidence from other military sites in Scotland goes cold. Then, its unique finds of fourth- and fifth-century artefacts reflect a Roman–native dynamic very different to the remainder of the country. Material from virtually all the great hill's excavations has shown it was much more than a simple trading partner servicing the nearby Roman garrison at Inveresk, 20km to the west, during the Antonine period. There is good archaeological evidence for its occupation for at least another 250 years as a power centre of the mighty Votadini, a formidable client kingdom that ruled the Lothians, and probably, as the complete absence of Roman bases in East Lothian suggests, as far south as the Cheviot massif itself.

To quote a previous author, Traprain Law is so prominent, it 'bulks like a harpooned whale on the East Lothian coastal plain' (Feachem 1963). The humpbacked hill, on which the fort is constructed, is a volcanic plug lying stranded like a leviathan in a sea of rich farmland almost 30km east of another, probably affiliated, major tribal centre, Edinburgh Castle Rock. As may be expected of one of the largest hillforts in Scotland, Traprain commands a dramatic vista of the surrounding fertile plain with the Bass Rock and North Berwick Law to the north-east, and Arthur's Seat off to the west (plate 17).

In a series of investigations from the first quarter of the twentieth century, supplemented by further assessments in the 1930s, '40s, '80s, '90s and the early 2000s, the 40-acre site was examined by means of field survey, excavation and aerial imagery. The latter technique showed that the hillfort did not stand alone, revealing signs of a rich hinterland of Iron Age farmsteads. Despite its importance, no overarching archaeological synthesis of the site has yet been produced, probably because of its size, the piecemeal nature of its investigation and the relative expense of such an undertaking. But it is not for the lack of academic investment: this hill has attracted some of the greatest names in Scottish archaeology ranging from Curle, Cree, Feachem and Bersu, to Armit, Dunwell and Hunter who have all at one time or another investigated the fortress.

Traprain can however be reasonably described as the most important site in North Britain with respect to the richness of Roman–native interaction – the wealth of material found on the hill is unparalleled in Scottish archaeology. More than three millennia of human activity has ensured the presence of objects as diverse as neolithic flint arrowheads and rock carvings, to the greatest concentration of Roman material from any indigenous site north of Hadrian's Wall. The perfection of the site is spoiled only by the ugly scar of the vast quarry on the north-east slope which perniciously

107. Traprain Law viewed
from the north. Multiple
ramparts can still be traced as
low earthworks. At its zenith,
the hillfort, which was likely to
have been the *oppidum* of the
Votadini, extended to 40 acres.
Note the 20th-century quarry.

ate away at this archaeological wonder until the 1980s. In concert with
the complete destruction of other great hillforts such as the Dunion in the
Borders and Dumbuck on the Clyde, it is a stark reminder of why regulatory
bodies such as Historic Environment Scotland are so important to our
heritage.

In its lifetime, the hillfort of Traprain witnessed several phases of expansion and contraction. At its greatest extent of 40 acres, it was comparable
to Eildon Hill North and in this phase the rampart was over a kilometre
in length. Largely due to the irregular nature of investigation its sequential
history, and how that relates to some of the finds, has been difficult to
reconstruct resulting in calls from leading academics for a large-scale excavation using modern techniques to help draw together the many loose ends.

What can the material already discovered on the hill tell us of the nature
of the interaction with Rome and what light can it shed on our understanding of fourth-century Scotland in general? From the outset, it should be
emphasised that Traprain was atypical in comparison with most other
indigenous sites. There can be no doubt from the quantity, range and quality
of material found there that the Votadini were, at least for a significant
portion of the Roman occupation, either pro-Roman or part of a full-blown
client kingdom. Dwellings continued in the roundhouse vernacular, but the
portable and disposable culture became recognisably Roman in terms of
personal adornment, table wear and luxury items.

After the departure of Antonine troops in the 160–80s the coin list from
Traprain shows a distinct hiatus until the late third/fourth century. This is

Client kingdoms

Control of the outer limits of occupied territories varied across the Roman Empire – some borders were defined by solid linear barriers and others were formed by more ill-defined geographic features such as mountain ranges or deserts. Beyond these structural borders, the Romans were adept at establishing controlling influence by creating buffers known as client kingdoms. A puppet ruler chosen by his Roman overlords to maintain peace and mediate tribute frequently led these polities. The client king would in return receive variable Roman military support, often against a historic tribal enemy. The creation of a client kingdom was usually a temporary holding position – such as that of the Iceni in East Anglia – until it suited the Romans to incorporate the territory fully within the wider imperial portfolio. Similar client kingdoms were also to be found in areas of colonialist expansion in the heyday of the modern British Empire.

paralleled by the pottery evidence, and it has been suggested, although not universally accepted, that the site was temporarily abandoned. An alternative reading of this could be that there was conflict following the withdrawal of the protective support of Roman forces, brought to the hill by war bands from the north taking revenge for the treachery of a 'Quisling' state that had facilitated Roman occupation. Or possibly the opposite, that Traprain had been caught up in indiscriminate Roman retribution during the Commodan War or the slightly later Severan genocidal purge.

Although either of these conflict hypotheses might fit the available data, there are two observations that may favour the latter option. Firstly, the abundance of Severan material at Cramond in the late second/early third century does not appear to 'drift' to Traprain, as it does for other time periods, which is a bit odd for a client kingdom which lay just down the coastline. And secondly, the hitherto unrecognised finding from the Traprain summit of a very characteristic triangular profile ballista bolt. This artefact, the significance of which has not been fully explored, requires some explaining as it is exactly the type of ammunition one might find at a site that had been on the receiving end of a Roman assault. This form of projectile tip is characteristic of the Antonine period or later, for example at Harzhorn, and unlike the armour-piercing 'bodkin' type head of earlier missiles. Investigations at Burnswark have shown, however, when there is an absence of projectiles, particularly lead and stone ones that are durable in Scottish soil conditions, an assault is exceptionally difficult to prove. As we have seen, it is unrealistic to expect incontrovertible proof of conflict

in all instances since the evidence of warfare is frequently fleeting and sparse.

Notwithstanding the possibility of a Commodan or Severan assault on the hill, some form of friendly contact recommenced in the fourth century with the telling appearance of a significant number of randomly dropped coins, spanning the periods of Constantine to Theodosius.

Traprain Treasure

One more superlative characterises the site – sometime in the early decades of the fifth century, during the period of turmoil which prevailed as the Western Roman Empire drew to a close, an extraordinary hoard of Roman silver plate was concealed below the floor of one of the roundhouses on Traprain's western plateau. The 23kg of silver, derived from at least two Roman dinner services, represents the largest deposit of hacksilver to be found anywhere beyond the frontier of the empire (plate 18).

The silver plate, in its crudely chopped and folded state of more than 150 pieces, was initially considered by Alexander Curle and his contemporaries who uncovered it in 1919, to represent booty awaiting smelting and casting into jewellery or other more conveniently portable wealth. And this may still be the case. However, assiduous comparison of weights and sizes of the folded components with other similar hoards from across the empire suggests that the assemblage would also fit with an official donative to a local powerbroker to keep the peace. In effect, this fabulous hoard could be the fifth-century equivalent of the caches of silver coinage used to stabilise (or destabilise) states beyond the empire's frontier during earlier epochs. It is sobering to speculate on the sequence of events that might have led to such a high-status dinner service being smashed up by agents of the state to pay for trans-frontier mercenaries.

The likely date of the concealment of the treasure is in the very late fourth or early fifth century, as indicated by the style of the silver plate and the inclusion of four Roman silver coins. This would have taken place about the time of the final withdrawal of Roman troops and central fiscal support from the south of Britain. As a final thought, the date of minting of the latest of these coins, an issue of Honorius, lies between 397 and 402, bracketing the period when Stilicho could have been in Britain.

Stilicho's downfall

If Stilicho did come to North Britain at the beginning of the fifth century, his entourage may possibly have brought hacksilver with them, though not specifically the Traprain hoard, to influence buffer states and to stave off further conflict. South of the Wall, soon after Stilicho's return to Gaul, the

OPPOSITE. 108. The Traprain treasure, which comprises 23kg of 'hacked' vessels including feasting, drinking and washing bowls.

military situation again became unstable with a string of usurpers in quick succession: Marcus, Gratian and Constantine III were proclaimed in quick order by the army in Britain and consequently troops were withdrawn from the island to fight in power struggles with Honorius in Gaul.

Stilicho's military prowess made him appear almost invincible at this time of uncertainty, dealing successfully, on behalf of Honorius, with sequential outbreaks of invasion and rebellion across the empire. However, like many powerful figures before and after him, he ultimately fell foul of court intrigue. In 408 he was accused of treason and executed on the orders of his son-in-law, the twenty-four-year-old emperor. The turbulent period that ensued saw the Roman Empire split once more between East and West with the latter falling prey to almost continuous incursions from across its frontiers. Eventually, in 410, Alaric, the first king of the Visigoths, reinvaded Italy and sacked Rome while Honorius fled to Ravenna, effectively casting Britain adrift and bringing the Western Empire to a close.

And what then of the great hill of Traprain? Archaeological evidence of continued occupation into the fifth century and beyond is at the moment scanty – this period is frequently materially elusive – but the finding of the hacksilver hoard and a Pictish neck-chain suggest that the site had a significant life after the departure of Rome. It is highly likely that it became one of the tribal centres, together with *Dun-Eidyn* (Edinburgh Castle Rock), of the emerging power of the Gododdin. These Brittonic peoples, centred in the Lothians, would give rise to the scion that would eventually assimilate with the tribes of north Wales and be memorialised in *Y Gododdin*, the earliest surviving Welsh poem.

CHAPTER EIGHTEEN

Entering the darkness

The non-linear nature of cultural evolution is difficult to perceive due to the generally slow pace of change. For many, the demands of everyday survival and the immediate grind of mundane circumstance obscure the uneven march of history. Our insensitivity is further exacerbated by an innate optimism that things will improve and move forward. Those living through an epoch, however, may not recognise a retrogressive step until the facade of continuous progress spectacularly crumbles. What second-century Roman would have correctly predicted the dystopia of the subsequent millennium? This can be graphically illustrated by two coins: compare the classical image and precise lettering of a Trajanic denarius with the primitive artwork and illegible text of a silver penny of King Harold, struck almost 1,000 years later.

Random global downturns are not the only forces at work: the peaks and troughs of 'large' and 'small' society also permeate all cultures and all times. Extending this observation of societal oscillation to smaller-scale archaeological interpretation of Roman Iron Age Scotland, may explain why for example, some settlements are 'defended' in some areas and 'open' in others. The phenomenon possibly reflects the nature, size and reach of the contemporary overarching powers. When we encounter hillforts bristling with ditches and compare them with open settlements, we are probably seeing polar responses to the effects of local versus pan-regional potentates: when relatively minor forces of warring neighbours were at play, during anarchic downturns, warfare may be characterised by the defensive architecture of smaller fortified farmsteads. In other times, protection provided by irresistible regional powers may have obviated the need for local defence and would have resulted in open settlements. So, for many reasons, the cultural, political and material landscape was probably set for major change on the departure of Roman forces at the end of the fourth century.

109. Silver *denarius* of Trajan (top) compared with the crude symbolism of a silver penny of King Harold minted a thousand years later.

110. The kingdoms of post-Roman Scotland.

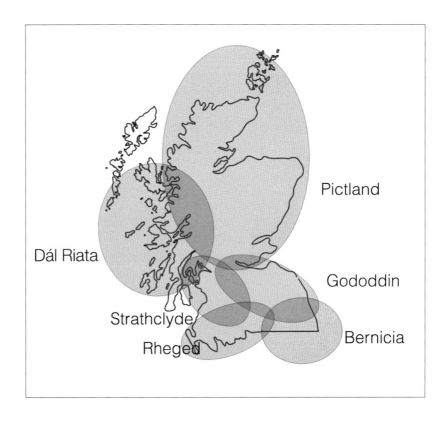

Dark Ages versus Early Medieval

The period after Rome's disengagement from Britain, spanning roughly from 400 to 900, was known until relatively recently as the 'Dark Ages'. This term, which has a long pedigree stretching back as far as Petrarch (1304–74), tends to inferiorise the societies of western Europe that had struggled to make ends meet after the halcyon days of classical Rome and Greece had passed. The epithet is now eschewed by historians and archae-ologists in favour of the more acceptable 'Early Medieval' period. Apart from being temporally correct, there is the feeling that this new descriptor is deliberately worded to show that things were not so grim after all. However, it is possibly unduly optimistic to suggest society actually improved after the implosion of the empire. Across much of Europe, the loss of centralised governance from Rome, strategic military control, stable monetary policy, and fine art and literature made possible by the largesse of empire almost certainly resulted in some form of 'darkness'. No matter how one frames the rough beauty of primitive aesthetics there is little doubt about the deterioration in much of the material culture of southern Britain (Saxon jewellery is perhaps the exception) in the centuries following the collapse of the Western Roman Empire.

111. Class II cross slab with 'Celtic' knotwork from St Vigeans in Angus.

But was this the same experience in North Britain, which had never been exposed to intense Romanisation and had not come to rely on continental patronage in any significant way? Could this period have been one of paradoxical growth under the unified overlordship of the Picts who had beneficially evolved in response to the existential threat of Rome? Did this interval, which has been portrayed as endless gloom for the rest of Europe, represent a halcyon period for the consolidated northern tribes?

The production of refined art in most cultures is dependent on society being sufficiently developed to support artists and this equally applies to Early Medieval Scotland. Indeed, art historians George and Isobel Henderson, in their monumental work *The Art of the Picts*, point out in their preface that: 'historians and archaeologists must now in their "models" allow for a political maturity and economic infrastructure adequate for the production of such art'. Pictland was benefitting from improved social and military organisation as evidenced by the numerous references to the Picts and their activities by their contemporaries – there are almost as many references in Bede's *Ecclesiastical History of the English People* to the Picts as there are to St Peter. In terms of archaeology, the poor survival of organic artefacts in the harsh climate of Scotland makes some of the more ephemeral aspects of Early Medieval life difficult to demonstrate, but stone tells a different story. Now converted to Christianity, the new religion was embraced by the peoples of North Britain as the numerous Class II symbol stones testify. These works of religious art, which were erected from Fife to Orkney, compare favourably with the best of Europe for artistic novelty and skill, and reflect a rich cultural hinterland that is materially invisible for all the reasons stated above.

Other evidence continues to emerge. Carver's work at Portmahomack between 1994 and 2007, unearthed a plethora of pointers to a monastic complex which was clearly thriving in the centuries after the departure of Rome. With strong evidence of manuscript production as well as other ecclesiastical and secular indicators, this site would not have been alone in taking advantage of the positive effects of its Pictish heritage.

What literary sources do we have to put more flesh on the bones of this period of sub-Roman Scotland? Essentially, there are only two British authors who shed any light in the darkness: the sixth- and eighth-century monks Gildas and Bede.

De Excidio et Conquestu Britanniae (*On the Ruin and Conquest of Britain*), the book by the monk Gildas (500–70), is a good example of useful historical information that requires to be teased out from an envelope of religious polemic. Gildas, who is reputed to have been born in the Lowlands of Scotland, provided a general description of Iron Age Britain in the same format repeated by Bede a couple of centuries later. He tells that the British people were subdued by the Romans 'not so much by fire and sword and war-engines, like other nations, but threats and terror alone'. This may go a little way to explain the absence we have already noted of Roman siege-works in southern Britain. With considerable invective, he covered the mutiny of the British army under the leadership of Magnus Maximus, who was proclaimed emperor in 384. Gildas claimed that in his failed attempt against Theodosius, Maximus robbed Britain of its best soldiers and left the

Early Christianity in Scotland

The small but significant corpus of early Christian inscriptions – thirteen were highlighted by Thomas (1991) – from southern Scotland shows that Christian influence was already well established by the fifth century, particularly in the south-west of the country. The form of the chi-rho monogram on the Latinus Stone from Whithorn for example, and the small group of stones from nearby Kirkmadrine, suggests that Christian symbolism and Latin writing were understood by at least a portion of the general population by the 450s. Despite the evocative archaeology and the direct references by Bede, St Ninian's place in this evolution has been challenged recently by the suggestion that he did not actually exist (and has been conflated with a later missionary, St Finnian). However, his foundation in 397 of *Candida Casa* – literally the White House – which gives Whithorn its name, remains the current understanding. The scatter of other early Latin inscriptions up the more easterly aspect of the country, from Chesterholm to Kirkliston, confirm that this influence wasn't simply due to Galloway's physical proximity to Ireland, although there can be little doubt that the *floruit* of the early Church in Scotland owed much to the travels of Celtic evangelists such as Ninian and Columba.

What is much less clear is how much of the evangelical ground had already been prepared by the late-Roman military presence in the north of England. Since Constantine had adopted Christianity as the official state religion in the mid-fourth century, it is reasonable to hypothesise that military personnel and their families may have provided a kernel of the new faith, which could have survived into the post-Roman afterlife of the northern garrisons. Supportive evidence is slight but the recent discovery at Vindolanda of the remnants of a lead chalice bearing Christian motifs, buried within the rubble of what is suspected to be a sixth-century Christian church is encouraging.

southern part of the island exposed to the 'cruel mercy of the Scots and Picts'. An appeal was made to Emperor Honorius who sent a legion which drove the Picts back beyond the frontier 'and the humiliated natives were rescued from the bloody slavery which awaited them'. At this point Gildas suggested that on Roman advice the natives built a turf wall across the narrow part of the country, but this proved ineffective. Once more, Roman forces returned to assist the hapless locals repel the barbarians but, on this occasion, when the Romans departed for the Continent, they announced that in future the Britons would have to fend for themselves.

'No sooner were they gone [the Romans], than the Picts and Scots, like worms which in the heat of the day come forth from their holes' hastily carried out an attack on the Wall garrisons. Gildas claimed the garrisons were ineffectual and panic-stricken, and 'slumbered away days and nights of their unprofitable watch'. An appeal was made to Rome: 'the barbarians drive us into the sea and sea drives us back against the barbarians'. The Romans this time were unable to help and British forces for the first time managed to temporarily drive out the invaders. Gildas went on to describe the Picts reaching the extremity of the island (the southern extremity, presumably Essex/Kent area) but thereafter the work essentially becomes a polemic with little historical detail. We can clearly see that in Gildas's writing, the Picts were consistently portrayed in a very negative light and treated with the same disdain as the dreaded Saxons. The same attitude was not true of the Venerable Bede.

Bede (the title 'Venerable' was added after his death) was a Benedictine monk at the monastery of St Peter and St Paul at Jarrow to which he was apprenticed in 680 as a *puer oblatus*, a boy dedicated to the monastic life. By the age of thirty, having narrowly survived a major plague, he was elevated to the status of priest with special scriptorial duties. He was a prolific and exacting writer, completing over sixty books, and showing a level of precision for facts and dates that greatly enhanced his reputation, becoming the only British cleric to be recognised by the Papacy as a 'Doctor of the Church'. He is also credited as the person who first promoted the 'BC/AD' dating system.

Bede's work is significantly less polemical than the writings of Gildas, concentrating more on the history of the Church and associated temporal events, although he does generously recognise Gildas's contribution. In his *Ecclesiastical History* Bede, like Gildas, commenced with a general description of Britain and the history of Roman involvement. Bede makes specific reference to Severus' campaign in the north because of 'the rebellion of the tribes'. This leads on to an unusual statement about Severus building a wall from coast to coast to separate the recovered part of the island from the unconquered tribes – Bede presumably making the same error as other early historians because of the prevalence of Severan inscriptions. However, Bede was emphatic that this wall was not of stone but of turf surmounted by a wooden palisade and a wide ditch. Bede placed it on the Tyne–Solway isthmus and it's hard to see how he could be confused about its siting – during Bede's lifetime, Hadrian's Wall was still extant and lay just 1 mile as the crow flies across the Tyne from his monastery in Jarrow. Since he spent his whole life in the immediate neighbourhood, it is exceptionally unlikely he was referring to the Antonine Wall, so it is probable he was ascribing the Vallum to Severus.

Bede, as Gildas had done before him, also told the story of the stripping of Roman troops for wars of succession on the Continent. He described the subsequent early fifth-century abandonment of the island in almost the same words as Gildas, and reiterated that Roman advice was to build another wall, this time across the Forth–Clyde isthmus. He states that this was also a wall of turf, indicating he was aware of the details of the position and existence of the Antonine Wall system although getting the date and motivation for its creation wrong. He then says that Roman forces came back one last time to rescue the locals from an incursion of the northern tribes. According to Bede, the Roman forces generously helped the hapless population to replace the Tyne–Solway turf wall this time in stone. In his words 'at public and private expense, they built a famous wall 8ft wide and 12ft high which can be seen to this day'. This then explains Bede's interpretation of the Vallum and sequencing of the two Walls. He goes on to say that as soon as the Romans had left for the final time, the Scots and Picts came back again and devastated the land as far south as the Wall: 'The Britons deployed their dispirited ranks along the top of the defence,' but this appeared to be no match for the hooked weapons (poles?) that the Picts used to pull the defenders from the battlements. There followed a period of chaotic retreat of British forces that subsequently gave rise to famine.

112. Pictish barrow cemetery from Garbeg near Loch Ness. Note the numerous characteristic ditched barrows of both round and square configuration – sheep for scale.

When Bede's story moved closer to the fifth and sixth centuries, and he found himself on firmer ground in terms of his sources, he began to concen-

trate on the transformational effect that the early Church had on North Britain and its relationship to the Pictish nation. He tells the story of St Ninian, who he says was the first missionary to attempt to convert the southern Picts. Since he died in 432 Ninian will have been preaching to the immediate descendants of those Picts who assaulted the Wall in the dying days of the Roman occupation. Bede also reflected on the letter sent by St Patrick, from Ireland, to Coroticus, the warlord of Alt Clut (Dumbarton Rock) beseeching him to stop slaughtering Christian converts (plate 19).

He went on to describe the coming of St Columba in 563 to Iona, the island given to him by the king of the Picts. He tells of Columba's power as a diplomat as well as his gift as a missionary, for he was well received by the northern Picts as he proselytised among them with impunity, pointing out that the southern Picts had already seen the error of their ways a considerable time before and had converted to the true faith in advance of their northern kindred. By Bede's time of writing, one has the impression that while not exactly benign neighbours, the Picts were being viewed from the south as a Christianised people who could be negotiated with.

Even if the benevolent influence of the early church has been exaggerated, we can now move beyond Bede and Gildas, as the historical chasm of the Early Medieval period slowly infills with new discoveries made almost yearly as part of a renaissance in Pictish studies. This has begun to peel back mysteries of places like the royal centre at Rhynie, which lies in the shadow of the great hillfort of Tap o'Noth. We are learning that the Picts, far from being an isolated mystery race, were connected to the rest of Britain and showing signs of extensive communication with Rome's successors on mainland Europe. Perhaps the apparent rejection of Rome by these northern peoples had, for them, resulted in a form of darkness that was not so gloomy after all.

CHAPTER NINETEEN

Conclusion: the Eagle and the Bear

The account of Scotland's interaction with Rome has evolved considerably over the last 300 years. Historians, archaeologists, artists and social commentators have spun their own versions from the thin yarn available, influenced by the zeitgeist of their times. The eighteenth century saw the rediscovery of the Roman period in Scotland as a time of growing antiquarian wonder at how and why the Roman Empire came to North Britain. As the Hanoverian grip tightened, Roman roads and installations were mapped with precision by men like General Roy for intellectual and personal interest, before the plough erased them completely from the landscape. Ditches and ramparts were carefully measured and admired from a military perspective – to the Georgians it seemed the Romans really knew how to put down a rebellion. In the nineteenth century conflations were perhaps unavoidable between the undeniable might and majesty of Rome and the expansion of Britain's own dominions – in which Scots were now playing a prominent part. Over these centuries the impressive scale of the Roman incursion was slowly pieced together by scholars plotting surface traces against an evolving historiography.

In the Victorian era, a blind eye was turned to the negative effects of imperial greed – occupation of foreign lands and the rapacious extraction of other people's resources were excusable if they could be softened by the illusion of an improving mission to grateful barbarians and 'noble savages'. And so began a curious relationship between the intellectual and social elite of Scotland and ancient Rome, permeating literature, politics, church and classroom. A blurring of the distinction between the oppressor and the oppressed, which has in some ways persisted to the present day.

By the twentieth century, archaeology was producing more reliable information, which although considerably more refined than the techniques at the disposal of the antiquarian, was still projected through the academic lenses and cultural contexts of the day. In the latter years of this trajectory, the portrayal of Rome's interaction with the local population has frequently been softened by deliberate underestimation of indigenous resistance to Rome's imperialist intentions. Despite attempts in recent years by some academics to redress the balance, the dominant narrative remains somewhat Romanocentric. The nature and sophistication of pre-Roman indigenous culture and the systematic investigation of the zones of contact and conflict are just some of the areas that would benefit from more focus and resource. It is a telling fact that despite southern Scotland's incredibly rich landscape of literally hundreds of Iron Age forts, only a single site (Broxmouth) has undergone anything of the sort of area excavation that allows reliable and meaningful synthesis.

The motivation behind this imbalance is less clear. It could be seen as a function of the relative quantities of material which scholars have been left to work with – the by-product of the rich residue of Rome's disposable culture contrasting with the sparse pickings from indigenous sites. Or the direction of travel being dictated by institutional biases with some actions masking old allegiances to more imperialist perspectives. There are academics who have opened the interpretative door to theories with a lesser colonial emphasis, but they are currently in the minority, and their work has not yet reached a wider audience. They have gathered evidence that disrupts Romanocentric views of Iron Age Scotland and challenges the myth of Rome as a casual visitor to North Britain.

Some have ventured to say that the Roman invasions of Scotland had no lasting effect whatsoever and rural life returned to much the same 'primitive' state after the Romans left. This view could be seen to promote a systematic trivialisation of the effects of conflict, particularly of the post-Agricolan and post-Severan periods and the failure to imagine the psychological and sociological impact of this form of trauma on potential refugees, a phenomenon now better understood from more recent war zones. If we have learned anything from Josephus' experience, this must have been a hellish period for local populations. Yet through adherence to treasured theory, the dominant narrative unconsciously supports a form of cultural inferiorism. As such, it compromises the Iron Age foundations of Scotland's language, culture and nationhood.

A restatement of the primary evidence may therefore be helpful in understanding what the experience of having the Roman Empire on the doorstep may have meant for the early Caledonians. Firstly, no matter how it is framed, this was no mere interlude in Scottish history. The Roman Iron Age in Scotland spanned over 300 years of many recorded episodes of interaction, mostly violent, with one of the world's most powerful and expansionist empires. A third of a millennium that saw the presence of one of the highest concentrations of Roman military personnel – it has been estimated at the height of occupation, at least one in eight Roman soldiers was serving in North Britain. The building of two great walls, the larger of which was maintained for a 300-year period and both with offensive and defensive characteristics of a magnitude not shared by any other Roman frontier of its size. Unlike other zones of interaction, there is little evidence of regular trade and no manifestation of any meaningful civic development.

In the context of resisting invasion by larger and more powerful nations, Scotland seems to have been Rome's Afghanistan. A small, stubbornly resistant, culturally asymmetric, geographically remote nation, abutting a larger and wealthier polity – like a thorn in the empire's back, North Britain appears to have largely rejected and resisted the allure of Rome. A seemingly insignificant but persistent irritant that Rome could not ignore, and which, in a limited but effective way, would ultimately become a force capable of holding the superpower at bay.

The conclusion I have reached then, is that whatever the Romans were doing in Scotland, it was certainly not playing out an imperial vanity project or practising marching or introducing the locals to Latin and hot baths. Nor does it seem, as those with inferiorist tendencies might believe, that the land was worthless: the density of settlement revealed by modern archaeology suggests the agricultural output of the arable portions of Scotland produced a rich bounty of cereals and livestock including cattle and horses. And there was mineral wealth too and more archaeologically ephemeral benefits like fabrics, hunting dogs and the assets of last resort – hardy young conscripts and potential slaves.

The Romans were certainly not here either as improvers, leaving no civilian legacy. In fact, if all the dregs of everyday Roman material culture from native sites in the whole of Scotland (excluding the silver hoards which had a special purpose and the unique situation at Traprain), including every fragment of broken pot, brooch and stray coin was heaped together it would barely fill a kitchen larder. Compared with the rich trans-frontier activity in other provinces, the Romans in Scotland could not be considered role models for aspirational natives.

A non-intentional but no less significant catastrophe will almost certainly have followed in the wake of Rome, a culture renowned for its wide-ranging contacts and rapid intercontinental transport. Those companions of mass troop movements, disease and plague, to which the insulated indigenous population would have previously been at least partially shielded, will have entered the country with the swiftly moving armies. It is possible, and indeed probable, that from time to time these pandemics will have devastated local populations in the same way measles and smallpox did in the Americas following their introduction by the Conquistadores and white settlers.

The Roman army almost certainly entered Scotland thinking it would be there for a limited period only: 'get the conquest done' and then let the procurator's henchmen tax whomever was left. It clearly didn't work out that way. The building of barriers, conflagrations of forts, siegeworks and desertions of native settlements plus depositions of metalwork and silver hoards are all evidence of stress. These stress signs cluster around four main periods: the reigns of Hadrian and Pius, and late in the reigns of Commodus and Severus. The artefact record is less strong for later years, and we must rely on literary sources for what was clearly major warfare in the fourth century as the Picts coalesced and found their voice.

The tribes of North Britain, as they themselves well recognised, were backed into this extremity of Europe, and were, in the words given to Calgacus 'the last of the free, shielded by our very remoteness . . . with nothing behind us but the sea'. But as Tacitus presaged, even the sea would not protect them from what in the end would be volatile contact with an empire that had aggressive expansion at its core: 'Plunderers of the world, they are not simply content with the land but also ravage the sea. If an enemy is rich, they desire its wealth, if it is poor, they wish to dominate it. They are not content with either the East or the West. Alone among peoples, Romans covet the poor as well as the rich. To rape they give the deceitful title of empire, and everywhere they create a desolation and call it peace.'

Such was the near-continuous assault on Caledonia, for over three centuries, at the hands of an empire that embodied these ideals as a divine right. A persistent long-distance martial retribution not to be rivalled in Scottish history until the comparatively short Hanoverian period when redcoats marched to the extremities of the island and planted fortresses of control at Forts William, Augustus and George. It is also easy to become

The Antonine Plague

Although local outbreaks of infectious disease were rife in the ancient world (infant mortality of 50 per cent or more was commonplace) a number of classical authors record episodes of larger epidemics. These were exacerbated in Roman times by the squalor of developing urbanism and the intercontinental movements of trade and massive armies. One of the greatest of these, which would today merit the title of pandemic, was the Antonine Plague (sometimes known as the Plague of Galen) that was recorded during the reign of Marcus Aurelius. Thought by modern authors, based on Galen's description, to be smallpox, this disease rampaged throughout the empire from the 160s to the 170s, killing approximately 10 per cent of the population. Dio recorded a further outbreak, with an even higher estimated death toll, in the late 180s. It is highly likely that this and other diseases were brought to mainland Britain by the Roman army.

overly focused on the direct actions of the Roman army, and to ignore the archaeologically ephemeral consequences of invasion such as famine and pestilence.

The long period of attrition of the Roman Iron Age must surely have affected the collective psyche of early Scotland. If nothing else, the evidence supports the contention that it eventually alloyed a Pictish identity that led to a pan-Caledonian polity capable of facing up to the empire on its own terms. A long view of the largely negative impact of Rome on the peoples of North Britain also introduces the possibility that a sense of 'resistance' – however that concept is characterised – may have become an indelible trait of northerners.

Places to visit

National Museum of Scotland, Edinburgh.

The Early Peoples Gallery contains an internationally important collection of indigenous and Roman artefacts, including the Traprain treasure, displayed alongside many Bronze Age and Pictish antiquities.

The Hunterian Museum, Glasgow.

Situated in Glasgow University, the museum displays the majority of the Antonine Wall distance sculptures and many other finds from Roman sites predominantly in the west of Scotland.

Trimontium Museum, Melrose.

The only museum in Scotland dedicated to the Roman Iron Age. Good collection of Roman and indigenous artefacts, including rare militaria. Excellent audio-visuals.

Smaller but significant collections of Roman Iron Age material can be found in: Elgin Museum, including the Birnie collection and many Pictish stones; Inverness Museum and Art Gallery; McManus Galleries, Dundee; Perth Museum and Art Gallery; Callendar House, Falkirk; Biggar Museum, including many scale models; Moffat Museum; and Dumfries Museum with many sculptures from Birrens fort and the surrounding area.

Pictish and Early Medieval Collections

Most of the museums listed above also display artefacts from this period (the National Museum has the Hilton of Cadboll stone for example) but specialist collections can be found in:

Tarbat Discovery Centre, Portmahomack. Many finds from the excavations at the site of the Pictish monastery there.

Groam House Museum, Rosemarkie. An independent museum, with a significant collection of Pictish art including the Rosemarkie Cross.

Meigle Sculptured Stone Museum, Meigle. Internationally important collection of Pictish art, including crosses and grave markers.

St Vigeans Sculptured Stones Museum, Arbroath. Impressive collection of stone carvings including the Drosten Stone.

Govan Old Parish Church, Glasgow. The church houses a nationally important collection of thirty-one Early Medieval sculptures including several massive hogback tomb markers.

Indigenous Sites

North of Hadrian's Wall there are literally hundreds of hillforts and other Iron Age structures, many in a good state of preservation. A few of the best are:

Hillforts

Barry Hill, Angus	NO 2623 5041
Brown Caterhun, Angus	NO 5550 6690
Burnswark Hill, Dumfries & Galloway	NY 1860 7870
Chesters, East Lothian	NT 5076 7286
Dunsinane Hill, Perthshire	NO 2136 3168
Eildon Hill North, Scottish Borders	NT 5545 3280
Hownam Law, Scottish Borders	NT 7962 2200
Hownam Rings, Scottish Borders	NT 7907 1942
Traprain Law, East Lothian	NT 5800 7470
Walls Hill, Renfrewshire	NS 4117 5881
White Caterhun, Angus	NO 5480 6610
White Meldon, Scottish Borders	NT 2193 4283
Woden Law, Scottish Borders	NT 7664 1237
Yeavering Bell, Northumberland	NT 9292 2934

Souterrains

Ardestie, Angus	NO 5030 3444
Carlungie, Angus	NO 5110 3597
Castlelaw, Midlothian	NT 2290 6385
Pitcur, Perthsire	NO 2529 3738
Rennibister, Orkney	HY 3971 1259
Tealing, Angus	NO 4121 3816

Northern brochs

Carn Liath Broch, Sutherland	NH 5894 6656
Clickimin, Shetland	HU 4643 4082
Dun Carloway, Lewis	NB 1899 4122
Dun Telve, Glenelg	NG 8290 1725
Gurness, Orkney	HY 3818 2685
Kilphedir, Sutherland	NC 9943 1891
Midhowe, Orkney	HY 3716 3061
Mousa, Shetland	HU 4573 2366

Lowland brochs

Bow Castle, Scottish Borders	NT 4615 4172
Edin's Hall, Scottish Borders	NT 7723 6031
Torwood (Tappoch), Stirlingshire	NS 8334 8498
Torwoodlee, Scottish Borders	NT 4657 3848

Roman sites north of Hadrian's Wall

(AW = Antonine Wall)

Ardoch fort	NN 8392 0991
Bar Hill fort and AW	NS 7075 7592
Bearsden bathhouse and AW	NS 5470 7211
Bothwellhaugh bathhouse	NS 7297 5789
Burnswark siege camps	NY 1860 7870
Callendar Park and AW	NS 8979 7961
Chew Green fort and camps	NT 7885 0854
Croy Hill fort and AW	NS 7332 7655
Duntocher fort	NS 4953 7267
Kirkbuddo camp	NO 4918 4404
Lyne fort	NT 1876 4056
New Kilpatrick Cemetery Wall base	NS 5573 7241
Pennymuir camp	NT 7546 1391
Rough Castle fort and AW	NS 8432 7987
Seabegs Wood AW	NS 8135 7930
Trimontium fort	NT 5696 3442
Watling Lodge AW	NS 8646 7983
Ythan Wells camp	NJ 6551 3818

Museums on Hadrian's Wall

Several of the forts on the line of Hadrian's Wall have excellent museums containing almost exclusively Roman artefacts:

Birdoswald Roman Fort; Housesteads Roman Fort; Corbridge Roman Town; Chesters Roman Fort; South Shields Roman Fort; Wallsend Roman Fort.

Great North Museum, Newcastle, has a large collection of Roman and indigenous material.

Roman Army Museum, Carvoran, is affiliated with Vindolanda Museum and contains a good collection of original artefacts and reproductions specifically related to the Roman army. Good audio-visuals.

Tullie House Museum, Carlisle, houses an extensive collection of Roman material from the western end of the Wall. The basement gallery is given over exclusively to the Roman period.

Vindolanda, which often has active digs on public view, has a large museum that houses an internationally significant collection of finds from the site including some of the famous Vindolanda writing tablets.

Open Air Sites

Some open sites, including several of the Hadrian's Wall forts/museums mentioned above, incur an entrance charge. On open sites, please use common sense and good manners – if a site lies on private land, please seek permission where necessary and close all gates behind you.

Hadrian's Wall

Many of the surviving sections of the Wall, ditch and Vallum are accessible to the public and the Hadrian's Wall Path is an excellent way of experiencing them. For those with limited time, here is a small selection of interesting parts of the Wall/structures not immediately associated with the forts or museums listed above:

Brunton Turret 26b	NY 9266 6968
Carrawburgh fort and *Mithraeum*	NY 8592 7117
Limestone Corner ditch and Vallum	NY 8758 7151
Milecastle 37	NY 7850 6868
Milecastle 39 and Sycamore Gap	NY 7606 6774
Milecastle 42 and Vallum	NY 7157 6669
Great Chesters fort	NY 7037 6680
Turret 44b	NY 6814 6670
Willowford bridge abutment	NY 6222 6647
Milecastle 49	NY 6200 6634
Section of Turf Wall	NY 5979 6560

Glossary

Augustan Histories the *Historia Augusta*, a late-Roman collection of biographies of the Roman emperors by a variety of authors

ballista a generic term for a catapult; may shoot bolts or stone balls

Batavi a Germanic tribe from the Rhine Delta, fabled for their horsemanship. Batavian infantry fought at Mons Graupius

berm the strip of land between Wall and ditch occasionally studded with obstacles

broch circular drystone tower-house fortification/dwelling with chambered walls. Unique to Iron Age Scotland

carnyx bronze animal-headed war trumpet favoured by the Celtic tribes

centurion officer in command of a century of Roman infantry (eighty men)

crannog roundhouse lake-dwelling founded on wooden piles

cropmarks the differential ripening of crops or grass growing over buried ditches or stone structures such as roads and walls, often visualised on aerial photographs during droughts

cursus honorum sequence of public and military offices expected to be held by a high-status Roman aspiring to senatorial service

dendrochronology dating of wooden structures and climate assessment by tree ring analysis

diploma double-leafed bronze document recording an auxiliary soldier's twenty-five years' service and conferring on him and his family Roman citizenship

dun small, fortified stronghold, usually circular in plan and often set on a rocky promontory. Most numerous in west of Scotland

ethnography the scientific investigation and description of peoples and their cultures

excarnation disposal of human remains by exposing them to scavenging wild animals

expeditio the Latin term used for a major military campaign, usually in a time of war, which implies the personal presence of the emperor

hillfort fortified settlement often situated on a hilly prominence and surrounded by concentric ditches

legate high-ranking Roman officer, often of the status of patrician or knight who was in charge of a legion for a period of up to four years

LiDAR laser imaging technique which amplifies small changes in the level of terrain

lynchets cultivation ridges produced by ploughing along the slopes of hills

magnetometry non-invasive technique which assesses magnetic properties of subsoil structures – detects evidence of burning

Mithraeum temple dedicated to the worship of Mithras

oppidum Latin word for town or tribal capital. In Britain it may refer to a large conurbation of indigenous habitations often surrounded by earthen ramparts. In essence a proto-town

osteology the study of ancient bones, which can provide clues to dating, geographic origin, nutrition and previous violence

palisade defensive wall made from wooden stakes often directly planted in post holes in the soil surface

patera bronze cooking casserole/drinking vessel common in the Roman world but especially part of a Roman soldier's personal mess-kit

prosopography a method which can be used to establish dating sequences derived from the study of the career trajectory of personnel

roundhouse circular domestic dwelling often with stone base and wooden superstructure common in Britain – may be two storeys high

singulares mounted bodyguard of a high-ranking Roman officer

sesquiplicarius junior cavalry officer paid one-and-a-half times the standard rate of pay

souterrain underground curving passage/storage facility often tunnelled into the soil in close relationship to roundhouse settlement

tetrarchy system of governance instituted by Diocletian in 293 whereby the Roman Empire was split between four rulers, two senior emperors (the *augusti*) and two junior (the *caesares*)

Tungri Germanic tribe from the north-west of the River Meuse (often conscripted into the Roman army), which was centred on modern Tongres area. Tungrian infantry fought at Mons Graupius

Vallum Latin word for an earthen rampart: in the context of Hadrian's Wall, the complex linear earthwork that lies immediately to the south

Varusschlacht The battle of the Teutoberg Forest in AD 9, described by Roman historians as the Varian Disaster, in which an alliance of Germanic tribes won a victory over three Roman legions

vexillation a detachment of Roman soldiers, usually referring to a subunit of legionary infantry

Further reading

A selection of general sources including some texts referred to in this volume.

Iron Age Scotland

Armit, I. 1997. *Celtic Scotland*. Birlinn, Edinburgh.

Armit, I. 1999. 'The abandonment of souterrains: evolution, catastrophe or dislocation?', *Proceedings of the Society of Antiquaries of Scotland* 129: 577–96.

Armit, I. 2012. *Headhunting and the Body in Iron Age Europe*, Cambridge University Press, Cambridge.

Armit, I. 2012. *Towers in the North. The Brochs of Scotland*. The History Press, Stroud.

Armit, I. and McKenzie, J. 2013. *An Inherited Place. Broxmouth Hillfort and the South-East Scottish Iron Age*. Society of Antiquaries of Scotland, Edinburgh.

Armit, I. and Büster, L. 2020. *Darkness Visible. The Sculptor's Cave, Covesea, from the Bronze Age to the Picts*. Society of Antiquaries of Scotland, Edinburgh.

Blackwell, A., Goldberg, M., Hunter, F. 2017. *Scotland's Early Silver*. National Museums Scotland, Edinburgh.

Campbell, L. 2011. *A Study in Culture Contact: The Distribution, Function and Social Meanings of Roman Pottery from Non-Roman Contexts in Southern Scotland*, unpublished PhD dissertation, Department of Archaeology, University of Glasgow.

Campbell, L. 2016. 'Proportionalising Practices in the Past: Roman Fragments Beyond the Frontier' in Pierce, E. et al. (eds) *Creating Material Worlds*. Oxbow Books, Oxford.

Cook, M. and Dunbar, L. 2008. *Rituals, Roundhouses and Romans. Excavations at Kintore, Aberdeenshire 2000–2006*. Scottish Trust for Archaeological Research, Loanhead.

Curle, J. 1911. *A Roman Frontier Post and its People*. Glasgow.

Feachem, R.W. 1963. *A guide to prehistoric Scotland*. London.

Harding, D.W. 1976. *Hillforts: Later Prehistoric Earthworks in Britain and Ireland*. Academic Press, London.

Harding, D.W. 2004. *The Iron Age in Northern Britain. Celts and Romans, Natives and Settlers*. Routledge, London.

Hill, J.D. 1995 'How should we understand Iron Age societies and hillforts?' in Hill, J.D. and Cumberpatch, C.G. (eds) *Different Iron Ages: Studies on the Iron Age in Temperate Europe*, 45–66. Oxford.

Hingley, R. 1992. 'Society in Scotland from 700 BC to AD 200'. *Proceedings of the Society of Antiquaries of Scotland* 122:7–53.

Hodgson, N. 2009. 'The abandonment of Antonine Scotland: its date and causes' in W.S. Hanson (ed.) *The army and frontiers of Rome*. JRA Suppl. 2009, 74:185–93.

Hodgson, N., McKelvey, J. and Muncaster, W. 2012. *The Iron Age on the Northumberland Coastal Plain*. TMW Archaeology and the Arbeia Society, Newcastle.

Hunter, F. 2007. *Beyond the Edge of the Empire – Caledonians, Picts and Romans*. Rosemarkie.

Hunter, F. 2008. *Excavations at Birnie, Moray, 2007*. National Museums Scotland.

Hunter, F. 2009. 'Traprain Law and the Roman world', in Hanson, W.S. (ed.) 2009. *The Army and Frontiers of Rome*. Portsmouth, Rhode Island.

James, H. 2011. 'Castle Craig: SERF, Perth and Kinross (Auchterarder parish), excavation'. *Discovery and Excavation Scotland*, 12: 144–5.

Jobey, G. 1978. 'Burnswark Hill, Dumfriesshire'. *Trans Dumfriesshire Galloway Natur Hist Antiq Soc* 53: 57–104.

Macinnes, L. 1984. 'Brochs and the Roman occupation of lowland Scotland'. *Proceedings of the Society of Antiquaries of Scotland* 114: 235–49.

Macinnes, L. 2020. 'The impact of the Antonine wall on Iron Age society' in *The Antonine Wall: Papers in honour of Professor Lawrence Keppie*. Archaeopress, Oxford.

MacKie E.W. 1982. 'The Leckie broch, Stirlingshire: an interim report'. *The Glasgow Archaeological Journal* 9: 60–72.

MacKie E.W. 2016. *Brochs and the Empire: The impact of Rome on Iron Age Scotland as seen in the Leckie Broch excavations*. Archaeopress, Oxford.

Mercer, R. 2018. *Native and Roman on the Northern Frontier*. Society of Antiquaries of Scotland, Edinburgh.

Miket, R. and Burgess, C. (eds) 1984. *Between and Beyond the Walls: Essays on the Prehistory and History of North Britain in Honour of George Jobey*. John Donald, Edinburgh.

Oswald, A., Ainsworth, S. and Pearson, T. 2006. *Hillforts. Prehistoric Strongholds of Northumberland National Park*. English Heritage.

Piggott, C.M. 1948. 'The excavations at Hownam Rings, Roxburghshire'. *Proceedings of the Society of Antiquaries of Scotland* 82: 193–225.

Piggott, C.M. 1949. 'The Iron Age settlement at Hayhope Knowe, Roxburghshire'. *Proceedings of the Society of Antiquaries of Scotland* 83: 45–67

Piggott, S. 1953. 'Excavations in the broch and hill-fort of Torwoodlee, Selkirkshire, 1950'. *Proceedings of the Society of Antiquaries of Scotland* 85: 92–117.

Rideout, J.H., Owen, O.A. and Halpin, E. 1992. *Hillforts of Southern Scotland*. AOC, Edinburgh.

Tipping, R. 2010. *Bowmont. An Environmental History of the Bowmont Valley in the Northern Cheviot Hills 10,000 BC–AD 2000*. Society of Antiquaries of Scotland, Edinburgh.

Toolis, R. 2021. 'Shifting perspectives on 1st-millennia Scotland'. *Proceedings of the Society of Antiquaries of Scotland* 150: 24 72–88.

Wainwright, F.T. 1953. 'Souterrains in Scotland'. *Antiquity* 27: 221.

Wilson, A. 2010. *Roman and Native in the Central Scottish Borders*. BAR 519, Oxford.

Romans in Britain

Beard, M, 2015. *SPQR: A History of Ancient Rome*. Profile Books, London.

de la Bédoyère, G. 2013. *Roman Britain: A New History*. Thames and Hudson, London.

Birley, A.R. 2005. *The Roman Government of Britain*. Oxford University Press, Oxford.

Breeze, D.J. 1988. 'Why did the Romans fail to conquer Scotland?' *Proceedings of the Society of Antiquaries of Scotland* 118: 3–22.

Breeze, D.J. 2014. 'Two Roman Britains'. *Archaeological Journal* 171: 97–110.

Breeze, D.J. 2019. *The Frontiers of Imperial Rome*. Pen and Sword, Barnsley.

Butler, R.M. (ed.) 1971. *Soldier and Civilian in Roman Yorkshire*. Leicester University Press, Leicester.

Buxton, K. 2001. *Bremetenacum: Excavations at Roman Ribchester 1980, 1989–90*. English Heritage.

Campbell, D.B. 2003. 'The Roman siege of Burnswark'. *Britannia* 34: 19–33.

Campbell, D.B. 2010. *Mons Graupius AD 83. Rome's battle at the edge of the world*. Osprey Publishing, Oxford.

Campbell, D.B. 2019. *The Fate of the Ninth*. Amazon.

Collingwood, R.G. and Myres, J.N.L. 1936/1975. *Roman Britain and the English Settlements*. Oxford University Press, Oxford.

Crawford, O.G.S. 1949. *Topography of Roman Scotland, North of the Antonine Wall*. Cambridge University Press, Cambridge.

Elliot, S. 2018. *Septimius Severus in Scotland: The Northern Campaigns of the First Hammer of the Scots*. Greenhill Books.

Frere, S. 1999. *Britannia. A History of Roman Britain* (4th edn). Pimlico, London.

Hanson, W.S. 1987. *Agricola and the Conquest of the North*. Batsford, London.

Hanson, W.S. (ed.) 2009. *The Army and Frontiers of Rome*. Portsmouth, Rhode Island.

Higgins, C. 2014. *Under Another Sky*. Vintage Books, London.

Hodgson, N. 2008. 'The development of the Roman site at Corbridge from the first to third centuries AD'. *Archaeologia Aeliana* 37: 47–92.

Hodgson, N. 2014. 'The British Expedition of Septimius Severus'. *Britannia* 45: 31–51.

Hodgson, N. 2021. 'The End of the Ninth Legion, War in Britain and the Building of Hadrian's Wall'. *Britannia* 52: 97–118.

Hoffmann, B. 2013. *The Roman Invasion of Britain. Archaeology Versus History*. Pen and Sword, Barnsley.

Hunter, F. and Keppie, L. (eds) 2012. *A Roman Frontier Post and Its People Newstead: 1911–2011*. National Museums Scotland, Edinburgh.

Jones, R.H. 2011. *Roman Camps in Scotland*. Society of Antiquaries of Scotland, Edinburgh.

Keppie, L.J.F. 1989. 'The fate of the Ninth Legion: a problem for the eastern provinces?' in French, D.H. and Lightfoot, C.S. (eds) *The Eastern Frontier of the Roman Empire*. British Archaeological Reports International Series 553, Oxford, 247–55.

Keppie, L.J. 1991. *Understanding Roman Inscriptions*. Batsford, London.

Keppie, L.J.F. 2000. 'Legio VIIII in Britain: the beginning and the end', in Brewer, R.J. (ed.) *Roman Fortresses and their Legions*. London, 83–100.

Keppie, L. 2004. *Scotland's Roman Remains*. John Donald, Edinburgh.

Keppie, L.J.F. 2009. 'Burnswark: native space and Roman invaders', in Hanson, W.S. (ed.) *The army and frontiers of the Rome*. JRA Suppl. 74: 241–52.

Keppie, L.J.F. 2013. John Horsley and the Britannia Romana (1732): the road to publication; the Tenth Horsely Memorial Lecture. *Archaeologia Aeliana* 42: 1–34.

Mattingly, D. 2007. *An Imperial Possession*. Penguin Books, London.

Maxwell, G.S. 1989. *The Romans in Scotland*. The Mercat Press, Edinburgh.

Mommsen, T. 1885. *The Provinces of the Roman Empire* (1996) Barnes & Noble, New York.

Poulter, J. 2009. *Surveying Roman Military Landscapes across Northern Britain. The Planning of Roman Dere Street, Hadrian's Wall and the Vallum, and the Antonine Wall in Scotland*. British Archaeological Reports British Series 492, Oxford.

Reid, J.H. and Nicholson, A. 2019. 'Burnswark Hill: the opening shot of the Antonine reconquest of Scotland?' *Journal of Roman Archaeology* 32: 459–77.

Richmond, I.A. 1955. *Roman Britain*. Penguin Books, Harmondsworth.

Russell, M. and Laycock, S. 2010. *UnRoman Britain*. The History Press, Stroud.

Russell, M. 2011. The Roman Ninth Legion's Mysterious Loss. BBC New website. https://www.bbc.co.uk/news/ magazine-12752497

Sommer, S. 2006. 'Military Vici in Roman Britain Revisited', in Wilson, R.J.A. (ed.) *Romanitas: Essays on Roman archaeology in honour of Sheppard Frere on the occasion of his ninetieth birthday*. Oxbow, Oxford. 95–147.

St Joseph, J.K.S. 1970. 'The camps at Ardoch, Stracathro and Ythan Wells: recent excavations'. *Britannia* 1: 163–78.

St Joseph, J.K.S. 1973. 'Air reconnaissance in Roman Britain, 1969–72'. *Journal of Roman Studies* 63: 214–16.

Woolliscroft, D.J. 2000. 'More thoughts on why the Romans failed to conquer Scotland'. *Scottish Archaeological Journal* 22: 111–22.

Woolliscroft, D.J. and Hoffmann, B. 2006. *Rome's First Frontier: The Flavian Occupation of Northern Scotland*. The History Press, Stroud.

Romans in Judea

Faulkner, N. 2011. *Apocalypse. The Great Jewish Revolt Against Rome*. Amberley, Stroud.

Goodman, M. 2008. *Rome and Jerusalem*. Penguin Books, London.

Mor, M. 2016. *The Second Jewish Revolt: The Bar Kokhba War 132–136 CE*. Brill Reference Library of Judaism.

Yadin, Y. 1966. *Masada*. Weidenfeld and Nicolson, London.

Yadin, Y. 1971. *Bar-Kokhba, the Rediscovery of the Legendary Hero of the Last Jewish Revolt Against Rome*. Weidenfeld and Nicolson, London.

Hadrian's Wall

de la Bédoyère, G. 1998. *Hadrian's Wall: History and Guide*. Tempus.

Bidwell, P. 2005. 'The system of obstacles on Hadrian's Wall: their extent, date and purpose'. *Arbeia Journal* 8: 53–76.

Breeze, D.J. and Dobson, B. 2000. *Hadrian's Wall*. Penguin, London.

Breeze, D.J. 2006. *J. Collingwood Bruce's Handbook to the Roman Wall*. The Society of Antiquaries of Newcastle upon Tyne.

Bruhn, J. and Hodgson, N. (2022). 'The Social and Economic Impact of Hadrian's Wall on the Frontier Zone in Britain'. *Britannia* 53: 125–57.

Corby, M. 2010. 'Hadrian's Wall and the defence of north Britain'. *Archaeologia Aeliana* 39: 9–13.

Graafstal, E.P. 2012. 'Hadrian's haste: a priority programme for the Wall'. *Archaeologia Aeliana* 41: 123–84.

Hodgson, N. 2008. 'The development of the Roman site at Corbridge from the first to third centuries AD'. *Archaeologia Aeliana* 37: 47–92.

Hodgson, N. 2017. *Hadrian's Wall. Archaeology and History at the Limits of the Roman Empire*. Robert Hale, The Crowood Press, Marlborough.

Moffat, A. 2008. *The Wall. Rome's Greatest Frontier*. Birlinn, Edinburgh.

Southern, P. 2019. *Hadrian's Wall. Everyday Life on a Roman Frontier*. Amberley, Stroud.

Symonds, M. 2018. *Protecting the Roman Empire*. Cambridge University Press, Cambridge.

Symonds, M. 2021. *Hadrian's Wall: Creating Division*. Bloomsbury Academic, London.

Antonine Wall

Abdy, R. 2002. 'A survey of the coin finds from the Antonine Wall'. *Britannia* 33: 189–217.

Bailey, G.B. and Moore, M. 2003. *The Antonine Wall: Rome's Northern Frontier*. Falkirk.

Breeze, D.J. 1982. *The Northern Frontiers of Roman Britain*. Batsford, London.

Breeze, D.J. 2015. *The Antonine Wall*. Birlinn, Edinburgh.

Breeze, D.J. and Hanson, W.S. (eds) 2020. *The Antonine Wall: Papers in Honour of Professor Lawrence Keppie*. Archaeopress, Oxford.

Brickstock, R.J. 2020. 'Pre-Antonine coins from the Antonine Wall' in Breeze & Hanson.

Campbell, L. (2020). 'Polychromy on the Antonine Wall Distance Sculptures: Non-destructive Identification of Pigments on Roman Reliefs'. *Britannia* 51: 175–201.

Campbell, L. 2020. 'Reading the writing on the wall: discovering new dimensions to the Antonine Wall distance sculptures'. *Journal of Ancient History and Archaeology* 7: 46–75.

Gillam, J.P. 1976. 'Possible changes in plan in the course of construction of the Antonine Wall'. *Scottish Archaeological Forum* 7: 51–6.

Hartley, B.R. 1972. 'The Roman occupations of Scotland: the evidence of Samian ware'. *Britannia* 3: 1–55.

Hodgson, N. 1995. 'Were There Two Antonine Occupations of Scotland?' *Britannia* 26: 29–49.

Hodgson, N. 2009. 'The abandonment of Antonine Scotland: its date and causes' in Hanson, W.S. (ed.) *The army and frontiers of Rome*. Journal of Roman Archaeology Supplementary series 74:18 5–93.

Keppie, L.J. 2012. *The Antiquarian Rediscovery of the Antonine Wall*. Society of Antiquaries of Scotland, Edinburgh.

Macdonald, G. 1934. *The Roman Wall in Scotland*. Clarendon Press, Oxford.

Macinnes, L. 2020. 'The impact of the Antonine wall on Iron Age society' in *The Antonine Wall: Papers in Honour of Professor Lawrence Keppie*. Archaeopress, Oxford.

Mann, J.C. 1988. 'The history of the Antonine Wall – a reappraisal'. *Proceedings of the Society of Antiquaries of Scotland* 118: 131–7.

Poulter, J. 2018. 'New Discoveries Relating to the Planning of the Antonine Wall in Scotland'. *Britannia* 49: 113–46.

Robertson, A.S. 1990. *The Antonine Wall: a handbook to the surviving remains*. Revised by L.J. Keppie. Glasgow Archaeological Society.

Romankiewicz, T. et al. 2020. 'New perspectives on the structure of the Antonine Wall' in *The Antonine Wall: Papers in Honour of Professor Lawrence Keppie*. Archaeopress, Oxford.

Swan, V.G. 1999. 'The twentieth legion and the history of the Antonine wall reconsidered'. *Proceedings of the Society of Antiquaries of Scotland* 129: 399–480

Steer, K. 1963. 'John Horsley and the Antonine Wall'. *Archaeologia Aeliana* 42: 1–40.

Picts and Early Medieval Scotland

Carver, M. 2008. *Portmahomack: Monastery of the Picts*. Edinburgh University Press, Edinburgh.

Clarkson, T. 2016. *The Picts: A History*. Birlinn, Edinburgh.

Foster, S.M. 2014. *Picts, Gaels and Scots: Early Historic Scotland*. Birlinn, Edinburgh.

Fraser, J.E. 2009. *From Caledonia to Pictland: Scotland to 795*. Edinburgh University Press, Edinburgh.

Henderson, G. and Henderson, I. 2011. *The Art of the Picts. Sculpture and Metalwork in Early Medieval Scotland*. Thames and Hudson, London.

Hunter, F. 2005. 'Rome and the creation of the Picts', in Z. Visy (ed.) *Limes XIX: Proceedings of the XIXth International Congress of Roman Frontier Studies*, 235–40.

McHardy, S. 2010. *A new History of the Picts*. Luath Press, Edinburgh.

Noble, G. et al. 2013. 'Between history and prehistory: the archaeological detection of social change among the Picts'. *Antiquity* 87: 1136–50.

Noble, G. and Evans, N. 2019. *The King in the North. The Pictish Realms of Fortriu and Ce*. Birlinn, Edinburgh.

Indigenous Peoples, Nationalism, Colonialism, Imperialism and Psychology

Ascherson, N. 2002. *Stone Voices*. Granta, London.

Berger, J. 1972. *Ways of Seeing*. Penguin, Harmondsworth.

Beveridge, C. and Turnbull, R. 1989. *The Eclipse of Scottish Culture*. Polygon, Edinburgh.

Bradley, M. 2010. *Classics and Imperialism in the British Empire*. Oxford University Press, Oxford.

Ferguson, B.R. and Whitehead, N.L. 1992. 'The Violent Edge of Empire' in Ferguson, B.R. and Whitehead, N.L. (eds) *War in the Tribal Zone*. James Currey Ltd, Oxford.

Hingley, R. 2000. *Roman Officers and English Gentlemen: The Imperial Origins of Roman Archaeology*. Routledge, London.

Maslow, A. 1943. 'A theory of human motivation', *Psychological Review*, 50:370–96.

Montgomery, A. 2017. 'Resisting the "Conquerors of the Universe": Celebrating the Rejection of Rome in Early-Modern Scotland'. *Journal of British Identities* 1: 35–58.

Piggott, S. 1958. 'Native economies and the Roman occupation of north Britain', in Richmond, I.A. (ed.) *Roman and Native in North Britain*. Nelson, Edinburgh.

Sharples, N.M. 1996. 'Nationalism or Internationalism: the Problematic Scottish Experience', in Atkinson, J.A., Banks, I., O'Sullivan, J. (eds) *Nationalism and Archaeology: Scottish Archaeological Forum 7*: 7–88. Cruithne Press, Glasgow.

Wells, P.S. 2001. *The Barbarians Speak*. Princeton University Press, Princeton and Oxford.

Conflict archaeology

Campbell, D.B. 2006. *Besieged. Siege Warfare in the Ancient World*. Osprey, Oxford.

Campbell, D.B. 2003. 'The Roman Siege of Burnswark'. *Britannia* 34: 19–33.

Ferguson, R.B. and Whitehead, N.L. (eds) 1992. *War in the Tribal Zone. Expanding States and Indigenous Warfare*. School of American Research Press, Santa Fe.

Fernández-Götz, M. and Roymans, N. 2018. *Conflict Archaeology: Materialities of Collective Violence from Prehistory to Late Antiquity*. Routledge, London.

Keeley, L.H. 1996. *War Before Civilization*. Oxford University Press, Oxford.

Reid, J. H., Müller, R. and Klein, S. (2022). 'The Windridge Farm *Glandes* Revisited: Clues to Conquest?' *Britannia* 53: 323–46.

Roymans, N. and Fernandez-Götz, M. 2019. 'Reconsidering the Roman conquest: New archaeological perspectives' *Journal of Roman Archaeology* 32: 415–20.

Sullivan, P.L. 2007. 'War Aims and War Outcomes: Why Powerful States Lose Limited Wars'. *Journal of Conflict Resolution* 51: 496–524.

Classical and historic period texts

Bede. *The Ecclesiastical History of the English People*. Farmer, D. (ed.) and Sherley-Price, L. (trans.) 1990. Penguin Classics, London.

Camden, W. 1586. *Britannia*. London.

Dio. *Roman History*. Carey, E. (trans.) 1927. Vol. IX. Loeb Classical Library, London and Cambridge MA.

Gildas. *On the Ruin of Britain*. Giles, J.A. (trans.) 2009. Serenity Publications, Rockville.

Herodian. *History of the Empire*. Whitaker, C.R. (trans.) 1989. Vol. I. Loeb Classical Library, London and Cambridge MA.

Historia Augusta (Augustan Histories). Magie, D. (trans.) 2022. Vol. II. Loeb Classical Library, London and Cambridge MA.

John of Fordun. *Chronicle of the Scottish Nation*. Skene, W.F. (ed.) 1871–2. Historians of Scotland 1. Edinburgh.

Josephus. *The Jewish War*. Goodman, M. (ed.) and Hammond, M. (trans.) 2017. Oxford University Press, Oxford.

Pliny the Elder. *Natural History*. Healy, J.F. (trans.) 1991. Penguin, London.

Tacitus. *Agricola and Germania*. Rives, J. (ed.) and Mattingly, H. (trans.) 2010. Penguin, London.

Tacitus. *The Histories*. Wellesley, K. (trans.) 2009. Penguin Books, London.

Online Sources

Many specialist papers are also available free online by the generosity of:

Cumberland and Westmorland Antiquarian and Archaeological Society
https://cumbriapast.com/cgibin/cwaas/cp_main.pl?action=cp_transactions_content_search

Dumfries and Galloway Natural History and Antiquarian Society
http://www.dgnhas.org.uk/tdgnhas_online_volumes

The Society of Antiquaries of Newcastle upon Tyne
https://archaeologydataservice.ac.uk/library/browse/series.xhtml?recordId=1001112

The Society of Antiquaries of Scotland
https://archaeologydataservice.ac.uk/archives/view/psas/volumes.cfm

Index

Page numbers in **bold** refer to illustrations

Keeping the peace: a Caledonian warlord examines the latest
offering of silver *denarii* from a Roman military envoy.